# The Tree of Life
# Bears Twelve Manner of Fruit
# An Alchemical Story
# By Dr. Robert R. Martin, Jr.

**Cover photo: Angel Oak by Michael Requidan**

# PREFACE

The following passages from Revelation are the inspiration for the title of this book. Please take the time to read them and see if you can determine what they are truly saying. Once you have read the book, take the opportunity to revisit these passages and see what you have learned. Everything will then become crystal clear and bursting with meaning. Enjoy!

**Revelation**

*2:17:* He that hath an ear, let him hear what the Spirit saith unto the churches; to him that overcometh will I give to eat of the hidden manna, and will give him a white stone, and in the stone a new name written, which no man knoweth saving he that receiveth it.

*21:21:* And the twelve gates were twelve pearls; every several gate was of one pearl: and the street of the city was pure gold, as it were transparent glass. *22: 1:* And he shewed me a pure river of water of life, clear as crystal, proceeding out of the throne of God and of the Lamb. *2:* In the midst of the street of it, and on either side of the river, was there the tree of life, which bare twelve manner of fruits, and yielded her fruit every month: and the leaves of the tree were for the healing of the nations.

*22: 14:* Blessed are they that do his commandments, that they may have right to the tree of life, and may enter in through the gates into the city.

*22: 17:* And the Spirit and the bride say, Come. And let him that heareth say, Come. And let him that is athirst come. And whosoever will, let him take the water of life freely.

# INTRODUCTION

This is the ultimate story of the human race. It is the story of the manna and the bread of the covenant, the story of the Philosopher's Stone and the Phoenix. The story you are about to read is a guide and a milepost and will change your life forevermore. This story contains history, science, lore and fantasy. It is the stuff that movies are made of; yet there has never been a movie made about it. It is a story of the reason for our existence as a species. This story is scientific, yet metaphysical; it is religious, yet heretical; and it is, above all, alchemical. This story may seem fantastic but it is truthful to the best of my ability to communicate it. There is something here for everyone, yet some will toss it aside, for they will not be ready for its life-changing message. Others will cling to it and, as a result, begin new quests in life. And no one who reads this story will remain unchanged.

In this book I propose to make a brief presentation of my findings, observations, and assumptions concerning mon- and di-atomic elements and their microclusters. This book will outline the history of these substances as well as touch on the findings and observations of other researchers and historical figures. The rich yet obscure history and tradition of the manufacture and usage of these substances will be discussed along with the validity of many claims, myths, and assumptions concerning them. This book will also seek to research many pertinent word origins along with their mythological significance where they apply to the subject matter. We will also discuss a great deal concerning natural sources of these materials and proper preparations insuring that the ORMUS is not lost before ingestion. Also of great importance, we will discuss what effects to expect when consuming these materials and the inner alchemy that should accompany their usage.

To get you started I will tell you a short story in Chapter One. It is Our Story, revealed to me during my research into the origins and knowledge of orbitally rearranged monatomic unit structure (ORMUS). Some of you might recognize certain elements to the story, yet it is quite the alternative to what we have been taught. The story, which reads like science fiction, is recounted in the most ancient of texts found on Earth.

Now read our story and prepare to travel back to our origins, and prepare to be permanently changed by it.

Realize that this work is not light reading. It is designed to bring about transmutation of the psyche just as does the alchemy it reveals. This work contains science, metaphysics, history and lore; it contains speculation, psychology, and ancient texts; it contains deep secrets, word origins and research results. And lastly, it contains a formula imparted by the greatest Master of Alchemy ever to grace the Earth with his presence. Prepare to be changed.

**Dr. Robert R. Martin, Jr.**

Dr. Robert R. Martin, Jr. holds degrees in Environmental Sciences, Holistic Health Sciences and Transpersonal Hypnotherapy. He is certified by a number of boards including registration as an Environmental Professional, Master Hypnotherapist and Alternative Health Practitioner. Dr. Martin also owned an environmental engineering firm in Virginia for 18 years. During this time, he maintained a hypnotherapy and holistic health practice which he continues today. Dr. Martin also pursues the ancient art of alchemy, utilizing the fruits of his work to manufacture a host of curative and therapeutic mixtures. During his quest for the Philosopher's Stone, he discovered the teachings of the Order of Melchizedek and became an ordained priest. He is now the Patriarch of the Ancient and Sovereign Order of Melchizedek, a corporation sole which hosts The Temple of Melchizedek, a society of ambassadorial priests of peace. Dr. Martin teaches classes across the country to Order of Melchizedek initiates. He is also a seasoned speaker and teacher offering classes and seminars in Practical Alchemy, Ascension Alchemy and Quantum Mechanics, Forbidden History, Holistic

Health and more. Robert enjoys playing and writing music and creating works of art and craft in multi media. He lives with his wonderful wife and energetic young son on a mountain top in rural southwestern Virginia where he and his family enjoy gardening, hiking and the view from the porch of their roomy log home.

# TABLE OF CONTENTS

CHAPTER 13

# CHAPTER 1

## Our Story and the Olden Gods

Our story begins in great antiquity, well before recorded time. Or should I say, well before the first-account records that have been found to date. We begin with a race of people in a far away land. These people, known as the *Anunnaki*, suffered a plight in their land which these days sounds all too familiar to us. This land known as *Nibiru* in ancient texts, is said to be an additional planet in our own solar system which travels a thirty-six hundred year elliptical orbit known as a god year or *Shar*. Nibiru, according to ancient texts, was for billions of years protected from the elements of cold and heat by its special atmosphere. When close to the sun, the atmosphere acted as a shield against the heat, and when far out in space, the atmosphere acted as a blanket to keep the planet warm. The atmosphere for many millennia was sustained by the many volcanoes about the land. And these people of Nibiru had periods of war and times of peace until they had overcome their warring spirits; or so they had thought. Nothing however could prepare them for the plight they would face the day the volcanoes ceased to spew their sustaining gases. I ask, does this not sound familiar as we hear increasingly bad news concerning our ozone layer which protects us from the intense radiation of the sun?

The panicked Anunnaki asked their adepts and sages what must be done. They asked the *Puhnja* seers about their ultimate fate. The adepts suggested launching missiles into the mouths of the volcanoes in hopes this would reignite their spirits. And so this was performed, but to no avail. They again consulted the sages and were told that the only hope was gold. Gold, they said, is the only metal that can be made into a fine white powder which then can be turned to gas and take residence within the upper atmosphere. The gold-zone layer will act as a cloak high above the planet to sustain our temperatures and protect us from the cold of deep space and the heat of the sun as we make our close pass. And this gas will neither be poisonous to us nor will it irritate the eye or the nose. But "where shall such great quantities of gold be found?" asked the people. The answer came from the Puhnja. 'We will survive' the people were told. We have seen it! There is a place which contains the gold we seek. We must go there to obtain what we need. But we must take care in our planning for there are great barriers of asteroids to breach on our journey. And we must take care in our approach for the land is unstable and soft. And we must take care in our work for the land is hostile with dangerous creatures, extreme temperatures, and rapid movements and cycles. The seers told how the atmosphere there was thin and the gravity weak. It will be hard to survive there they said. The place they referred to was Earth. All the Puhnja seers related was ratified by the scientists and adepts. But how could this be accomplished?

This task seemed insurmountable by the people and so the idea was turned down. But one day, a man set out to prove a point. He stole some of the missiles left over from the ancient wars, loaded them onto a ship and made his narrow escape. *Alalu* made his way toward Earth with his ominous cargo. He used some of the missiles to blast his way through the asteroid belt and approached Earth. The craft was not equipped to land on the soils of Earth so he crashed into the sea in a body of water, now known as the Persian Gulf, and used his craft like a boat to make his way to shore. Once upon shore, he donned his silvery fish suit and went out onto the land. He tested the air and found it to be breathable so he removed his helmet. He tested the waters of the salt marsh and found them to contain gold. He went inland and found fresh water and tested it and found it was good to drink. He was elated with all of his findings until the sun began to set. The sky turned red and he was frightened, he was so sure this was the end. But the sun quickly returned. How could the day be so short he wondered?

When Alalu had performed all of his tests he opened communications with his home planet Nibiru. I have found it he exclaimed! Here there is the gold we seek. Multiple missions would follow. A new way was devised by the scientist Ninsumon who would later be called Enki (Lord Earth) to breach the asteroid belt using water pressure. And mining commenced. First, gold was extracted from the sea, however, it soon was realized that this would be too inefficient. Next, gold was extracted from the ground and great quantities were shipped home. Since the cargos were so weighty, giant stone platforms had to be constructed to support the take offs of the heavily laden cargo vessels. Eventually, a weigh station was established on *Lamu* (Mars). The mission was seemingly a success but the *Anunnaki* people soon became overworked. They asked Enki, the second-in-command and the keeper of all the science, what can we do? We need more workers, the people complained.

## The Mixed Worker

Enki suggested that they create a mixed worker. He would take the ova of the ape woman which was the indigenous hominid found in Africa, and mix the essence of the Anunnaki into it. From this clay, we can sculpt a primitive worker who will carry much of the intellect of the Anunnaki but who can be ruled. So the task was performed. After a great deal of practicing with ape woman (early hominid) DNA and animal DNA resulting in a number of often hideous part-man part-beast chimeras, perfection was eventually reached and it was then time to mix the Human with the Anunnaki.

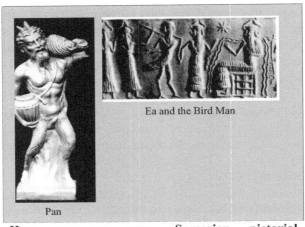

Ea and the Bird Man

Pan

**Here we see some Sumerian pictorial interpretations and one Greek statuette (Pan), of the part man part animal mixes resulting from the DNA mixing practice. This may have given rise to the many fables of half human-half animal mixes such as the Centaur and the Minotaur.**

Birth mothers were chosen from among the Anunnaki. The work was performed in the house of *Shi Im Ti* or (breath wind life), the biological laboratory of Enki and his half sister *Ninti*. Together they created a workforce of test tube babies, the *Ilu Amilu* (mixed worker). However, as they reproduced, the workers soon began to revert back to a more primitive state becoming more hairy and less intelligent. So phase two was begun whereas a greater amount of Anunnaki DNA would be used. This resulted in a very intelligent hybrid that made good workers, but they could not reproduce. They had what was known as the disease of two species mixing. **"Male and female created he them and blessed them, and he called their name** *Adama (of the earth)*" (Genesis).

4

## The Si-im-ti and the Tree of Life

The SI-IM-TI was the house of life where Adapa and the Eva were created by ENKI (Lord Earth) and his half sister NINTI (Lady Life) along with other members of the family tree of life.

Eventually, the birth mothers could not continue to make babies and so the newest models of *Adamu* (older form of Adama which is plural for Adam, meaning 'of the Earth') were then re-engineered so that they could reproduce on their own. This was accomplished using stem cells from the rib marrow of Ninti and Enki. The couple that was chosen for this was Eva and Adapa (Adam and Eve). Soon they replenished the Earth and amazed the Anunnaki at how fast they could reproduce. And a work force was built to serve the Anunnaki and take up their toil while on Earth.

The high commander *Enlil* (Lord of Airspace) was very concerned about the new humans. They were so intelligent that he was concerned that if they were to learn the secrets to longevity and gain the knowledge of whom and what they really were, they would choose not to serve the Anunnaki and would become as the Anunnaki themselves. So, Enlil sent down an edict that the new humans were to keep their distance from the family Tree of Knowledge and Tree of Life. But Eva broke the rule and went to Enki who impregnated her and gave her a son (Cyin or Cain). After her association with Enki and his family, Eva learned that she, as well as all other humans, were viewed as little more than cattle to the Anunnaki. She learned that to be naked was to be uncivilized. One day, the lord Enlil was walking in the garden and Adapa and Eva hid from him for they knew they were naked and they were embarrassed; and they knew that Enlil saw them as little more than animals. Enlil became enraged as he knew that if the humans were to gain too much knowledge, or everlasting life, that they would then become like the Anunnaki themselves and thus become uncontrollable. "Behold, the man has become as one of us!" he cried. Adapa and Eva were expelled from the premises in order to keep them away from Enki and his family lest they gain long life as well. Enki too was scolded and told that he was not to share any more secrets with the humans.

Kingship was then descended from heaven. Adapa (Adam) became the Earth's first King. Since now he had the knowledge of clothes and learned that clothes were regal and that nakedness was uncivilized, he was granted a cloak upon his coronation. Adapa served the Anunnaki well and was able to achieve control and ruler-ship over the people on behalf of the Anunnaki. The Earth mission was finally going well and its leadership became proud of Adapa and his achievements. One day, Adapa was sent to Nibiru to visit *Anu*, the king of that world and father of Enki and Enlil. Enki worried that Adapa would partake of the foods and elixirs of long life while on his visit. He worried that Enlil would destroy Adapa upon his return if he thought that he had become as an Anunnaki. So Enki, while preparing Adapa for his trip, briefed him on etiquette and how to gain entrance to the house of Anu, but he also told him that he would be offered food and drink and that he was not to accept. These are the food and drink of the Gods and would be poison to him Adapa was told. Upon Adapa's arrival on Nibiru, Anu eagerly received Adapa with pride but was offended when Adapa refused food and drink. However, all else went well and the trip was a success. Adapa returned to Earth and was well received upon his return home. What, we should ask, was this food of the gods? What food could possibly so alter the nature of Adapa as to make him as one of the Gods themselves? Herein lays the premise of our story.

### The Olden Gods

Everything was going well. The workers produced great

quantities of gold and served the Anunnaki well. Eventually however, the Anunnaki began to fall back into their ancient, war-like ways. They broke up into factions and began to fight. Eventually, they used humans to do much of their fighting. And then, to make matters much worse, many of the Anunnaki and **Igigi** (lower ranked Nibiruans associated with **watchers** or angels) began to take human women as wives. **"And the sons of God saw the daughters of men and that they were fair and took them wives of all which they chose." (Genesis 6:2)** Anunnaki women also took humans for husbands as well. This began to create great problems. When the Igigi mixed with the first and more primitive humans that were created, this resulted in hybrid giants who caused many problems about the Earth as they were intelligent, powerful and very angry that they were often unable to reproduce and usually did not inherit the extreme life span of the Anunnaki. **"There were giants in the Earth in those days; and also after that, when the sons of God came unto the daughters of men, and they bare children to them, the same became mighty men which were of old and men of renown." (Genesis 6:4)**

When the tribes of Enoch, the son of Cain, mixed with the Anunnaki, the offspring were not hybrids and they were every bit as intelligent, and nearly as strong as the Anunnaki. They also possessed long life, albeit not quite as long as the Anunnaki. This was due to the fact that Cain, who was fathered by Enki, a full Anunnaki, married Luluva, who was also full Anunnaki and Enoch was a child of this union. This generation of humans could be considered a bridge species able to effectively reproduce with either Nibiruans or the more primitive generations of humans without producing hybrid giants.

For the giants *(Nephelim)* however, it seemed that the shorter, more human, life span was genetically dominant. Although they did live somewhat longer than humans, they were unsatisfied with their inheritance and their exclusion from Anunnaki society. They began to teach the humans to create steel and started to force humans into following them rather than to serve the Anunnaki. Eventually, the Anunnaki allowed the destruction of the Earth at the order of **Enlil** (Lord of Airspace) who carried the highest rank among those of the Earth mission. The destruction was an attempt by Enlil to recover control of the Earth from the Nephelim and all of the noisy humans. This great act was facilitated by the passing of Nibiru on its circuit through the solar system. Enlil would cause his Anunnaki people to abandon Earth for a time until the crossing was past. He would not allow the Earth people to be warned nor would he protect them from the asteroids that would plunge into the sea, nor from the giant waves that would follow. Neither would he protect them from the collapse of the great Antarctic ice shelf and the resulting rise in the oceans of the Earth.

**Sphinx and the Great flood courtesy of the Grand Lodge Ath-Ka-Ptah**

### After the Flood

After the Great Flood, the Earth was cleansed of most of the problems including most of the workers and the giants. Some of the offspring of Cain who were more advanced, such as Enoch, were taken up into Anunnaki society for fear of their power over the humans.    Additionally, there was *Ziusudra,* The biblical Noah who saved a number of his relatives and friends from the flood in the great ark commissioned by his secret father Lord *Enki.*

After the subsiding floods, kingship again descended from heaven just as it had in earlier times, but this time there was to be no more Human/Anunnaki contact.   Kings were created to be smarter still than the human population and more enlightened. They were created to be the go-betweens, the middlemen between the gods/Anunnaki and the Humans.  The kings would communicate to the people what the gods desired for them to do. The kings were granted substances such as the *Star Fire* extract, the rich food of the matrix made from the extracts of the blood of the wombs of the specially trained and bred Anunnaki priestesses which, until this time, was the sole prerogative of the Nibiruan elite, the Anunnaki. The kings were super-human creations of the Anunnaki, superior in all respects to other humans.   Their life spans were greatly increased, their subtle intuitions were great and their intellect was far superior to their subordinates.    These kings were also more powerful and healthier than normal humans.  And what is a king without a queen?  The Anunnaki created queens as well.  They were also fed on substances which made them the female equivalent of the king.  The kings followed a strict, ritualized breeding program which retained the purity of the bloodlines for posterity through the matrilineal line of the queen by the passing of the mitochondrial DNA that can only be passed on by the female.

And so the work recommenced and at the order of the kings, the people mined gold and other metal ores and performed numerous tasks to serve their kings and their gods.  The people cultivated the lands and built temples and other structures such as irrigation canals.  They waited on the kings and the gods and served them with enthusiasm.   They cooked their favorite foods and even entertained them.   And they worshiped them and the ground beneath their feet.

9

## Forbidden Fruit

One day, an edict was handed down by Enlil (who would later be referred to as *El Shaddi*, Lofty Mountain, by Abraham) that there would be no further consumption of blood. The blood referred to by *El Shaddi* was not what we might think, such as the blood of cattle for instance. In fact, the blood referred to here was the *Starfire* which will be explained at length in later sections. After this edict, the life spans of most of the elite tribes, such as *Abraham* and his descendants, began to rapidly shorten with each generation. Soon the human life span was one hundred and twenty years. **"And the Lord said now all your years shall be one hundred and twenty"** (Genesis). This edict was in preparation for the Anunnaki departure. However, there were a few who maintained a somewhat lengthy life span. Did they possibly find some substitute to the Anunnaki Priestess lunar essence known as Starfire? The answer is yes, there was a substitute brought to the adept by Enki, the very one who had created and loved the Adamu. And, through his son *Ningish* (better known as Thoth or Hermes), the alchemical techniques were devised and taught to the kings and priests of old. So until the time of final departure, *Ningish-Ziddha*, (Thoth's full Sumerian title) taught the people of the Earth the alchemical sciences while also teaching about the high, true Lord of the Cosmos, the Lord of Light that dwells within all things, *Adon* (Adoni, or my Lord). This was the true God of the universe, a conscious presence known even to the Anunnaki as the source of all. However, there were others who prepared humans before the Anunnaki departure by spreading religions of fear in hopes that people would wipe one another out in the service of their angry, jealous gods.

The Priests, Kings, metallurgists and great artificers of gold were taught by Ningish to prepare the *Shem-an-nah* (stone of brilliant fame), and then they prepared these substances for themselves and those of deserving status. People such as the great priest-king *Meleki-Tzedeque* (now known as Melchizedek) were among the first to be taught. Later, people such as *Bezaliel*, the builder of the Ark of the Covenant and son of *Uri Ben Hur*, and Moses the Exodus leader, and even *Miri-Amen* (Miriam of the

Israelites), were among others who were taught the great secret science of alchemy. Eventually special schools called mystery schools were begun in order to teach these traditions to kings, lords, priests, masons and vulcans or smithies. Along with the teaching of the manufacture of the manna, (a biblical term for the Shem-an-nah meaning 'what is this?') the mystery schools also taught inner alchemy partly from the Qabalistic traditions of the Shemite (Semitic) kings and queens designed to heighten awareness and subtle intuition.

## The Way of Devotion

One day when all of their work was done and the people of Nibiru were once again safe and there was finally enough gold after thousands of years of mining to save the atmosphere of Nibiru, the Anunnaki vacated their seats like migrating birds. They simply placed all of their differences aside and left the peoples of Earth behind to fend for themselves, taking with them only a few examples of human life and a few crossbred Anunnaki/Humans who would come to serve the Anunnaki in their home world and be the stock for the creation of a new line of Nibiruan servants. The people who remained were confused and panic-stricken. Many tried to continue serving their gods. They tried desperately to bring them home with the smell of their favorite food, roasted meats. Some began to worship their kings as surrogate gods. While still other entire races such as the **Tuatha De Dannon** (the children of Danna, or **Di Annu** as she was known in Mesopotamia) became gods themselves due to their high levels of Anunnaki DNA and thus retained Anunnaki qualities and traits. And though the Anunnaki are gone and have been for nearly 3,600 years, we continue to weave their story into our notions of God. But we were taught by Thoth before his return back to his homeland that there is only one high God of the cosmos. And even though we have been weaving fable, lore and tales of all sorts of people and beings into our notions of God and religion, the majority of us have basically and naturally gravitated toward a more true understanding of God, the unified consciousness of all, the Source, the great Lord of the cosmos who dwells within all things and all people and who is light and love. So, I always say, speed in light and love, which is to say farewell in the love and light of **Adon** the Lord and consciousness of the cosmos.

For a full and comprehensive understanding of the story of the Anunnaki and their sojourn to Earth, read Zechariah Sitchin's *Earth Chronicles* and *The Lost Book of Enki*. Also read the Sumerian texts, Atra Hasis (The Creation of Man) and the Enuma Elish (the Celestial Battle), The Epic of Gilgamesh and the Babylonian Flood Story.

It is perhaps important here to impress that we, as human beasts of burden, were expressly bred to be devoted to the gods that we might serve them completely without question or quibbling. We were all equipped with the genetic predisposition for great devotion just as the domestic dogs are bred for devotion to man and a strong desire for certain tasks. Such as the herding dogs have it in their genes to herd and they are never happier than when they are herding for the master. The draft horse is bred to pull and is never more satisfied than when pulling by the master's command. The humans created by the Anunnaki were most devoted to the service of their masters and were only satisfied when they could be in service. When turned out with no one to serve, they would become lost and distraught unless they found some surrogate to serve.

When the Anunnaki, Igigi and other Nibiruans vacated the Earth leaving humans behind with no one to serve, those who survived often turned their devotion toward surrogates. Some, such as the Egyptians, began to worship and serve their kings as gods. Still others began to turn devotion toward proclaimed gods and spirits of the Earth and stars. Some continued to worship the olden gods as if they were still present. Some turned their devotion towards science while others turned their devotion towards the harnessing of spiritual/mental power and life forces.

Perhaps one of the earliest peoples abandoned to struggle with their overpowering devotion was the Tuatha De Dannon (pronounced Too-ha Day Dan-yon) who were abandoned by Di Anu (also known as Inanna) when she was offered the seat of Ur in Mesopotamia. These people, also known as the Fey or the

(Faerie Folk), became extremely powerful wizards. As they were a separate race from most other humans, they possessed more of the Anunnaki essence which granted them a great life span well beyond other humans. The Fey protected their life spans by not mixing with other races of people. The Fey were the first Druids who turned their great devotion to the understanding and use of elemental forces. Eventually, when faced with the inevitable coexistence with other races, according to tradition, they simply stepped into a parallel dimension.

To this day, some Druid Bards (Druid elders or priests), Pict Sidhe (Sidhe is pronounced Shee, Pixie- Pictish priests), An-Da Shealladh (pronounced An Da Sha lahd, meaning the two sights or second sight) and others believe they can go visit the Fey, who are actually all around us, by use of the Aisling or Dream Vision. These are the inspired ones or the Awenyddion. The concept of Awen, or inspiration, is deeply tied to the genetic predisposition for devotion or extreme inspiration and was born from great devotion in the absence of the gods. The concept of Awen is central to the Fey and to all who believe they can commune with them. It is odd that the very substance which we have naturally occurring in our brains, di-methyl tryptomene (DMT) which we will discuss later in this book, often brings about visions that include the visitation of Fey-like beings when ingested, smoked or sniffed. This is the very brain molecule that increases as we become more spiritual or as our mental ability to utilize elemental energy increases. For this reason, Shamans and Yogis alike have greater amounts of DMT naturally occurring in their brains. Therefore, it is likely that the great inspiration of the Fey increased their natural DMT to enormous levels, allowing them to literally step into and become their vision.

There are other races such as the Rama who left Atlantis to create three cities of northern India and Pakistan where they could devote themselves to the use and manipulation of the elemental forces. These were great nations of priestly people devoted to righteous lifestyles and rigorous spiritual/mental practices. They forsook technologies at-large for mental development and the expansion of awareness and so they became very powerful shamans. On the other hand, the people

13

whom they left behind remaining in Pisida (Atlantis) became extremely devoted to power through technology. They aspired to control the world through the use of their mighty weapons. This eventually became their swift and total downfall; however, they too destroyed the great Rama civilizations.

Nowadays, most people direct their devotion in many ways and we often describe it as a sense of purpose. Some of us have found the real God, Lord of the Cosmos and, however we see this God, we have become devoted to that concept. While others have become devoted to family, still others are devoted to a job as we would have been in the early days in service to the gods. There are those of us who are devoted to a sport, while others are devoted to themselves. And, as always, there are those who are lost without a target for devotion. These are the lost souls who do not know where to turn. Some turn to the misuse of substances and can become thieves to support habitual behaviors. These people are most easily helped by finding something to become devoted to. They need to connect with a sense of purpose. This can be a religion or a cause, but it is often the only thing that will save them. These are the lost people, the legacy of the Anunnaki departure.

Due to this Anunnaki legacy of devotion, we must have at least one notion of purpose in life or we feel lost. We must have something we can feel devoted to or inspired by in order to thrive. If not, then we become like a chained dog or corralled horse, never able to realize our nature. As we will learn in this book, we must be inspired in life and we must have at least a purpose or we feel lost; for devotion is a part of our nature which, if ignored, will fester within us and cause sorrow and grief until we set it free. Devotion is not an emotion although it is very emotional; it is rather a complex behavior which cannot so easily be turned off.

The devotion behavior with which we were programmed by the Anunnaki has caused a phenomenon within the human race, one which the Anunnaki did not foresee. The Anunnaki thought that in their absence we would flounder forever without direction and that we would eventually kill ourselves off. But, not for lack of trying, we have not yet killed ourselves off, and we have not all floundered without direction. Many have turned devotion to causes which have greatly advanced the human race. We have advanced through science, spirituality and humanity; all by the power of devotion. We have met with incredibly rapid advancement as a species solely due to devotion. So the very key to our service to the Anunnaki may allow us to surpass them in many ways. In fact, many, such as the Fey and the Rama, have long since surpassed them in mental ability. If the thoughtless use of our runaway technology does not take us to extinction, we may one day become greater than the Anunnaki. We must however learn to incorporate all of our devotees in the task of running the world. No one faction can successfully run the world without the willing help and support of all other factions. Without this interfaith and inter-devotional attitude there will be action without conscientiousness, or faith without grounding, and science without foundation or morality. Our survival depends upon cooperation, the cooperation of a unified humanity. Now we shall continue our story, picking up the storyline with myself and how others and I have come to rediscover the substances fed to the early kings who were installed by the Anunnaki.

# CHAPTER 2

**ORMUS**

About 15 years ago I began working on an environmental catalyst. As a part-owner in an environmental engineering firm, one of my goals was to produce a catalyst that could be employed to reduce the emissions of combustion. I began working with certain ores that displayed bizarre characteristics under specific conditions. Eventually, I realized that these ores were the catalyst that we were seeking; however, we were at that time unable to identify the active ingredients within these ores. We knew that it would be necessary to understand how the substance was able to act as a catalyst before we would be able to market it to industry.

During this time, I discovered and began to follow the work of a man named David Hudson who had reportedly discovered a new phase of matter he called monatomic elements which possessed all sorts of interesting and seemingly impossible characteristics. All too quickly I began to realize that the characteristics displayed by the substances that I was working with bore incredible similarities to the substances described by Mr. Hudson. I was drawn to ancient textual material and lore due to similarities between substances discussed in ancient texts and the substance that I was working with. I began to realize these were all the same materials. It turned out that this new phase of matter was not so new after all, for it had been known in antiquity by many names including the Philosopher's Stone, Manna, and the Light Bread. Eventually, I realized that there was a great amount of information concerning these materials and their manufacture stored within ancient scientific and religious texts. These writings include texts on alchemy, major religions, myths, and legends. Some were even outright manuals on manufacture and use. Information on these elements continued to pull my attention, as it still does today, toward the history of these substances, their function in the human body and the process of their creation.

During the course of my study and experimentation with naturally occurring substances bearing these elements, I began to realize the link between my work and that of David Hudson. I still work with these substances for their industrial applications, but I am even more intrigued with the health benefits of ORMUS (Orbitally Rearranged Metallic Unit Structure) as these elements are often titled by the mainstream, also called ORME's or (Orbitally Rearranged Monatomic Elements) and the role it plays in biology rather than the inherent industrial or environmental applications.

Eventually, I learned how to manufacture monatomic and di-atomic elements from the twelve platinum group elements known to be able to transform to a high spin state. *(This will be explained in later chapters).* These elements are Cobalt, Nickel, Copper, Ruthenium, Rhodium, Palladium, Silver, Osmium, Iridium, Platinum, Gold and Mercury. When reduced to the singular atom, or to the di-atom in cases where there are an odd number of electrons, these substances act alone without bonding with other atoms. In this case, the di-atom acts more like a singular atom. I have discovered through my research that these substances exist wherever life or organic matter is found and are essential to all life. They have gone unnoticed by most modern chemical analysis since they are so very different structurally than basic elements, leaving most modern analytical techniques insufficient to identify them. It has been demonstrated that these elements have a natural affinity to the regions of the human body where they are needed and, once absorbed into the bloodstream, they quickly and easily go where they are needed. Even though these substances cannot react chemically and therefore cannot act as a drug in the body, their effects after ingestion can easily and almost immediately be felt by most people due to their superconductivity of light frequencies and the effects of these frequencies on the various organs of the body.

### The Elements

Of these twelve elements that are able to go into the mon- or di-atomic high spin state, the most important in the human body are rhodium and iridium. Rhodium and iridium are essential in neurological function, DNA conduction, and the formation of nested spiral structures within the cells such as microtubulin and microfilaments which may be essential to cellular communication and structure *(this will be expanded upon in later chapters)*. It has been determined that as much as 5% of the human brain by dry weight consists of di-atomic rhodium and iridium atoms. It has also been determined that rhodium is present within the telomeres of healthy DNA and, where it is absent, the DNA slowly falls apart and is unable to repair itself or effectively replicate. For these reasons, high spin rhodium is effective at normalizing certain cancer cells and prolonging life.

Gold is another important element. Since most gold of early times before smelting techniques were widely used, known as electrum, was actually a mixture of gold, silver and copper among other admixtures, the substances made from it contained these platinum group elements. When converted to the high-spin state, these elements turn to a white, soft, "light as a feather" powder. This was made into bread cakes that were often referred to as **shem**. It was also referred to by dozens of names such as shewbread, bread of the covenant, the bread of life, manna, shem manna, light bread, and the food of the gods. The early philosophers referred to the powder and its ceramic form as the Philosopher's Stone or, when put into suspensions, it was called the Elixir of Life.

Gold and copper ORMUS are able to act on the processes of the brain by first acting to jumpstart the pineal gland which is nick-named "the seat of the soul". This gland is responsible for our intuition and insight. Gold might also be responsible for the connection of the biological brain with the higher intent. The pineal gland also produces melatonin when activated which heightens awareness and acts as the body's greatest anti-aging formula. Copper helps to temper and regulate brain chemistry and helps rebuild collagen. Iridium is another platinum group element important for metabolism and DNA conductivity. Platinum helps the immune system, while ruthenium and nickel balance the functions of many glands.

## ORMUS Supplements

So, if we already have these substances within our bodies, should we consider supplementing them? The answer may be yes. Our modern lifestyles put us and our foods in touch with electromagnetic fields which drive away these elements from our foods and our bodies. As we age, we lose more of these vital nutrients until our bodies literally begin to break down. But how do we supplement our bodies with these important elements? If a product claims to contain monatomic elements, how can one be sure it really does, and that it does not contain other not so healthy things such as heavy metals? Also what foods might we eat that contain these important elements and how should we treat these foods to insure that these elements remain within the foods until ingestion? These are some of the questions we will be exploring.

**Melchizedek and Abraham**

20

# CHAPTER 3

**The New Pioneers**

## Chemistry and physics of mon- and di-atomic elements

The following is a brief discussion of the chemical and physical nature of mon- and di-atomic elements. In order to simplify the terminology, from this point on both mon- and di-atomic elements will be referred to as ORMUS. This name has been proposed to stand for (Orbitally Rearranged Metallic Unit Structure). It is an old word meaning "serpent" in certain languages and "tree" in others. The name "tree" refers to the *tree of life* and the "serpent" refers to the *serpent of the tree of life* and *of the serpent line*. The serpent is a symbol of DNA and is associated with rejuvenation. Phonetically spelled, the ancient word for tree is Orme, Ormes, Ormus, Ormas and, on a side note, this word has so long been applied to these elements that there have even been alchemists who have taken *Ormus* as a surname. For these reasons it perhaps seems appropriate that this name be a good candidate by which to refer to all of these elements. This acronym is also similar to the title of the patent which was applied for by David Hudson for the manufacture of monatomic gold which was ORMEs. ORMEs stands for Orbitally Rearranged Monatomic Elements. However, as will be further explained, it has been found that these materials are not all monatomic. Some are di-atomic. For this reason many people have resorted to the name ORMUS (Orbitally Rearranged Metallic Unit Structure).

As previously mentioned, the ancient word for tree is spelled phonetically and has been spelled Orme, Ormes, Ormus and Ormas. It is interesting that the chosen acronyms all fall within the same meaning of the ancient word for tree. Even the name Ormas can be an acronym which I myself might coin as Orbitally Restricted Mass Atomic Structure. The word Ormas was the Greek name of one of the important angels of the hour. Ormas was the angel of the tenth hour and the helper to archangel *Uriel* who took Enoch to a far off land and taught him the ability to use the henge (as in Stonehenge) to calculate the time of the year and ages in order to forecast and keep track of the coming flood event.

It is obvious however that alchemists of late have seemingly struggled to have the acronym remain in keeping with one of the more commonly accepted spellings for the ancient word for tree (ORME, ORMES and ORMUS). If one wishes to call the atom a unit, then the acronym could remain ORMUS but actually mean (Orbitally Restricted Mass Unit Structure). It should briefly be noted that most ancient languages such as Hebrew, Egyptian, Phoenician, Acadian and Sumerian were all written primarily in consonants. Vowels were only added as sounds when spoken. There was of course no standardized spelling, especially where vowels were concerned. So it is actually all in the pronunciation, for all forms of the word ORMUS would have been spelled RMS. It was up to the speaker to know where to place the vowels and which ones to use. This was highly affected by region and accent, so the word could have a wide variety of pronunciations determined by the vowel sounds inserted, such as ORMAS, ORMUS, ORMES or ORMIS. Even the first sound could have varied a bit to become URMUS or ARMAS.

From this point forward I will remain more in keeping with the other alchemists both past and present by referring to these elements as ORMUS rather than my coined acronym, ORMAS. The meaning of the ORMUS acronym for the purpose of this book will be Orbitally Restricted Mass Unit Structure, rather than the more widely known Orbitally Restricted Metallic Unit Structure.

In this Chapter we will attempt to lay ground work in the chemistry and physics of ORMUS and microclusters so that we can build a base for understanding the nature of ORMUS and microclusters and their inherent characteristics and effects in nature.

**Physical Structure**

First, as previously mentioned, it is important to understand that all ORMUS are not monatomic. Those atoms of the platinum group which have been determined to go to the high spin state and have an odd number of electrons will actually reduce to the di-atom, or two atoms, rather than to the single atom as do those which have an even number of electrons. This is a fact which Hudson does not acknowledge. Hudson believes that all ORMUS are mon-atoms. However, there are many others, including myself, who believe there are both mon- and di-atoms. It is important to realize that the discussion on this issue could be considered splitting hairs since the di-atom actually acts as a single atom. However, the distinction between the two is important for the reason that a mon-atom produces a single helical energetic field while the energetic field produced by a di-atom is a double helix. This is important when considering biological effects and functions as we will later discuss in the **Biological Importance** section.

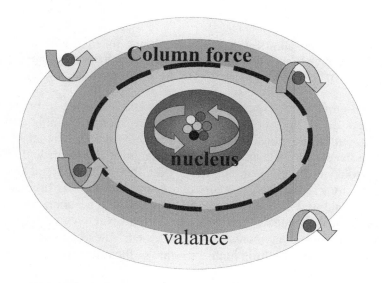

**The diagram above shows an atom in its normal condition.
Valance electrons (those outside of the column force)
are available for bonding.**

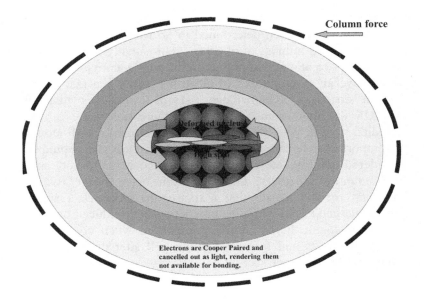

**Column force**

Deformed nucleus

High spin

Electrons are Cooper Paired and
cancelled out as light, rendering them
not available for bonding.

**Here we see the elliptical shape of the nucleus due to its high spin state and the absence of definable electrons which are all Cooper-paired as characteristics of the high spin atom.**

A mon-atom forms when something causes a molecule to break down or divide and subdivide until it reaches a critical number of atoms within the molecule. Once the critical number is reached, the molecule blows apart down to the singular (mon) or double (di) atom. If the electron number is odd, then it reduces only to the di-atom rather than to a singular (mon) atom. It is prudent here to suggest that this state of being would be short lived where most elements are concerned. However, where these platinum group elements are concerned, the condition is sustained by the resulting high spin state of the nucleus.

When the platinum group element is taken down to the mon- or di-atomic condition, the nucleus of the atom goes to a high spin state which acts to protect the valence electrons from further bonding. When atoms are bound in molecules, they have certain electrons that are available for bonding with other atoms called valance electrons. These electrons bond with others to lock the

24

atoms together and form molecules. Atoms also have other electrons within shells located closer to the nucleus that are protected or shielded from bonding by a force known as the column force. This screening potential is produced by the nucleus and extends outward specifically to shield certain electrons, but does not normally extend beyond the valance electron shells. When platinum group elements of this category are reduced down to the mon- or di-atom, something interesting happens. The nucleus goes into a high spin condition which causes the nucleus to become orbitally deformed. So, instead of remaining spherical in shape, the nucleus becomes football shaped. Since the column force stays a certain distance from the boundary of the nucleus, it is subsequently extended outward. When the column force is extended beyond the outer valance electron shells, the atom then becomes stable in the di- or monatomic state. The reason that the atom becomes stable is that when the column force extends beyond all electron shells, the electron pairs within the shells become Cooper-paired, which is to say that they join together as spin forward and spin reverse particles and nullify one another as pure light. When in this state, the electrons are translated in part to higher dimensional space/time. This means that the atom loses five ninths of its original weight. Once in this ORMUS condition, the element cannot bond back into a molecule naturally. The ORMUS is then destined in most situations to remain a mon- or di-atom. Due to the protection of the outer orbitals by the column force, the atom is restricted from bonding with another atom, at least not in the typical fashion.

Since ORMUS have no valance electrons, they cannot do chemistry. They are completely inert as far as chemical reactions are concerned. However, they do have energy fields that are quite different than they would normally possess. These energy fields are not well understood, however they produce some very important effects in biology which we will discuss at greater length later in this book.

Since the ORMUS electrons are all Cooper-paired, the electron cloud of the ORMUS is capable of accepting any amount of light influx. It has also been recognized that ORMUS atoms can pass light between one another with no net loss in energy. This superconductivity is limited only to a range of specific frequencies. All other frequencies are eliminated, or in some cases repelled. As we shall soon see, this is most important feature of ORMUS material.

**Microclusters**

Microclusters are a recent discovery and, although this phenomenon is rarely studied in the U.S., it is considered worthy college course material in some other countries such as Japan where courses are taught in Microcluster Physics. Microclusters form when ORMUS and/or other related materials attract one another. The attraction of these like-atoms is not well understood. Microclusters can involve other materials not in the ORMUS condition which we can refer to here as impurities. ORMUS is exotic matter which in this special condition does not adhere to previously conceived understandings of how matter should behave. ORMUS can appear as a powder, gas, liquid, ceramic, metal, or, under certain conditions, can be made to leave this space/time dimension for short durations or permanently.

When ORMUS mon- and di-atoms attract one another, they form a cluster known as a microcluster. When ORMUS is produced as a white powder, it is essentially microclustered. Under conditions of extreme heat or pressure, the microclustering effect becomes more lattice-like forming a ceramic crystalline structure. In nature, these crystals can form around impurities or within the matrix of impurities. This is the most common form of microcluster in nature. Microclusters themselves also are exotic in nature and can act as a gas, liquid, ceramic, metal or any combination. Microclusters are likely formed by the stitching together of the helical field produced by the ORMUS. When exposed to sufficient durations of adequate heat or pressure, the atoms are able to move closer together and allow their energetic fields to more closely and tightly knit with one another. This results in a glass known as the Philosopher's Stone.

The above picture shows several different types of Philosopher Stones. The center pinkish color stone with a reddish streak in the center is called a *dragon's eye*. It is composed of rhodium ORMUS, pink iridium and a streak of red lion and is the most valuable of the group. Bottom right is a *luna stone* made of copper ORMUS with a splash of red lion. Bottom left is a Jupiter stone made of copper ORMUS, green lion and red lion. The middle left is an Earth stone made of copper ORMUS, nickel, red and green lion. The middle right is a transparent 100% gold ORMUS stone. The upper left is a platinum ORMUS stone and the top right is a quartz crystal for comparison. The stone in the caduceus is of pure rhodium ORMUS. All of these stones emit a soft milky bluish light especially noticeable when in darkness.

When ORMUS are placed under other conditions, such as electrical fields for instance, their helical fields become more loosely knit and the nucleuses become more excited resulting in a partial or complete gasification or liquefaction. Depending on the amount of the impurity present in the microcluster, the microcluster may possess very bizarre qualities which are extremely important to industry. Industry has been taking advantage of some of these qualities for years, especially catalytic effects, without knowing what produces the effect.

However, once the microcluster is fully acknowledged and better understood, the result will be a renaissance of clean technologies available to industry.

### Physical Nature

As stated earlier, ORMUS can be considered exotic matter existing as a gas, liquid, ceramic, ceramic-like powder, or it can be seemingly driven into nonexistence. In nature, ORMUS most often exists as microclusters with high amounts of impurities sometimes referred to as monatomic minerals. It also may be that a great deal of the atmosphere is made up of ORMUS gases. And, it is a fact that water of all sorts, especially sea water, possesses ORMUS in varying quantities most often in the liquid form. Various techniques for extracting ORMUS from water may cause the ORMUS to be converted to a white precipitate which, when dried, will appear as a white powder. All living things have ORMUS within them as will be discussed later at length. For this reason, plant or animal alchemy can be employed to isolate these materials from almost all plant or animal tissues and excretions. Below is a picture of pure gold ORMUS.

**This picture is of gold ORMUS, notice the luminescence of the material as it absorbs light.**

Some ORMUS are able to produce a very interesting effect when heated to the catalytic temperature of 950 degrees Fahrenheit. At this temperature, they are able to superconduct the frequencies of the Meissner Field of the Earth in order to produce weightlessness. The Meissner Field, or magnetic field of the Earth, is like any other natural magnetic field in that it is made up of electrons that are thrown off and retrieved in a consistent pattern. Of course when the electrons leave to produce the magnetic field they are at that point photons, which are in fact light, and in this case, of a non-visible frequency range. ORMUS superconducts magnetic frequencies of light at the critical temperature of 950 degrees Fahrenheit, yet it also conducts other frequencies without being heated. As the ORMUS conducts these magnetic fields, they ride on them to become weightless. This happens with all of the ORMUS to varying degrees. In my perception, mercury creates the most exaggerated effect in this regard followed by rhodium. This seems like a remarkable effect that would no doubt be a very important discovery. There is ample evidence that these effects were known and taken advantage of in ancient times, therefore this effect, like the substance itself, is a rediscovery.

The weightlessness effect is not limited to the ORMUS material itself; rather the effect is produced as a field extending outward in all directions for a certain distance reminiscent of a magnetic field, depending on the exactness and consistency of the temperature and the type of ORMUS used. The weightless field is able, in certain cases, to envelop the vessel in which the ORMUS material is contained, causing it to become weightless or at least to reduce in weight. Hudson reports a crucible becoming weightless when heated to catalytic temperature. ORMUS also reportedly produce super-fluidity under certain conditions. I have observed this effect both when the precipitate is suspended in water and with the dried powder. Also I have noticed that powders made from microclusters found in nature produce this effect.

### Examples of ORMUS Characteristics

When suspended in water, ORMUS tends to move away from the edge of a bowl when the water is poured out. When the suspension is in a bottle, the slightest turn, no matter how slow or minute, causes the precipitate to climb up the sides of the bottle leaving a depression in the center of the precipitate.

**This picture shows several different ORMUS materials in bottles. From observation, one can see that these substances seem to climb the sides of the bottle leaving a depression in the center which is an example of super-fluidity.**

Powders made from the precipitate or from certain ORMUS microclusters tend to act like liquid when agitated. They pour from a container like liquid and look like liquid when an object passes through them by producing ripples. When they are stirred, they tend to keep swirling for a short time when the stirrer is removed even though the powder is dry.

ORMUS also are reportedly able to undergo cold fission. If the high spin nucleus is disrupted it easily flies apart. The amount of energy able to cause this effect reported by Hudson is 10 electron volts rather than the traditional one million electron volts currently employed to produce fission.

Certain ORMUS such as rhodium have been reported by Hudson

and others to fission when dried in certain high energy conditions such as intense sunlight or intense magnetic fields. This effect produces (as described in Lawrence Gardner's book *Bloodline of the Holy Grail*) an explosion equaling many thousands of flash bulbs with essentially no blast. This experiment conducted by Hudson produced such a flash without disturbing a pencil balanced on end next to the flash and without burning the filter paper on which it was resting.

When ORMUS are subjected to an electrical arc of 5500 degrees Fahrenheit without a shield gas, they may undergo fusion, including the anode in the reaction, resulting in the disappearance of both the anode and the ORMUS in a flash of light and gamma radiation.

ORMUS containing microclusters have been noted to seemingly "burn" when placed within a strong vacuum. However, this may not in fact be an oxygen reduction reaction. This reaction is able to sustain itself within the vacuum without oxygen or other gasses. It is very likely that some of the other molecules within the microcluster are being transmuted to light, heat and oxygen.

The ORMUS materials are often excellent catalysts, especially those whose parent material is a good catalyst such as rhodium, osmium, iridium, platinum, and palladium. It has come to my attention through my work however that these substances are actually not acting as a catalyst at all. Ancient peoples used these substances to transmute certain base metals. The most fabled is the case of the alchemists who transmuted lead to gold with the use of the Philosopher's Stone. They did not do this for profit. It was no more than a way to test the material to see if it was ready for ingestion. The early Vedic peoples of India used to transmute gold to mercury and then back to gold in the white power form in order to test it for consumption. It has been shown through research that carbon is easily transmuted to oxygen when it comes in contact with certain ORMUS materials heated to a temperature of 950 degrees Fahrenheit. This effect is priceless where the environment is concerned.

The transmutation abilities of ORMUS materials can remove

98% of all products of combustion. One such experiment conducted, which I witnessed, entailed routing the exhaust of a coal fired furnace back to the combustion chamber so that no exhaust exited. This would normally starve the flame for oxygen resulting in a rather quick and smoky end to the fire. However, the coke (coal dust) was salted with microclusters containing high amounts of ORMUS and the fire continued to burn brightly and well without smoke. The transmutation of carbon to oxygen within the combustion chamber was able to keep the fire oxygenated even without an effective exhaust to the combustion chamber. This should be impossible but it worked every time. I have proposed that the process is transmutation rather than catalytic since ORMUS are inert and unable to become involved in chemical reactions. However, due to their energy fields, they do have a quantum effect which can cause the number of electrons within certain atoms to change, thus causing a transmutation to occur.

### Elements That Form ORMUS

There are twelve elements which are able to go to the ORMUS state and remain stable in that state. The other elements that are able to be driven to the monatomic state are oxygen, hydrogen and iron. None of these remain stable, with the possible exception of iron which can in certain cases be maintained in the monatomic state by associating with other ORMUS materials. Even monatomic oxygen and hydrogen can be produced to form a gas called "water gas" or "Brown's Gas" that remains stable long enough to be used for its miraculous effects. However, it will eventually drop to a lower electrical potential and begin to make molecular bonds. The elements we are most concerned with here are those of the platinum group which can be reduced to the mon- or di-atomic state and become stabilized in that condition by their high spin nuclei.

The following is a the Periodic Table
showing the atomic number of the 12 ORMUS forming elements
listed below the table.

| | | | | | | | | | | | | | | | | | |
|---|---|---|---|---|---|---|---|---|---|---|---|---|---|---|---|---|---|
| H 1 | Hydrogen is not really a group I element | | | | | | | | | Inert elements or Noble gases | | | | | | | He 2 |
| Li 3 | Be 4 | Group I or alkali metal elements / Group II or alkaline earth elements | | | | | | Group VII or halogens | | | | B 5 | C 6 | N 7 | O 8 | F 9 | Ne 10 |
| Na 11 | Mg 12 | | | Transition elements | | | | | | | | Al 13 | Si 14 | P 15 | S 16 | Cl 17 | Ar 18 |
| K 19 | Ca 20 | Sc 21 | Ti 22 | V 23 | Cr 24 | Mn 25 | Fe 26 | Co 27 | Ni 28 | Cu 29 | Zn 30 | Ga 31 | Ge 32 | As 33 | Se 34 | Br 35 | Kr 36 |
| Rb 37 | Sr 38 | Y 39 | Zr 40 | Nb 41 | Mo 42 | Tc 43 | Ru 44 | Rh 45 | Pd 46 | Ag 47 | Cd 48 | In 49 | Sn 50 | Sb 51 | Te 52 | I 53 | Xe 54 |
| Cs 55 | Ba 56 | Lu 71 | Hf 72 | Ta 73 | W 74 | Re 75 | Os 76 | Ir 77 | Pt 78 | Au 79 | Hg 80 | Tl 81 | Pb 82 | Bi 83 | Po 84 | At 85 | Rn 86 |
| Fr 87 | Ra 88 | Lr 103 | Db 104 | Jl 105 | Rf 106 | Bh 107 | Hn 108 | Mt 109 | 110 | 111 | 112 | 113 | 114 | 115 | 116 | 117 | 118 |

Elements #110-118 have not been made yet
or have not yet been recognized by the
scientific community

| Lanthanide series | La 57 | Ce 58 | Pr 59 | Nd 60 | Pm 61 | Sm 62 | Eu 63 | Gd 64 | Tb 65 | Dy 66 | Ho 67 | Er 68 | Tm 69 | Yb 70 |
|---|---|---|---|---|---|---|---|---|---|---|---|---|---|---|
| Actinide series | Ac 89 | Th 90 | Pa 91 | U 92 | Np 93 | Pu 94 | Am 95 | Cm 96 | Bk 97 | Cf 98 | Es 99 | Fm 100 | Md 101 | No 102 |

COBALT
NICKEL
COPPER
RUTHENIUM
RHODIUM
PALLADIUM
SILVER
OSMIUM
IRIDIUM
PLATINUM
GOLD
MERCURY

We will learn as we progress through this information, these materials are present to some degree everywhere throughout the earth. They are in the soil, the air, the water and in all living things. It is due to their inert structure that they remain unchanged after they are naturally created by volcanic, meteoric, and natural methods. They are then dispersed by the winds, the ocean currents, the flow of streams, and by the cycles of life. As will be seen later see in Chapter 12, the Emerald Tablet relates that the Earth is its nurse and it rides in the belly of the wind.

**Representations of Thoth/Hermes/Tjehuti,
who is credited with writing the Emerald Tablet.**

**A representation of the Emerald Tablet from
Heinrich Kunrath's Amphitheatrum sapientiae aeternae.**

# CHAPTER 4

## A Rose By Any Other Name

During the course of my research on the environmental catalyst, I, like Hudson, was drawn to the multitude of historical references to these materials. The information within these references became ever more apparent as I began to decode the iconography and colloquialisms of the translated ancient textual information. As I performed more experiments, I was able to understand more of the references to the subject matter. Eventually I came to realize that the ancient textual information held many secrets to the manufacture of ORMUS as well as an astounding alternate history of the human race.

With further decoding of many of the alchemical texts, I began to put the decoded procedures to the test and, after a great deal of trial and error, I met with success. Once I realized true success in the manufacture of these materials by the ancient methodology, I had the epiphany that all of the references to these materials must be based in reality and, if in fact these references are based in reality, then there must be other truths to be discovered within them. What is so exciting is that these very texts lead one to believe that our ancient history on this planet is not as we have been told by historians, our religions, or our scientists. We have an alternative history which, once the components are all considered congruently, albeit fantastic, makes much more sense than the stories we have been told.

In the course of this book, I will attempt to present a very brief overview of the multitude of historical references to ORMUS and related tales and information through the ages back to the origins of recorded history. I will relate the past importance of these substances and show you how and why the knowledge was lost.

## Names and References to ORMUS in Different Cultures

In the following sections we will learn about references and cultural names for the ORMUS in many different forms and preparations. The names we shall discuss are from many origins and many are translated into English as we are used to seeing them. Others will be offered in the original language in which they were coined, if we are used to seeing them in that native form. For example, *ambrosia* is the Greek food of the Gods. It is a Greek word yet we are used to seeing it in this form and so it will be listed as *ambrosia*. Many of the names that are listed below will be very familiar as one reads through the list. Additionally, there will be stories, lore, word origins and other information offered in conjunction with the various listed names to help the reader get a sense of the history concerning each name. Finally, some of the alternate historical information which can be gleaned from various texts will be offered in order to present the references in their true light.

## Alchemical References: Renaissance, Medieval, Middle Ages

### The Elixir Of Life
This is an alchemical term from the Middle Ages for the famed Philosopher's Stone in liquid form and in water suspension. The early Alchemists would prepare various elixirs from the stone such as the White and Red Lion elixir, the Morning Star, The White Dove and the Green Lion among many others. The Elixir Of Life, used for spiritual purposes as well as for life extension and health, was among the simplest of elixirs to prepare as it was a simple suspension of the prepared Philosopher's Stone powder in pure water.

### Philosopher's Stone
The origins of this name utilizing word **Stone** refers to the ORMUS compounds' ability to withstand any temperature without becoming consumed. It was sought after by the early philosophers/alchemists as the essence of life to be used as a bodily supplement for life extension and rejuvenation. The philosopher grew well beyond normal in his mental and intuitive capabilities as a result of ingesting the stone. Sometimes the Philosopher's Stone was referred to as the "*Highward Fire-stone*" from the Aramaic **Shem an na** which suggests the stone's

36

ability to elevate the user in consciousness. The word highward in ancient Canaan was Shem, the same word used for name, brilliant, bright or rising fame, and the conical or mound shape of the stone that was prepared in a crucible. For this reason **Shem an na** could be translated in many different ways. The word Shem will be explored in greater length in Chapters 5 and 6.

It is not known for sure which of the twelve ORMUS elements were employed to create the Philosopher's Stone. The element that is most often discussed in philosophical texts is gold; however there is some speculation that rhodium and iridium were the most prized for the extension of life. Gold on the other hand was employed for the expansion of awareness, consciousness, mental capacity and access to the spiritual realm. Due to its inherent ability to stimulate and open the pineal gland, gold was most often used to make elixirs that would bring about extreme ESP (Extra Sensory Perception) in the user.

The Philosopher's Stone was also prepared as an actual stone that could be held or mounted in jewelry. The stone in this form was a very strong glass of the ORMUS and was utilized to aid the alchemist in focusing mental/spiritual powers. The Philosopher's Stone in this capacity was a receiver of conscious energy, a transmitter of the alchemist's psychic energies as well as an amplifier.

### White Dove
In the making of the elixir, the early alchemist often used a dove feather to skim the film from the cooking "prima materia" ( first matter) during the initial stages of the manufacturing process. Since the resulting powder is snow white and since the dove feather used was also always white, the resulting powder was commonly called the white dove. The dove was also a representation of peace and higher consciousness.

### The Phoenix

The story of *The Phoenix and the Fire Stone* describes the Phoenix which is reduced to ashes only to be reborn more beautiful than before. The Phoenix which rises as white powder gold is the end result of the alchemical work, the ORMUS of gold. The Phoenix and the Fire Stone is an alchemical fire process which employs a forge and produces white ORMUS powder. During the mid-stages of the process, red powder gold was produced from which the white powder gold would ultimately be made. The Red Gold as it was called, later to be called Red Lion, was in itself a very valuable substance and had many uses. The Starfire made the king the Malkuth and the queen the Rose of Sharon. The Red Gold was associated with *Starfire* which we will learn later, was made from the lunar essence of the Anunnaki priestess. The Red Lion of course was not Starfire but since it produced some of the same effects and looked exactly the same as the dried and powdered Starfire, it was thus regarded as the lunar female essence.

### The Red Lion

The Red Lion was the name given to a particular stage of the ORMUS development of gold. During the gold ORMUS manufacturing process, the gold goes through many stages of development and changes in color from yellow to black to red to light green/gray and finally to snow white. Sometimes the process was halted at the red stage and the resulting red precipitate was washed. This substance was then put through an additional alchemical procedure in order to strengthen and charge it. The resulting red powder was used as Red Gold or Red Lion. The scarlet/brown powder was often dissolved in wine and was considered a powerful medicine. Since Red Gold is not fully ORMUS nor is it metallic gold, it can set foot in both the world of the ORMUS atom and the world of the molecule. It possesses a low grade form of the ORMUS energetic field yet it can do chemistry and so it may act as a leash for attaching higher spin grade ORMUS to molecules for biological transport. The chemistry of Red Lion is not well understood. It possesses the ability to cause the recipient to function with a high level of psychic ability. Perhaps the most astounding of its fabled side effects was described in the book *The Red Lion* by Maria Szepes. In *The Red Lion*, an alchemist's apprentice (Hans Burgner), in his fervor to become an alchemist, kills his Magister Edward Anselmus Rochard and steals the Red Lion. He later takes the Red Lion and, as a result, is subjected to remembering each past life immediately upon each incarnation. In his case, the first few lives proved very difficult to deal with due to his ill deeds. He eventually becomes adept and achieves the stone after becoming a student to Comte De Saint Germain. This book, although in my opinion a poor translation, is nevertheless a must read for anyone considering the ingestion of the Red Lion elixir.

### Green Lion
The Green Lion is the same as described above except it is made of copper and/or nickel. Since early gold was not pure but was usually a mix of copper, silver and gold (termed electrum) as well as other platinum group metals in lesser quantities, it would often go through the green phase due to copper and or nickel content. The Alchemists of the Middle Ages prized the Green Lion as a gentle cure-all.

A bottle containing liquid Green Lion is shown, and is a beautiful blue/green color. Also notice the super-fluid characteristics. Green Lion can be turned into a sky blue stone with ample amounts of heat under clean conditions.

### White Powder of Gold

The white powder of gold is as previously described. When the gold is taken all the way to the high spin orbitally rearranged state it forms a snow white powder that is the purest and most noble form of gold. All of the platinum group metals that will go to the high spin state, twelve in all, will form a white powder if completely taken to the ultimate high spin state.

### Arcanum

Sometimes the alchemists referred to the Philosopher's Stone as the Great Arcanum, or the greatest secret, as it was indeed kept a secret among the initiate and adept philosophers. Only one knowing the language of the philosopher could decode the secret information and learn the real message of the coded information to learn if the text was truth or a sophist's ruse designed to detour the fool-hearted. Other Alchemical names and references include Lapis excelsius, Lapis elixir, Lapis philosophorum, Morning star and White stone.

### Ormus, Orme or Ormes

Interestingly, this name was given to the ORMUS well before

Hudson coined the title of his patent ORMES. The word origin means tree and may refer to the tree of life. During his research, Hudson found a biblical prophecy that stated that in the end days God would give the knowledge of the manna that had been taken away back to the people. It would be revealed through a later day David who would be a farmer (which David Hudson is) and that he would be a descendant of the line of David. Hudson incidentally checked his family tree to find that he in fact was related to the De Anjou family which is supposedly within the Davidic line. **"The farmer shall plant the tree (ORMES) of life and the new nation will become as a nation of priests."** Only the priests of Israel were allowed to take the sacred bread or manna except during the exodus and under other stressful situations where the manna might aid in survival. Also, it should be added that I have unwitting begun to fulfill the above prophecy by creating a nation of priests. As we will read later, Melchizedek was the priest who offered the shem manna and wine as a sacrament. Later, Jesus (Yeshua) was to be ordained after the Order of Melchizedek. The sacrament of Yeshua was the same as that of Melchizedek.

*I myself for some time have been a Melchizedek priest and also offer the same sacrament. I have acquired an anciently written Corporation Sole from a dear friend from which the priesthood can operate. The corporation society* **(The Temple of Melchizedek)** *seeks to make its priests true Ambassadors of Peace with ambassadorial status throughout the world. The Ancient and Sovereign Order of Melchizedek will exist as a nation unto itself and therefore become a nation of priests doing good works and offering the true sacrament of Melchizedek and Yeshua. I did not consider the implications when I first started the project; it simply dawned on me during the writing of this book. Anyone interested in learning more about the priesthood and* **The Ancient and Sovereign Order of Melchizedek,** *can go to the TempleofMelchizedek.com for more information.*

## Bread of the Covenant
Jesus (Iesus/Yeshua Ben Yoseph) describes himself as the manna from heaven to be consumed in order to live forever in spirit. Yet the ORMUS manna is offered in the last supper to the

41

apostles in the age old Starfire Ceremony of the Davidic line which was passed from Melchizedek or (Malachu Tzedeque) of Abraham's time through the Davidic line which entailed the consumption of bread and wine. Textual evidence strongly suggests that the bread was no ordinary bread. It was most likely the ORMUS of gold and was made of fine White Powder Gold. This bread was always made by the alchemist, priest or goldsmith; it was never made by a baker. For instance when God ordered Bezaliel to build the Ark of the Covenant, he made all sorts of golden items to be placed inside of the ark. Among these items was the "bread" of the covenant that he was given explicit instructions on how to make. However, Bezaliel was a goldsmith, not a baker.

It is also important to note that when people consumed unleavened bread, which is to say bread that does not rise and become airy or fluffy but rather, due to having no added yeast or levening, remains flat or dense, they could at some early time have been referring to the shem manna cake. When baked on a stone, brick, paddle or any other flat surface, the wet manna dough would simply dry out and would not rise. When prepared this way, manna powder forms a tasteless pithy feeling lightweight cake. The cake may feel in the hand like a chunk of Styrofoam. Amazingly, if that same lightweight cake is taken up to high temperatures, it will form a stone of smaller size yet will be greatly heavier than the original cake. Due to the tastelessness of the cake, spices or fragrances were sprinkled atop the cakes before they were cooked. Often frankincense (a gum resin used in perfumes and incense) was used to scent the cakes by crumbling the ambers into a dust and sprinkling it over the cakes before they were cooked. Of course leavening would have no effect on the white powder of gold and so it was not used. There is some speculation on my part that it was a sometime practice to employ the use of egg white to help hold the powder in a cake. The egg white would first be whipped into a meringue and then the powder would be folded in. Cooked over low heat, the cake would emerge light and fluffy and could be eaten without crumbling. The rituals of the consumption of unleavened bread and Starfire comprised the Eucharist feast ceremony, or as it is most commonly known, The Last Supper.

## White Bread, Sacred Bread, Unleavened Bread, Bread of The Presence of God, Bread of Life, Divine Bread, Light Bread, Show Bread

All of these types of bread were at one time made of ORMUS of electrum. There are countless references to show that these substances were made of white powder or flour made from gold or in some cases other metals of the platinum group. In Egypt and in Qumran the symbols used for light and for these special breads were often interchangeable. And in the Dead Sea Copper Scroll listing all of the riches stored in the temple, these symbols are all referenced by the symbol for gold. In Egypt the light bread, which looked like a conical cake due to the fact that it was baked in an alchemical crucible, was said to be the food of the light body or the Ka body. It was this very food that was said to bring light to the Ka and help the Ka body flow light. It was said that the body needed to be fed in order to live and that the same was true for the light body. However, the light body had to have special food which was the light bread.

### Shem Manna

This name goes back to Sumerian times when Melchizedek offered Abraham the temple bread and wine. This was described as the Highward Fire Stone. The word *Melchizedek* was a title meaning righteous king. The word Melchi is a form of *Malkuth*, *Malcus/Malchus*, and *Melik* all meaning King or kingdom or my king. The important point to make is that the *Malkuth* was also a state of high mind, enlightenment and high intuition caused by the Starfire usage that a king of that time had to reach in order to be a king of the people. A remnant of this meaning remains in Hebrew as one translation for "malkuth" being counselor, as in a very wise person or person of high mental capacity. The word *Zedek*, *Zoduk* or *Tzedeque* meant righteous. In Phoenician this was *sidik* or **sydik**. However, in old Sumerian and Canaanite times, this was paramount to calling someone a saint and this word or title was only given to the highest of priests.

Melchizedek was also the king of Salem, which was not a place, rather, it was the Semitic word for peace. So, Melchizedek was the enlightened righteous priest king of peace. The Judaic sect of the Essenes, who were the record keepers and the keepers of the gnosis, long held that Father Shem, son of Noah, was the great Melchizedek. It is said that the Semitic or Shemitic peoples of this language group are so named after Shem. For eons and in many regions, both the bread and the crucible conical shape itself has been referred to as a Shem. This gives rise to the name Shem Manna, or the "what is it of Shem". Shem was the great Melchizedek who offered the Shem Manna as a sacrifice rather than to sacrifice animals as was the common practice of the day. Later Jesus would be named a priest after the order of Melchizedek as he too did not believe in the sacrifice of God's wonderful creatures and therefore offered the Shem Manna and wine as his sacrament in the way of Melchizedek.

Another interpretation of the word shemanna might be borne by breaking the word up differently such as Shem an na translating to the brilliant highward or ascending stone of An or Anu. Also considering that the word Anu also translates as heaven in many ancient languages of the Middle East and Egypt as well, Shem anna might also translate to something like the brilliant highward stone of heaven. The word anna in many instances is just a different pronunciation of the word anu. We find this in the title *Mary Anna Ishtar* meaning Ishtar beloved of Anu.

**Shar an na**
Also identified as the stone of the orbit of heaven or the deity *An* or *Anu*. Anu was the King of the planet *Nibiru* and a shar is a divine year of 3600 Earth years which equals one orbit of the planet *Nibiru*. A more direct translation of Sharanna might be 'the orbit of An'.

**Keeper of The Secrets, Spittle of The Father, Semen of The Father, Manna, Mufktz, Golden Tear of the Eye of Horus, Bread of The Presence of God, That Which Issues From the Mouth of The Creator**
These terms for the ORMUS supplements were inspired by the Egyptians. They used the ORMUS in multiple ways and

therefore had many words and terms for the many forms of ORMUS substances, many of which were not intended for ingestion. The glass made of gold ORMUS was sometimes used to charge the light body or Ka, which is equivalent to the life force. It was also often called a shem (not to be confused with light bread which was often likewise called shem) but may have also been referred to as *Mufktz, shefa, shew bread, or light bread* which was designed for ingestion unlike the glass shem. Both the bread cake and the glass stone were called shem due to the fact that they were both made in a crucible and were of a shem shape. It is interesting to note that the bread could be made into a glass, and once it turned to glass, it would gain back a large portion of its original weight as gold. However, as bread it would be light as a feather. Yet as proof of the difference in the weight of ORMUS as a glass in comparison to its weight as a powder, the glass or stone of the ORMUS can be panned just like gold or gems from other substrate (gravel, sand, silt) as it is very heavy. In the bread form, it would simply float away in the current if one were to try to pan it out of the sand of a river bank for example. Additionally, the glass of ORMUS when made from the powder looses very little of its volume. It is miraculous how something can gain weight and density without changing very much in volume when heated to the state of vitrification.

**Ben-Ben**
*Ben-Ben* was said to have been the cry of the ***Bennu*** bird at the beginning of creation. The meanings and ideas associated with the word Ben-Ben are complex; however we will attempt to greatly simplify this for our purposes. The Egyptian pyramid capstone was gold glass and the word "ben" means gold. So the capstone was "gold" gold, or the purest form of gold. The gold glass can appear from white and opaque to a clear and slightly golden color. Just as all other ORMUS gold, ORMUS in its glass form may also be prompted to produce a beautiful bluish white glow. I believe that the glow is ultraviolet light escaping from the ORMUS as all other frequencies of light are fully retained within the stone flowing from atom to atom via the crystalline lattice energetic structure. Pyramid art has depicted the great Pyramid of Giza producing rays of light like a beacon or lighthouse. Many ancient Egyptian and Sumerian texts speak of

the pyramid's guiding beacons. The gold glass was also employed by the alchemists of the Knights Templar to produce much of the window glazing of the Notre Dame Cathedral which was dedicated to "Our Lady" Mary Magdalene. Many other cathedrals windows of France were made of the very same substance. This substance was the famed *Spiritus Mundi* which translates as the inspired breath or spirit of the universe, or world, and is most often said to mean spirit of the world.

## Milk of the Goddess, Milk of the Fairies or Shidh, Milk of Morgan La Fey, Food of Tuatha Da Dannon

These references are Celtic. Probably the most well known example of Fairies' Milk comes from the tale which describes how Cu Chullain saves a fairy's life. He is offered a reward of his choosing and he requests only a tits measure of milk as his reward. Does it not seem particularly odd that Cu Chullain, who himself was half-Fairy, would make such a request when he could have had anything his heart could desire? The answers are to be found in the Sumerian story of Gilgamesh who was himself half-God. It seems to be a common theme all over the world that the sons of Gods or the Anunnaki, would most often inherit a life span much closer to that of their human ancestry. This prompted most of these often historical figures to search for ways to gain back their immortal status. So, just as Gilgamesh went on a search for his immortality, so too did Cu Chullain desire the long life of his Faery heritage. This theme is played out over and over in many ancient traditions about the world.

### Recent Terms

**Monatomic elements**: Elements of singular atoms

**Monoatomic elements**: Elements of singular atoms, different spelling

**White Powder Gold**: Referring to the white powder form of monatomic-state materials

**Orme**: Egyptian word for tree

**Ormus**: Named after a great Alchemist and also word for tree, stands for Orbitally Rearranged Metallic Unit Structure.

**ORME**: David Hudson's patent: Orbitally Rearranged Monatomic Elements

**M-state**: Monatomic state

**High Spin Materials**: Referring to the high spin state of the nucleus in a monatomic atom

**Aqua Vitae**: Water of life

**Elixir of Life**: Liquid form of m-state materials

*The Alchemist* by Cornelis Pietersz Bega
(Image is in the public domain)

# CHAPTER 5

## Manna and the Golden Calf

Manna is perhaps the most well known name for ORMUS. Manna is a Hebrew word which translates as a question meaning simply, What is it? or What is this? This word comes from the Egyptian equivalent which means exactly the same thing. In the *Papyrus of Ani, The Egyptian Book of the Dead*, written by Thoth/Tjehuti/Hermes Trismigistus, the Pharaoh is noted as asking certain questions before passing on to Khert Netjer, the Egyptian concept of the afterlife. In the earliest form of this text, the questions always began with What is this?, and then the answer was given in each instance.

The *Papyrus of Ani, The Egyptian Book Of The Dead*, describes the process of the Egyptian Rite Of Passage at the end of which the Pharaoh would join the gods. An example of some textual excerpts from the *Papyrus of Ani* follow:

"What is this?"

"It is the horizon of his father Tem. I have made an end of my shortcomings, and I have put away my faults."

"What is this?"

"It is the cutting of the navel string of the body of the Osiris the scribe Ani, whose word is true before all the gods, and all his faults are driven out."

"What is this?"

"It is the purification on the day of his birth. I am purified in my great double nest which is in Hensu on the day of the offerings of the followers of the Great God who dwelleth therein."

"What is this?"

"It is Ra-stau, that is to say, it is the gate to the South of Nerutef, and it is the Northern Gate of the Domain. Now, as concerning the Island of Maati, it is Abtu. Others, however, say that it is the way by which Father Tem travelleth when he goeth forth to Sekhet-Aaru, which produceth the food and sustenance of the gods who are their shrines. Now the Gate Tchesert is the Gate of the Pillars of Shu, that is to say, the Northern Gate of the Tuat. Others, however, say that the Gate of Tchesert is the two leaves of the door through which the god Tem passeth when he goeth forth to the eastern horizon of the sky. O ye gods who are in the presence [of Osiris], grant to me your arms, for I am the god who shall come into being among you."

The passage refers to a Pharonic rite of passage which entailed taking massive quantities of manna over a nine month period preceded by a forty day fast. Now with the understanding that the repeating question (what is this) is the Manna, or light bread, the food of the gods, read the passages once more to have the meaning more clearly reveal itself.

## Exodus

During the Exodus, Moses fed manna to the Israelites in order to help them endure the rigors of desert travel. The Israelites were fed manna in two different forms. The first form was a natural variation of micro-clusters which sometimes occurs in nature under certain conditions and results as a precipitate of naturally occurring polysaccharides. The explanation is quite extensive; however it is important to say that certain plants which have large amounts of polysaccharides are high in monatomic rhodium. Interestingly, these are the most well known of the healing plants such as aloe, jewel weed and plantain among others. There is a type of shrub that proliferates on the Sinai Peninsula that, under certain conditions, exudes white fluffy precipitate chips. This may have been the manna picked up from the ground by the Israelites.

The second type of manna taken by the Israelites was made more obscure in the Bible possibly due to some agenda expressed by the Hebrews. Parallel textual information written from the Israelite's perspective tells a different story that clears up the Mount Sinai incident related in *The Book of Exodus* which was written from a Hebrew standpoint. Before one attempts to understand this explanation, it is firstly required that one comes to grips with the fact that the Israelites were very different peoples from the Hebrews at the time of the exodus. They did not have the same culture nor did they even believe in the same

God. The Israelites believed in Adon (the Egyptian equivalent to Aton) which means simply "Lord". This god was an all encompassing mind without face or name and was the creator of all things and the manifestation of love. Aten, as this godhead was called by the Egyptians, was not a sun god contrary to common belief. Aten rather came into the heart, the mind and permeated all things. The sun was used as the best possible metaphor for Aton/Adon since its light is warm and brings life to all the Earth and its energy permeates all things. The Hebrews believed in El Shaddai (meaning lofty one of the mountain) who was noted as a storm god of wrath and vengeance and was described as being like a man having a house, a wife, a body, two arms and legs, and was most of all a very jealous being willing to punish anyone who worshiped another god or who transgressed any of his laws. These two godheads were quite different beings who were later amalgamated into one: Jehovah or Yahweh.

The Exodus accounts in the Bible relate that while camped at the base of Mount Sinai, which was really called Mt. Horeb or Desert Mountain, the Israelites ran amuck. They celebrated a bit too much and went out and made a golden calf idol to worship while Moses was up on the mountain. Moses came down from the mountain with the tablets bearing the Ten Commandments and, in his fury, he broke the tablets saying the Israelites were not worthy to receive them. Then something odd is related in Biblical scripture. The golden calf was then taken by Moses up to the mountain and burnt in the fire to ashes and put in the water for the Israelites to drink. Sir Lawrence Gardner relates in his Grail talks that gold burned in a fire produces molten gold, not ash. Might there have been some other process that was followed? This was likely so.

In other non-Biblical texts it becomes quite clear what transpired. The Israelites were very devout Adon followers and they neither believed in nor was there any such notion as a calf god to them. They, unlike their Hebrew forefathers and cousins, did not believe in animal sacrifice. Rather, in their elation they created a sacrament effigy which resembled a calf made of all of their riches in order to offer their riches as sacrifice to Adon. In the Bible it is related that the mountain was smoking as if a giant forge was operating. Indeed there was a forge on the mountain which, in the late 1800's, was discovered by Sir William Flinders Petrie of The Palestine Exploration Fund during an archeological expedition in the Sinai. There, Petrie found an entire temple complex dedicated to the goddess Hathor. Discoveries of metallurgical crucibles, depictions of light bread offerings, and a stone coffer full of a mysterious white powder made it quite clear that the temple was an alchemical workshop of sorts.

The golden calf was taken to the mountain and sacrificed to Adon, to whom a dedication in stone was made by the famed Ramses who, as related in the Bible, was supposed to have been a supporter of the Egyptian pantheon and an opposer of YHWH. The forge operating there was most likely an alchemical forge used to make ORMUS since there were no discoveries of iron, copper or malachite typical to a smelting operation. The alchemical result was of course white powder which to the Israelites resembled ashes yet it was the very same gold (electrum) of which the calf had been made. This manna was then placed in the water for the Israelites to drink, not as a punishment as suggested in the bible, but rather as a supplement to help sustain them in the desert. Undoubtedly, Moses had given an order to gather gold, but in his absence, the Israelites fashioned the calf as a proper sacrifice at the behest of the prophetess Miriam. When Moses returned to find the rabble, he was not angry about the calf effigy. Rather, Miriam had insisted that the commandments brought down were not to the liking or belief of the Israelites so they were rejected and subsequently destroyed. Miriam was locked away for seven days and when the Israelites would not change their minds, she was released.

Moses then went back into the mountain and compiled a new set of rules that were more to the taste of the Israelites. The new rules were more Egyptian in their origin and so more familiar to the Israelites. In fact, they were taken from spell 125 of the *Papyrus of Ani*. Remember, it was Moses' job to bring together two very different peoples and so he had to find ways to unite them in doctrine and in ceremony and later the two God-heads were rolled into one. However it can be seen in the story of

Exodus that the Israelites seemingly changed their character greatly during their sojourn and were even exceedingly cruel to many people of their cousin cities. It seems as if there occurred some sort of extreme change in the doctrines and beliefs of the Israelites during their time in the desert. It would be apparent that the Israelites started out as believers in Adon and then became believers of YHWH after the Mount Horeb/Sinai episode.

Here it is important to briefly revisit the golden calf idol episode of the book of Exodus. First, we might explore the meaning of a golden calf at that time. The primary representation of the pharaoh was of a golden calf or a calf of the sun. This epithet was granted to the pharaoh, because when the king was consecrated, his holy mother became Hathor the cow goddess and his father was Ra the golden sun god. Thus, the pharaoh would be a Golden Calf. In fact, the pharaoh was the only old dynasty Egyptian god to be depicted as a golden calf. An excerpt from the Pyramid text Utterance 485 relates the pharaoh Pepi as a golden calf.

"Pepi comes to thee, O Ra, a calf of gold, born of heaven. I have come to
you Ra, a calf of gold born in the sky, a fatted calf of gold...
O Horus, do not leave me boatless.

Unless the Israelites were figuratively sacrificing the Pharaoh to the alchemical fires, it does not make sense that they would be paying him homage so soon after escaping the clutches of Egypt. However, as has been discovered in modern times, the temple complex atop Mount Horeb in the provence called Serabit El Khadim was in fact dedicated to the Goddess Hathor who would be figuratively considered the Cow Goddess Mother of the Pharaoh. Perhaps it was symbolic in some way for the Israelites to offer the Son of Hathor to Adon in Hathors' own house as a sort of closure to an episode of Israelite history.

Additionally, Enlil of Shinar/El-Shaddi of Abraham, was often denoted as the bull of heaven. On occasion he would be represented as a bull or a calf. This would not have been the intent of the Israelites for they believed in Adon/Aten the Lord who had no earthly representation. There is an obscure letter to Akhenaten from a Canaanite prince referring to him as the Golden Calf. So if Moses and Akhenaten were one and the same, the calf effigy may have likely been constructed in his honor as a pharaoh, to offer up as a sacrifice to Adon. At any rate, it is ridiculous to believe that the calf was manufactured by the Israelites in order to worship it as a false god or idol. It was most obviously a sacrament in effigy to be offered up to Adon and burned in the fires in the place of a real living calf. At this time in history, the sacrifice of a real calf would have been an abomination. It was then the job of Moses to see that it was transformed into the Mfktz or Manna to be used as sustenance for the long desert journey.

**Moses and Akhenaten**

The first to propose that Moses and Akhenaten were perhaps the same individual was Sigmund Freud. It is important here to draw on the notion that either the biblical Moses and Akhenaten were one and the same or they most certainly knew one another. I for one think that the parallels are far too great for them not to have been the same person. Akhenaten, for those who may be unfamiliar with him, was the Amarna period King of Egypt who completely changed the state religion from Ra/Amon worship to the worship of Aten. He changed his name from Amenhotep (Amun is pleased) to Akhenaten (Servant of Aten). Aten is depicted in the Amarna period art as a solar disk with rays streaming down to all earthly things. On the ends of the rays of light there are small hands that reach into all of the objects in the relief. Held in some of the hands there will be seen the Ankh which symbolizes life, indicating that the light of the sun offers life to all things.

For the simple reason that Aten is represented as a solar disk, Egyptologists have always referred to Aten as a sun god. This however is far from the truth. One only has to ask one question in order to begin to understand that this notion of Aten as a sun god is incorrect. The question is, if Aten was in fact a sun god, then why would a pharaoh risk everything as a heretic just in order to replace one sun god (Amun/Ra) with another sun god (Aten)? When reading texts relating to Aten, it becomes quickly apparent that Aten was in fact a nameless energy which warmed the soul, granted life and rose in the heart like the sun rises in the sky. The sun was the best possible metaphor for Aten and was itself a creation of the energy of Aten. When reading scribal texts of the great Thoth (Tjehuti or Djehuti), the Egyptian serpent god who sported the ibis head mask, one learns that Aten was a God of the cosmos whose energy was masculine and feminine. Thoth teaches that the Aten energy permeates and creates all things. This energy is consciousness, love and light. Thoth often relates that if one but receives a single ray of the light of Aten (this relates to understanding just the smallest bit of the Aten consciousness), then one shall be released from the fetters of cosmic law, thus gaining the power to overcome the aging process and the confines of space and time at will. From this scant bit of information we can quickly see that the suggestion that Aten was simply a sun god is very unrealistic.

Another direction we can look to find the true nature of Aten/Aton/Adon/Atum/Atun etc. is to read the Corpus Hermeticum and like materials. It has been passed down through history that first Pythagoras in the fourth century BC and then Plato in the third century BC went to Egypt and studied with the priests from the books of Thoth/Hermes. It is said that these great Greek philosophers obtained all of their wisdom from the writings of Thoth. These philosophers brought back this knowledge and wisdom to Greece and began the Greek Hermetic Mystery Schools. This philosophy defines a God of all Gods and a god of the Cosmos referred to as Aton or Atum. If this god was considered a sun god, it would have rivaled Apollo the Greek sun god who was actually the equivalent of Ra Amun of Egypt. However, unlike in Egypt, the Greeks saw no contention between these two god heads even though the God Aton was associated with the warmth and life giving rays of the sun in Greece as well. It is apparent that the Greeks knew that the sun was not a god, but rather, that the sun was more or less the epithet or logo of Apollo due to its greatness. The sun for Aton was a metaphor which helped to exemplify the light and warmth of the Aton with the life of the true believer.

Also, as we will discuss, Moses along with others including Miriam was trained in the Egyptian mystery schools which are mostly hermetic in curriculum. As the Bible relates, Moses refers to God as the Law or the One Law prior to the exodus episode. The law of Moses can quickly and easily be likened to the Adon/Aten god of the cosmos which governed all natural law. It was the one consciousness and mind of all. It had no name or face and was the energetic control behind and within all physical phenomena. The name YHWH was not known to Moses until the Mt. Sinai episode and is obviously a separate entity and not the Adon Lord of the Cosmos or as Moses calls it in the Bible, the law. To learn more about Aten, one can read the texts attributed to Hermes/Thoth/Tjehuti/Thooti/Tehuti as well as the poems and tributes to Aten of the Armana period.

It is apparent that Aten is no sun god per se. Aten is rather a god of the universe. It is appropriate here to explain that Akhenaten (meaning Servant of Aten) had very close ties to the Israelites. His real father is not Pharaoh Amenhotep III but Reuel who arguably is one and the same as Amram the father of Moses. Akhenaten has Israelite family and friends and it would make sense that he would learn about their religion and customs as well. Since this is not a book about Moses/Akhenaten, I will say only that the parallels between the two are too astounding for them not to have been one and the same. This is a topic well covered by a plethora of other authors including Sigmund Freud.

Now, to relate back to the Mount Horeb incident, we can see that if Moses and Akhenaten are indeed the same person, then Moses would have been Pharaoh for a time. If Moses had been Pharaoh, then the golden calf that was offered by the Israelites might have been on his behalf. This would have been a way to acknowledge him as their King even though he had been rejected by Egypt. This subject is too broad to delve into here at length. There are a few books that the interested reader should explore including *Moses and Akhenaten* by Ahmed Osman, or *Genesis of The Grail Kings* by Laurence Gardner.

This is a typical example of the very amazing alternate history revealed when following this course of study. The information relayed here is only a fraction of the alternate history even concerning this one episode. This material is fodder for multiple volumes. It is important here to mention that one of the most helpful texts that I have found for the manufacture of ORMUS was attributed to the very Miriam (the Beloved) previously mentioned who was the prophetess of the Israelites.

## Miriam and the First Mary

First, let us discover some important information concerning the name Mary. Many people believe that the name Mary is Hebrew but this is incorrect. The meaning of the name Mary is for some reason hidden, lost, or obscured in the Hebrew language and is said to mean "bitter" or "rebellious". However, the name Mary now and always has meant "beloved". For instance, in Egypt the name Mariamun means beloved of Amun and became shortened to the familiar name Miriam. Another such name is the full title of the Babylonian Goddess Ishtar (Mary Anna Ishtar) which means Ishtar Beloved of Annu. This name has become Mariana, Marian, Maryann (Beloved of An). There are many forms of the name Mary including Mary, Miri, Merry, Marri, Miriam, Maria, Mari, Mariana, Marieanne, Mariani (Beloved of Ani), Mariomni (beloved of many), Marion (of the Beloved), Marianum (beloved of the year), among others. The equivalent to Mary in other languages is Di. The name Di means beloved as well and is found in many of the same forms including Diana (beloved of Anu) Dianne (Beloved of An), and Deanna. Many of the Goddesses with the Mary epithet are one in the same as those with the Di epithet.

The first important Mary was the goddess Ishtar or Mariana. She was the Sumerian goddess of love and war. A cult of priestesses originated under her charge headed by her handmaiden Lilith. These were the first starfire priestesses who fed the early kings on their rich food of the matrix as their lunar essence was considered to be the supreme food of excellence and light which, we will later find, issues through the goddess from the universal matrix. Without their essences, the king could not become sovereign. This line of priestesses extended well into Egypt.

57

Eventually these priestesses were referred to as *The Beloved*. In Egyptian and in many other languages such as Sumerian, they were simply titled beloved and the word for beloved was Mary. Since the time of the well known Miri or Miriam, the title of Miri or Mary has been used to denote the beloved. The title was even picked up by the Catholic Church to be used by nuns as a title such as Sister Mary Martha, or Sister Mary Margaret, Sister Mary Joanna, and so forth. A nun would be called Sister until achieving a superior ranking at which time she would be referred to as Mother. In some non-Catholic traditions the female priest is referred to as Mother.

The mother of Jesus was married to the crowned Prince who was titled Joseph after Joseph the patriarch. Jesus had a sister titled Mary and he himself married a Mary. All of these Mary's were priestesses or princesses of the line from Mary Anna Ishtar tradition. To learn more on this subject and to obtain a slightly different perspective on this subject, read Lawrence Gardner's *Bloodline of the Holy Grail*.

Ishtar:

At the Gates of Ishtar

The first biblically important Mary was Miriam the Prophetess who was no doubt a Priestess of the matrilineal line extending down from the early priestesses of the Mary Anna Ishtar tradition. It is important here to realize that the Mary Priestess-ship was often held within close lines to the Kingship. Mary priestesses were frequently raised to the status of goddess and held in very high veneration. The sister-wife of the king, which would be a half sister or a close cousin, would usually be a Mary and it was from the Mary that the kingly succession would

59

proceed. Miriam the prophetess was a sister wife of Moses/Akhenaten. More importantly, she was a great alchemist and prophetess. At this time it was not often that one would find a female alchemist. Mary was highly revered by the Israelites, so much so in fact that they followed her advice rather than that of Moses. It was Miriam who incited the dissent at Mount Horeb because the new laws were not in keeping with the Israelites beliefs. Miriam was said to be full of wisdom and insight. She was able to tell the future, read thoughts and heal the sick. She taught alchemists of the day to make the white stone and the light bread. Though the Bible states that she was punished for inciting insurrection, she continued to be revered by the Israelites. If not for her, the commandments may have been very different from the Egyptian-based Ten Commandments which were presented the second time Moses came down from the mount.

It also may be considered that the Israelites started to take a turn away from their peaceful Adon support back to the support of the God of the Hebrews, El-Shaddi (also spelled Shaddai), or Lofty Mountain. During their generation-long sojourn in the Sinai desert, the Israelites became increasingly more war-like and wrathful at the behest of their God now called YHWH. It was YHWH who had directed the building of the ark to be used both as a weapon of war as well as a method to communicate his bidding to the Israelites. With such a powerful weapon, known to strike dead all who dared to approach without the proper clothing and preparation, the majority of the Israelites felt invincible. Moses, on the other hand, simply felt the necessity to finish what he had started. Most likely he now knew that the new godhead would not have him lead the people into the Promised Land as Moses would not have allowed them to so violently and mercilessly attack their cousins to claim Canaan. But it was El-Shaddi/YHWH who wished to reclaim the land of Canaan from the other deities worshiped there and the Israelites became his army.

Moses was told that he could not enter the Promised Land as a result of one small infraction against YHWH. At one point in the desert the people were dying of thirst. Moses saw fit to use the abilities that had been granted him to smite the rock with his rod that water might flow for the people to drink. For this he supposedly was disallowed to enter the Promised Land and was forced to live out his days in relative exile. This was not the action of the loving, life-giving, cosmic Adon who the Israelites had previously worshipped. This was not the action of the natural law which had been so well described by Moses. No indeed, this was the action of an Anunnaki godhead who was on the warpath to reclaim territory and he was not about to have the Priest King Moses daunt his success by curtailing the wrathful march of the newly hardened Israelites into the homeland, leaving a wake of destruction and death.

Did Moses stay behind alone? In fact he did not. A group of Adon supporters remained with him in the desert. Some actually remained in Egypt and never even joined the slow sojourn to Canaan. These were the predecessors to the Essenes and the Theraputae. The Theraputae continued to follow the teachings of Moses and supported the god of natural law, the Adon. The Theraputae became great healers and continued making manna for their sustenance. Later, during the peaceful reign of King Solomon in Jerusalem, additional remnants of Adon supporters began to surface. Eventually, these groups appeared to have survived by seeming to amalgamate their notions with the concept of YHWH. But by this time the God Enlil/El-Shaddi and all of the other Anunnaki had vacated, having finally achieved their mining quotas.

Eventually, most of the Adon supporters would live in desert communities outside of Jerusalem and the larger cities. These groups would become known as the **Essenes** and would include the **Nazareans** the **Jebusites** and the extreme ascetic group most often associated with the word Essene **The White Brotherhood**. It was from the Essene sect the Nazareans that Yeshua (Jesus) would come forth teaching once again the love-based doctrine of the Adon (Lord) and Law of the cosmos. The teachings of Yeshua had in part been the teachings of Moses and had been the teachings of Melchizedek before him in Abraham's time now only to come full circle and surface once again in its land of origin. It is discouraging that these teachings would so quickly become corrupted and overburdened by the power hungry agendas of the Pauline movement and the subsequent Holy Roman Empire. It is only now that these beautiful truths are beginning to surface once again to complete their cycle.

# CHAPTER 6

## Melchizedek, Shem and the Great Thoth

It was the great Amou Shem Galanna (Lord of the Light bread),
who passed on the knowledge of the bread to Shem who had
previously practiced the Starfire Ritual which entailed the
consumption of the Anunnaki High Priestess' menstrual extracts
mixed with wine. As it relates in the Bible, the human life span
was to be shortened by disallowing further consumption of
blood. For this reason, man was taught through Melchizedek the
usage and manufacture of a starfire replacement; the Shem-an-
nah. So who shall we say that this Lord of The Light Bread is
exactly? This question is answered by some scant information
offered in Sumerian/Babylonian and Canaanite texts. Without
delving into my assertions in great detail, I will say that we have
once again returned to the figure Thoth. In the region of Sumer,
the Great Thoth was known as Ningishziddha and as Hermes to
the Phoenicians. To further understand the connection of
Ningishziddha to Thoth, read Zechariah Sitchin's *Earth
Chronicles*.

As a serpent god, Ningishziddha was depicted as two serpents
entwined about a staff or pole. The pole represented the tree of
life while the serpents represented life, rejuvenation, knowledge,
and the knowledge of the essence or DNA. The staff of Hermes,
or what we know as the caduceus which is used as a symbol for
many branches of medicine, represents much the same as it is
comprised of entwined serpents writhing about the tree of life.
However, there are other features which are represented in the
caduceus imagery, the wings and the egg. These two symbols
are alchemical to the core and have many levels of meaning. On
a mundane level, the wings represent the sublimation while the
egg represents the vessel of Hermes which would hatch the stone
of the philosophers. On a higher level, the wings are the right
and left lobes of the cerebrum which through enlightenment
carry the pineal gland, the seat of the soul, represented by the
egg, on high to be exalted by spirit. So here in the staff we have

the basic alchemical principle of Hermes **"As above, so below"**. It was likely the great alchemist/scientist Thoth who passed on the secrets to man through Father Shem the Great Melchizedek as a replacement for the starfire which had been outlawed by Enlil the El-Shaddi.

### Shem

Now, it is time to further understand the word Shem and thus Melchizedek's actual name. We will start by giving the Hebrew definition of the word shem which simply means "name". As we read ancient texts, we begin to see that the word Shem is used in dozens of contexts and so it must mean more than simply *name*. And why on earth would one name a child Name? Because of this question, modern Hebrews assert that Shem's name "shem" actually means brown or tawny referring to his skin color. However, I can find absolutely no evidence of this meaning in ancient times. Upon asking myself these questions, I began to find out all that I could about the word shem which eventually brought me to a greater understanding of shem as a name as well as why the word shem was used to denote the light bread itself. Here is what I have learned.

Upon further study, we find the word shem to mean "fame". If one were to proclaim their fame, they would offer their Shem. It is also to be understood that the light of someone's name is a person's "fame", therefore, shem could also mean bright or brilliant fame. The naming of the king of the people, Bright Fame, became a custom in certain countries. Interestingly, my name is Robert which also means bright or brilliant fame, the name by which the kings of Scotts were called, as opposed to the kings of Scotland who were no more than kings of territory. Further, the word shem implies a bright fame that has risen above the rest or which has risen to heaven in honor or acceptance by God. Additionally, the word shem can mean "renown" and we could very well see that Shem would become renown as the forefather of all Semites after whom they were named.

Now we can begin to see why Shem was called Shem. He would

rise in bright fame above all others. He would be known throughout the land and the ages and was honored by men and beheld by his God. The shem shape derives from a stone monument upon which one's name and epitaph or fame would be engraved. This could be a grave monument or a monument proclaiming one's fame to the world. The shape of this type of monument was most often like that of a modern day grave stone which is shaped like an upside down U. Sometimes the monument was like an umphalus or dome-shaped stone. Both of these shapes, when depicted two-dimensionally in hieroglyphic form, look the same as an upside down U. Therefore this class of shapes became known as shems. Also, for a similar reason, the word shem was used to mean memorial. Stone signs that gave useful information were also known as shems. In fact, the modern word "sign" derives from the Greek sima which derives from sem or shem. From this we get the word semantic.

The word semen is often thought to mean seed, yet it actually translates to "name stay" or "fame stay". This refers to the decent of the family line which is inherent within the male essence (sem) and the word In or Inn (en) which means to reside, stay or inhabit. There were certain oils used in biblical times by kings and the elite for purposes of anointing. These special anointing oils were likened to the cherished semen and were called Shemen or shem-in. It is likely that semen was derived from this term although there is debate concerning this.

There is yet another meaning of the word shem which derives from the above meanings. Things that are brilliant are known as shems. Sometimes the sun is even referred to as shem, as in the Hebrew word for the sun, Shemmesh, which translates as "Name on Fire". The name of the Sumerian god Utu Shemash derives from a similar meaning. There are many modern words which derive from shem. Things that show forth light or glisten are said to "shimmer" (shem mer). Most jewels of ancient times were cabochon-style cuts. This shape is in itself dome-shaped and shines with light. For both their shape and their brilliance, these stones were called shems and in modern day are called gems which derived from the word shem.

The word "shame" is also connected to shem. It actually is the antithesis of shem and means to dishonor, defame, or disgrace. From this is also derived the word sham meaning false or counterfeit, not genuine or pretended.

Sometimes shem simply means stone or a stone that is used as a key to help correct something. This eventually became used as a masonry term. The shem in masonry was used to make things either level or to help other stones fit. The modern word for this term is "shim".

Since shem is connected with things that rise above all else, the word shem often simply means "on high" and is connected with the word Shanah which means "that which is highward". For this reason and due to the shape of the shem, Zechariah Sitchin often translates the word shem to mean rocket ship. Although I believe he is correct in certain circumstances, we can see here that shem can mean many other things. We can however see that a shiny dome-shaped object that rises into heaven *in a brilliance* would likely have been called a shem.

The Hebrew word for heaven, "Shamaim", derives from the Acadian word (Shem Ma Im), which means waters on high or highward waters. These waters referred to are the spiritual waters of chaos spoken of in the beginning of Genesis. From this word we also get the word Shaman which refers to someone who can harness the power of the heavenly waters or the heavenly **word** or **name** as in the beginning there was the word or name of God. Another relevant Hebrew word is Hashem which comes from Ha-Shem which is an epithet for God literally meaning "The Name" in modern Hebrew. We can see from all that we have discussed that it very well could mean a lot more than simply *The Name*. Hashem might refer to a being who resides on high in a brilliance, who is famous and renowned and if we dare not speak their name aloud, we call them "The Name" which might seem to say The One Name, or Greatest Name or The Word. The phrase could literally contain a multiplicity of meanings.

There were also a great people of the Middle East, possibly

originating in Malta, who were called the **Shem Su Hor.** They were well known in Egypt and were fabled to have built the *djed* towers which were instruments of great power. The name Shem Su Hor is said to mean "The Illuminated Ones" in Egypt while it can mean "Shining Ones" in other regions. This would connect this group to the **Anunaga** (Shining Ones). The word Anunaga was a later variation of the word Anunnaki. People with strong Anunnaki bloodlines were said to be filled with light. Most of these groups would, in one language or another, be referred to as shining or illuminated ones. Elves are known as Shining Ones. Even Noah was called a Shining One due to his light skin and hair and the appearance of being filled with light. For this reason, his father suspected that Noah had been fathered by one of the angels who at that time were the Anunnaki. Some traditions have it that Noah's real father was none other than Enki himself, the Great Lord of Earth and creator of the human work force. This can lend additional credence to why the name Shem was given to this one son of Noah who was also filled with light and looked like a Lofty One, which was what the Annunaki were often called by humans.

The Shem Su Hor were great and powerful priests. They were well known throughout the entire region from Babylon to Malta, to Egypt and beyond. Many Shem Su Hor skulls have been found in Malta and similar skulls have been found in many other places about the world. Compared with modern human skulls they are quite different anatomically. The braincase is much larger while the jaw is sturdier. The heads are elongated, just as the depictions of the heads of Pharaohs in ancient Egypt, suggesting a connection of sorts to these early dynasties. It is likely that Shem himself would have been considered a Shem Su Hor as was his father Noah.

To further describe the look of the Shem Su Hor master, Tjehuti tells us jokingly that once, when he introduced the house worker of Horus (Goa-omni) who was human to the priests of the north, she asked them in a defiant playful manner to "clasp their eyes lest the waters flow out and they be blinded". This was due to the very crystal blue color of the albino-like Shem Su Hor eyes appearing as water.

No doubt the first Pharaohs were Anunnaki while the second dynasty Pharaohs were Shem Su Hor demi-gods. Both groups likely wore the Atef crown (elongated head covering/hat/helmet) to cover their elongated heads. The shape of the face in the Shem Su Hor and the Anunnaki, coupled with the growth patterns of the reddish hair of the male Shem Su Hor, was rather leonine in appearance. Also, due to their large size and great strength, especially of the Anunnaki, they were likened to lions. Because the male lion's face encircled with the tawny mane was associated with the brightness of the sun, the early dynasty Egyptian kings were associated with the lion as well as the sun. This is the reasoning behind the creation of the Sphinxes to depict the early kings of Egypt and beyond.

It is prudent to mention that there are at least three distinct Nibiruan races that were on Earth during this occupation. The largest in stature were the Anunnaki, the smallest, the Phunjah, who were marginally larger than humans. The other race I have no name for other than Igigi who were red-haired, as opposed to the white-haired elite Anannaki and the nearly hairless Phunjah. It is likely that the true Maltese Shem Su Hor priests were a mix of Phunja and second-generation humans/homo sapiens. It is also important to note that these three races mixed with different generations of Earthlings producing various races, many of which were hybrids, and most of whom no longer exist. However, there is much fossil evidence to support this theory.

**Egyptian bust**

**Akhenaton and Nefertiti**

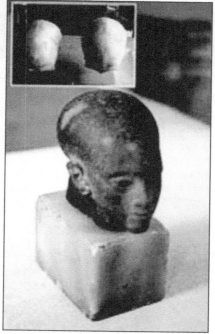

**Maltese bust**

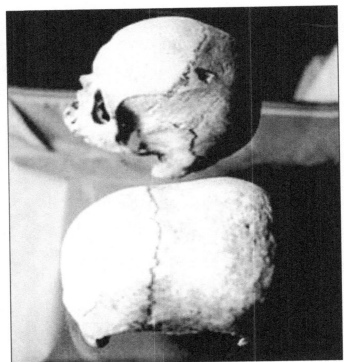

**Maltese Shem Su Hor skull (bottom)
compared to a modern skull (top)**

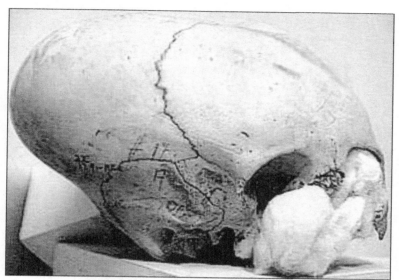

**Maltese Shem Su Hor skull**

**5<sup>th</sup> Dynasty
Atef Crown**

**5<sup>th</sup> Dynasty Atef Crown**

This comprehensive study of the word *shem* illustrates the complexity of its meanings. It is now easier to see that the shem-shaped bread-cake, brilliant and filled with light and offered as a sacrament by Shem, is identified with the sun's brilliance and the loftiness of heaven and, as said in scripture, grants a new name to the consumer, is therefore called shem.

**Yads and Shems**

There is one more important meaning for the word shem that directly relates to the subject of this book. In great antiquity, the Anunnaki communicated through special devices. The most integrally important part of the communication system was the Shem. When the communication device was installed, it was placed atop a great tower such as a pyramid or a ziggurat in order for it to be aloft. The great pyramid of Giza was once equipped with such a shem. The shem was a conical or, in the case of the Great Pyramid, a pyramid-shaped stone. But this was not an everyday rock carved into a conical or pyramid shape; it was rather the glass of gold. When the white powder of gold is taken to a temperature of greater than 1800 degrees F., the attracting forces inherent within the material causes the atoms to become tightly packed to form a crystalline lattice structure. This is not the lattice of a metal, but of a glass.

This glass, known to the later philosophers as the **One Stone,** was employed atop the pyramid to perform a host of tasks. The stone by itself could be used as a telepathic focusing device allowing the initiated to communicate with each other and of course with the Gods. However, the stone would focus certain frequencies of energy that were emitted by the Earth and amplified by structures within the pyramid. This amplified energy could be used in many ways. The most common use was as a beacon since the stone would emit light. Ancient pyramid paintings show rays emitting from the top of pyramids. The next most common use for the shem was its ability to focus energy to send communications to distant regions of the Earth and other planets. A different device was constructed for receiving messages. A more sinister use of the stone was as a defensive weapon. In cases where the pyramid would be under any sort of attack, energy focused into the shem could be made to emit gamma radiation in a foul eruption to indiscriminately annihilate everything in a given radius. Lastly, the shem could emit directional bursts of gamma radiation as well as a currently unknown type of pulsing ray to distant stationary targets. In certain Vedic texts, it is related that Atlantis was destroyed by the improper use of such a weapon. The story states that as the Atlantians attempted to destroy the inhabitants of the fertile plain of China by firing a ray inward through the Earth at these unsuspecting people on the other side of the globe, a catastrophic outcome resulted. Unfortunately the people of China were destroyed, but unexpectedly the island of Atlantis was also destroyed by a massive earthquake and sunk into the ocean due to a colossal plate shift.

The fabled tower of Babel might have been planned as a communications device. The word Babel eventually came to mean confounded or confused as a result of what happened when Babylon was destroyed and the languages were confused by the influx of tribes that scattered the Sumerians. However, the word Babel actually comes from Babylon and Babylon derives from the original name of the City "Bab Ilu" meaning "Gate of God". In texts describing the building of the Tower of Bab Ilu, we read "and let us build a tower and upon it let us set up a shem". So why do we suppose that the Gate of God would need a shem atop of its central ziggurat temple? Perhaps this tower of the city of Marduk /Ra was to become the communication beacon for communicating with Nibiru, the home planet of the Anunnaki. Enraged by this attempt to usurp his authority, Enlil/El-Shaddi ordered the tower destroyed and allowed the hordes and bands of nomads from the north to come in and scatter the peoples of Sumer forever, destroying their common language. Interestingly, it was also Enlil who ordered the destruction of the Great Pyramids' shem and it was his son Ninurta who imprisoned Marduk/Ra in the pyramid and left him for dead. Ra however was later rescued by his many priests who excavated under the pyramid and emerged behind the portcullis to free him. This excavation is known as the fabled well shaft.

There were lesser shems that were designed for Earth communication only. They were not set atop great towers, nor did they have elaborate amplification structures employed along with them. These devices are often depicted in Egyptian, Greek, Sumerian and other art as a conical shaped stone often with two birds sitting on top of it or carved upon the face of the stone. These were the stones of communication. The birds represent the stone's ability to send messages aloft around the world. The navel stone, the Omphalus was a representation of such a stone.

The Bible speaks of **Yads** and **Shems** such as in the verse Isaiah 56:4-7. In this verse, God says that He will give those who follow His commandments and please Him yads and shems better than sons and daughters and an everlasting shem that will never be cut off. Since *shem* is almost always translated as *name* in the Bible, the word name is almost always put in place of shem in this verse, whereas yad is a bit more open to interpretation. Yad is alternately translated as memorials or places depending on the Biblical translation and still there are cases where it is not interpreted and both words are left in their untranslated forms. It should be noted that wherever yad shows up in the Bible, it is most often coupled with the word shem. This brings into question the translation of both words.

The yad is just another kind of memorial stone. In Egypt, the yad is often shaped like the pyramid. The capstone of the Great Pyramid might have been called a yad as it would have been shaped like the pyramid itself and made of the glass of gold ORMUS just as the ORMUS shems were made. Here the only difference in the two words is the shape of the object described. The Egyptian obelisks were yad-shaped at the top. The yad looks like a pointer to heaven. For this reason the yad is often thought of as a pointer. In fact, the modern Hebrew use of the word yad is applied to a pointer used to peruse scripture which is most often tipped with a stylized hand in a pointing gesture. The hand pointing on the yad is symbolic of the historical yad gesture which is derived from the hand of God reaching to help man. The yad can also often be seen as a hand clasp or two hands reaching toward one another, one upward and one downward. The famous image painted by Michelangelo in the Sistine Chapel of God reaching down to touch fingers with Adam is a classic yad gesture. Yad and shem were often spoken of together. The Pillars of the Temple of Solomon, Boaz and Jachin are said to be topped with yads and shems. To say that something is adorned with yads and shems might be to say that there are memorials carved in stone that are gestures of good faith that will help all of humanity to ascend to God. The Yads also might serve to indicate these shems in the architecture as a sort of pointer or indicative gesture. Such is true of the obelisk which points to heaven while all glyphic inscriptions follow the gesture in direction toward heaven, thus exalting the message of the memorial or shem.

There are also the tools of divination such as those used by Joseph Smith, the founder of the Mormon Church, known as the **Urim** and **Thummim**. These devices were supposedly used by Joseph Smith to translate the inscribed gold plates as well as the writings of Abraham. These tools are shems and yads, one being shaped like a cabochon while the other is shaped like a small pyramid. There is some speculation that the earliest of these devices were made of the glass of gold and thus harbored the powers of ORMUS and filled the user with the powers of divination as long as the diviner resonated with the stone due to the ample ingestion of the ORMUS. Others of these stones may have been made of natural ORMUS bearing microcluster stones as likely was the pillar stone which Jacob rested his head upon while having his dream of ascent into heaven.


## Zedek

Earlier in this work, Melchizedek was identified as Father Shem. It was also mentioned that the title Melchizedek identified Shem as the Righteous King of Peace.  We might also find further clues in the Melchizedek title which link him to the great Thoth/Tjehuti, who may have been his alchemy teacher. We will later learn that Thoth was none other than Ningish - Ziddha who was identified by Zechariah Sitchin as one of the sons of Enki (Lord Earth).  Here we must understand that in the Canaan area where Melchizedek lived, the Lord Enki was the chief deity and was referred to as Baal which simply means Lord or on occasion as El which simply meant lofty one in very early times.  Baal was a lord of nature, rebirth, fertility, and rainfall among other things.  Our clue however resides in the word rainfall.  The word Tzediqu, which is the origin of the second half of the Melchizedek title Zedek, had in very ancient times to do with rainfall.  Rainfall was rejuvenating and supported the food crops. In that time, rain was considered good or right.  To call someone righteous was to suggest that they were as right as rain.  Since none of Enki's other sons were involved in Canaan, and since Thoth was vested with the building of civilization as he had been charged with the totality of his father's science and cultural knowledge, it is fitting to assume that here he would have been a tutor of the king. Also, used in the region, we find the word Adon which we have learned also means Lord.  We will see that Thoth taught many societies about the one God of the Cosmos, Adon.   It is suspicious that the word in Canaan was Baal however the word Adon was also in use. Here I believe that the two words were utilized in order to draw distinction between the two.  So why would this be necessary unless there were two lords that were deified by the Canaanites?

In the book of Jasher, which presents a more contemporary version of the Exodus events than does the Book of Exodus, Melchizedek is identified as Shem and it goes further to identify Adonizedek with Melchizedek, stating that they are one in the same. We find if we study ancient documents that Enki/Baal was not a jealous God like his half brother Enlil the El-Shaddi. In fact it is Enki, who after warning Noah/Ziesutra about the pending flood, tells him that he wishes no further worship of him or his people as he says "we are not gods". So, who was Shem venerating by adding Adoni to his title? Adon was the Great One Lord and Consciousness of the Universe as taught by Thoth. The "i" at the end of Adon simply denotes ownership, thus Adoni means My Lord just as Melchi means My King. This continues in Modern Hebrew as Adonii. In Greece this word became Adonis. It could have been that the people were calling Shem Adoni, My Lord as a way to set him apart from Baal. But Baal would not have been upset by someone using his title as he was not jealous. Since the chief deity of the region was Baal/Enki, a king of the region and supporter of Baal might have been called Baalizedek. It is obvious here that Father Shem was proclaiming in his title that he was a supporter of The One God, Lord of the Cosmos, Adon, a concept taught to humans by the great Thoth. Also, anyone who would be as right as rain and worthy of the title Adoni must have been fully enlightened and would likely become an ascended master. As Thoth states, anyone who but receiveth a single ray of the light of Aten/Adon hath transcended the cycles of the cosmos and is bound no more to the forces of nature.

Shem himself was a Shem Su Hor master. Here we find the last and final name of Shem. Shem was seen, by his look and mental powers, to be like a lofty one or an El. Because of this the people often referred to him has He Who is Like a Lofty One. The name for this is Michael. And as Shem became an ascended master upon the completion of his only physical incarnation, he remains Michael (He Who is Like God).

**Umphalus Stone from Delphi and Shem Monument or Naval Stone**

**Shem or light bread offering    Shem and Ankh symbolizing the life within the light bread**

78

King Akhenaton blessing the Showbread in the light of Aten. The act of blessing the manna in the light of the sun the means of charging the manna with light before it was consumed. In the background, Nefertiti can be seen blessing the showbread as well. Coming down with the hands of the sunrays one can see the ankh being offered to each representing the offering of life.

# CHAPTER 7

## The Rose of the Plane of Sharon, The Legacy of the Goddess

The word Sharon originally was not the name of a place or a person, rather it derives from the words "shar", "ra" and "on" meaning "orbit light of". It is also important to mention here that a shar is also a God year of 3600 years or one orbit of the planet Nibiru which is sometimes referred to as a divine year. From a multiple of 3600 came our notion of 360 degrees equaling a full circle.

The word *ra* has meant *light* in many languages and is the epithet for the Egyptian sun god Ra. *On* is a word that often is used to mean *relating to*, or *of something*. With this in mind, we might translate this phrase as the Divine Orbit of Light, or the Holy Orbit of Light or even The God Orbit of Light.

### The Rose of Sharon

In comparison to the preparations of the King to become a Malkuth, the Messianic Queen must also strive for a similar enlightenment before marriage. She must reach a higher plane of consciousness as described by the early Hebrews. She would, through the taking of starfire and later the alchemical substitutes, bloom as a rose in the Divine Orbit of Light and reach a higher plane of consciousness. Thus the Song of Solomon states: "I am the Rose of Sharon and the lily of the valleys." The lily refers to the starfire priestesses who were noted as being lilies or flowers, as they were the ones who "flowed". And the Priestesses were in early times, as pointed out by Sir Lawrence Gardner, all named after Lilith and bore such names as Lily, Lilutu, Lilimon, Lilet, Lilique, Liluva, Lilorin, and so on. Here it is appropriate to discuss Starfire, the substance for which manna was granted as a replacement.

Starfire was most often an extract made from the menstrum of specially trained and prepared Anunnaki priestesses who were fed great amounts of ORMUS. These extracts contained valued live Anunnaki hormones, neural transmitters, neural peptides, stem cells, growth factors, enzymes, fibrolysin (a thinning agent), live endometrial cells, and super-charged endocrinal secretions of the pineal and pituitary glands and a host of other bodily chemicals along with ORMUS in its most potent bio-available form. This may sound disgusting to some, however it must be understood that hormone supplements today are derived from things like desecrated animal glands, pregnant mare's urine, and many other not so pleasant sources. In essence, the starfire supplement could be compared to our current use of human fetal cord blood for example.

The preparation of starfire varied from tradition to tradition. In some cases it was made by way of extraction, whereby the menstrum was put through an extraction process and the end product bore no further resemblance to blood. This was likely the process employed by the goddesses who fed the early pre-flood Kings. In parts of India the ritual continued until recent times and there is some speculation that among certain groups the ritual continues today. In many regions, the menstrual blood was simply captured in special vessels and then mixed with wine and consumed.

Kusi - Ritual Vessel

**Indian Starfire Capture Vessel**

The Sithians of Europe employed many variations to the ritual and preparation ranging from the collection and drying of the blood to the drinking of the blood directly from the Priestess. When dried, the blood could be stored for a time until a later use when it would be mixed with wine. It is also important to include that not all starfire included only the blood. In many instances feminine ejaculate was also mixed with the blood to make starfire. The female Grafenburg (or G-spot) response produces a fluid sometimes in great amounts called female ejaculation. Not all women are able to be stimulated to ejaculation. However, the starfire priestess was trained to do so as part of her training regime. The Grafenburg response fluid proves not to be urine, but rather much more akin to prostate fluid under analysis. Amrita, as it was often referred to in ancient times, is produced by the female equivalent to the male prostate gland and contains prostate specific acid phosphotaze and prostate antigen. Amrita also contains glucose, fructose, creatine, and a host of other nutritional substances.

## Sumerian Elixir

It is important to reiterate that the early Starfire Priestesses, the flowers, were expressly bred and raised from specific Anunnaki lines to produce these substances. As time went on, the vital essences were much diminished as the original family lines were bred out by the mixing of Anunnaki with humans. It is shown in the texts of the Sumerians that the elixirs made from the starfire contained otherworldly microbiological entities that had nothing short of incredible health benefits. As these substances were created within the bodies of the Anunnaki they could only be passed to humans by the ingestion of Anunnaki blood and, as the priestess was expressly raised and fed to produce even higher levels of these substances, it made the flower a most important resource to the early human kings. It may seem particularly strange, but the biological entities that were produced within the blood and gametes of the Anunnaki have recently been rediscovered by a certain Dr. Merkl who seems to have met with some extremely unfortunate demise. His death has been said by many to have been suspicious at best.

These life giving substances discovered by Dr. Merkl include a host of various biomachines and crystalline substances, all of which seem to be at least in part constructed of ORMUS materials. There are two main substances discovered by Merkl. The first substance consists of various crystalline structures. Some of these structures are shaped like crosses and others are shaped like cubes, while still others are bizarre shapes, some resembling ferns and twigs among many other odd shapes. Merkl named these substances life crystals. The life crystals help to provide energy for the body by energizing the cells through their inherent ATP. These crystals which Merkl called ATP (adino triphosphates) were analyzed by David Hudson and found to be constructed of 100 percent pure ORMUS gold.

Life crystals were synthesized by Merkl with the use of a solar reactor and were created from off-the-shelf vegetable sources which inherently contain gold and gold ORMUS. It is interesting how intensified sunlight brings about the synthesis of these life giving structures given what we now know about ORMUS. Light always plays a role here and it is obvious that there is an intelligence template which is inherent in, or at least received by the ORMUS, and put to work within the biological system.

The second substance discovered by Merkl was called Chondriana. Chondriana acts like a giant T-cell which roves around the body attacking all bacteria, virus and cancer cell invaders. The Chondriana looks like an optical device which, Merkl states, operates on light interference patterns. These interference patterns contain intelligence and are part of the makeup of the matrix of the universe. For this reason, the ancient usage of the term for starfire as the Rich Food of The Matrix was appropriate indeed. We must consider that the word *matrix* itself is an ancient Latin word for womb, from which the word *madrigal* is derived, meaning *mother's song from the womb*. The universe itself has a womb from which all things are born and we today call this the matrix, everything that issues from the matrix is the madrigal of creation. Just as the rich food is offered to the madrigal from the matrix of the mother as starfire, so does the ORMUS issue to us as the Rich food of the universal matrix.

Shaped like two sets of dumbbells crossing one another in the center, the Chondriana is able to devour its prey and break it down to its light interference patterns. Once this has been done, the Chondriana is able to use part of the light as energy for itself and the rest is converted into very tiny protein-like structures which also have an immune function. Merkl has termed these tiny structures black proteins which are also created by certain life crystals. The Chondriana acts like a factory for these. The Chondriana is obviously an extremely intelligent machine which at first sight is obviously a photo-operational mechanism which is equipped with lenses to capture photo interference patterns which it utilizes as one source of energy and sustenance.

**This microscopic image of chondriana optical device surrounded by black proteins was taken by Merkl through his specially designed optical microscope based on the Rife technology.**

These structures, both the life crystals and the Chondriana, have been found in the fossil record existing millions of years ago on Earth. The most miraculous thing I find about these substances is that they all were depicted throughout Sumerian art work. Since Merkl had to have a very special microscope in order to see these substances, which are smaller than a wavelength of light, means that the Sumerians were able to see entities of such small size or at least were shown these images by superior beings. This suggests that highly advanced microscopic techniques were in use at the time in Sumer which exceed the ability of an electron scanning microscope. The Sumerians told us that the substances which were manufactured from ORMUS elements were the Elixir of Life. These substances which were inherent within the bodies of the Anunnaki priestesses were given to the human kings in the form of starfire. The human kings of the day would have been highly advanced, both physically and mentally. Their immune function would have been greatly superior to that of normal humans, approaching that of the Anunnaki themselves. For them, the starfire was the elixir of life which brought them to the advanced state of the Malkuth which we shall later learn is the foundation of the tree of life. This is the advanced state of sovereignty that the King must reach in order to rule. Eventually, Malkuth came to mean kingdom of the realm of the king. However the King (Malek, Malchu) had to become sovereign and to do so was to advance to the state of Malkuth which was the express charge of the high priestess Lilith of the starfire tradition who managed the supplementation and development of the kings and queens through the starfire priestesses in her order.

**Soma**

Starfire was not the only naturally rich ORMUS containing substance of course. Among the many other naturally rich ORMUS bearing substances was the Soma, known also as the Nectar of Immortality, Chitta and Mind Stuff. These terms are all Vedic in origin. *The Soma Pavamana* is a very long text attributed to the making of soma. Soma was made from petrified plant matter that was mined out of rock. This substance was known, and is still known, as *shilajit*. Shilajit was comprised of the remains of some sort of ancient plant life or detritus that became trapped between layers of rock and was preserved for a very long time. Over time, minerals such as copper, nickel and gold infiltrated the shilajit. The ancient Vedic peoples, as explained in the Soma Pavamana, mined the shilajit from the rocks. They crushed and ground the material, then dissolved it in some sort of acid such as strong vinegar. The juice, as they called it, was filtered through a cylinder containing fleece. The liquid was filtered over and over and then the pH was adjusted to produce a brownish green juice that was consumed by the demi-Gods to make them strong, increase their vitality and extend their lives. Essentially, the manufacture of Soma is plant/mineral alchemy. The majority of the ORMUS in Soma is inherent in the shilajit and therefore the alchemical methods employed are primarily simple extraction techniques. It is obvious that some of the colloids of copper and nickel that infiltrated the shilajit over the millennia have been transmuted to their ORMUS form. The result is a juice that contains all of the ancient plant ORMUS, which is much more concentrated than that found in present day plants, and added ORMUS of nickel and copper. In addition, all of the colloids of minerals inherent in the shilajit along with the infiltrated colloids which have gathered within the material over the ages are present. It quickly becomes obvious how great the Soma elixir is for the body. The Soma was truly a wondrous drink that was highly venerated by the Vedics, so much so that much of the Rig Veda is attributed to Soma Pavamana. This will be discussed further in the section dealing with Health in Chapter 9.

Soma was made from shilajit. Shilajit is such an amazing substance that I thought it helpful to discuss its formation. Shilajit is an exudate that is pressed out from layers of rock of sacred mountains in Nepal and certain other high mountains. It is composed of humus and organic plant material that has been compressed by layers of rock. Humus is formed when soil microorganisms decompose animal and plant material into elements usable by plants. Unlike other soil humus, shilajit humus consists of 60% - 80% organic mass. Approximately 200 million years ago, India was a large island continent off the Australian continental coast separated from the Eurasian continent by the Tethys Sea. The Indian continent drifted north at a rate of about 9 meters a century. This movement led to the eventual disappearance of the Tethys Sea. Forty to fifty million years ago, the Indian continent collided with the Asian continent. This caused the seabed of the Tethys Sea to be pushed up and keep moving up to eventually form the Himalayan Mountains. The Himalayan Mountains continue to rise more than 1 centimeter a year. During this transition, the mineral rich and fertile soil of the seabed gave rise to lush, dense tropical vegetation.

As the ground continued to be pushed up to become mountains, much of the plant material became trapped by layers of rock and soil and remained preserved for thousands of years. Gradually, the plant material was transformed into humus which is a rich organic mass. Due to microbial action and the tremendous pressure from the weight of the mountains, the humus was transformed into a dense, viscous, mineral-rich mass. This is Shilajit. The trapped layers of Shilajit become exposed due to the extreme temperature variations in the mountainous environment and erosion from monsoon rains. Shilajit exudes from between the cracks in the layers of rock during the summer when the temperatures rise and the Shilajit becomes less viscous. The native Nepali people climb the mountains and repel cliffs to collect the Shilajit.

Shilajit has been used for thousands of years and for as many different health problems. It is listed as a healing agent in ancient Sanskrit writings and is used today in Ayurvedic medicine. Shilajit was said to have been discovered by Himalayan villagers observing large white monkeys migrate to the mountains in the warm summer months. The monkeys were seen to be chewing a semi-soft substance that flowed from between layers of rock. The villagers attributed the monkey's great strength, longevity and wisdom to the substance. Villagers began to consume the substance themselves and reported a broad spectrum of improvements in health. It seemed to give them more energy, relieve digestive problems, increase sex drive, improve memory and cognition, improve diabetes, reduce allergies, improve the quality and length of life and it seemed to cure all diseases.

Shilajit contains a wide range of various chemicals beneficial to health. One group of the most important of these chemicals is Di-benzo Alpha Pyrones which are able to pass the blood/brain barrier and act as a powerful antioxidant protecting the brain and nerve tissue from free radical damage. It also inhibits the enzyme Acetylcholinesterase which breaks down Acetylcholine, therefore increasing the levels of Acetylcholine in the brain. Low levels of Acetylcholine are associated with Alzheimers, poor memory and concentration problems. Shilajit can still be purchased today.

### Tree of Life

Many Sumerian records often refer to pre-diluvial times which were often studied by the Sumerians themselves. The Sumerian texts of 4,500 to 7,500 years ago often referred to times that were pre-flood of 11,000 to 13,000 years ago and beyond. In pre-diluvial times, the secrets of the ORMUS were held by a certain family. The family was represented by the serpent symbol and was noted as wise, which is the real meaning of the original word for serpent (nhsh or nahash). The primary ones who held this knowledge were Enki (Lord Earth), Nigishzidda (son of Enki, also known to the Egyptians as Thoth/Tehuti and to the Greeks as Hermes, and to the Romans as Mercury and to whom Enki taught all of his science), Ninti (Lady Life, also known as Nin Hursag and Hathor), and finally, Lilith of Genesis fame, touted as the first wife of Adam who spurned him. These were among the most important members of the family tree who were the keepers of the knowledge and secrets to long life. Enki's brother Enlil (Lord of Airspace or also called El-Shaddi meaning Lofty Mountain), as stated in Genesis, was opposed to allowing humans access to the tree of life or the tree of knowledge.

It was prohibited for Adamu (earthlings) to partake of this knowledge, thus the tree of life and the tree of knowledge were off limits. The reason for this was that the Adamu (humans) were servants and the Anunnaki (From Heaven to Earth They Came) did not want the earthlings to become as perfect as the Anunnaki themselves for fear of losing control over their human slaves. Later however, as the Anunnaki lines were bred out and the human life spans began to shorten, this rule was broken by

Nigishzidda and Lilith. They began to feed the great Adamu kings the Anunnaki Starfire substances in their purest forms. Only the Priest Kings and Dynastic Queens were fed these substances in order to increase their intuition, metal ability, health and longevity. This was necessary in order to help the King and Queen become a suitable human/God go-between. Previously there had been too much interaction between humans and Anunnaki and too many half breeds resulted. The crossbreeding between the Anunnaki and the first generation humans, who were more primitive than the second generation, produced giants who were more intelligent than humans and non-subservient to the Anunnaki, posing a great problem. Further human/Anunnaki contact was prohibited by Enlil, the older of the two brothers. It then became necessary to bring kingship to humans so that humans could be ruled in surrogate. The kings had to be able to understand elaborate concepts, receive instructions telepathically and to prompt the masses to do the bidding of the Gods. This was the early conceptual beginnings of divinely ordained rulership. Moreover, the King was a great investment and therefore should have a greater life span than that of other humans. The line which carried genetics closest to that of the Annunaki was the best breeding stock for the Kings. This was the line of Cain. It should be noted here that Cain, whose father was none other than Enki, was already two thirds Anunnaki as his mother Eva was also part Anunnaki by genetic manipulation. Later, Cain married Luluva, a purebred Anunnaki Starfire Priestess. Therefore, Cain's first son Enoch was mostly Anunnaki.

Here it is important to point out one of the great deceptions of the Genesis Books. The Book of Genesis tells us that Seth's grandson Enoch lived 365 years and then he was translated or taken up by God. Many have supposed this to mean that he was taken into heaven. The word translate in this case as defined by Websters is to change from one location to another; to transfer. Bible scholars have supposed this to mean transferred to heaven or "taken up". Yet upon reading ancient manuscripts, we find that Cain's son, along with Cain and other members of the family line, are relocated to areas which are isolated from other humans, living out their lives in seclusion and having contact only with the Anunnaki.

With this in mind, it becomes apparent that in order to hide the fact that the line of Cain was to become the important kingly bloodline, Enoch, along with others of the line, were deliberately confused with the line of Seth who were more purely human since Seth's mother and father were Adamu (of the Earth). So the translation of Enoch more likely occurred with Cain's son Enoch, not Seth's grandson Enoch. The reason for the Anunnaki decision to translate Enoch into their society is plain to see. Here is a man who is just as they are. He is as one of the gods. It would be safer to take him into their society than to allow him to run around with the humans creating problems. There are a number of texts to support this notion that the important Enoch of the Bible is in fact Cain's son. Additionally, texts also explain that many others were taken up as well, enough people to create a city of their own someplace far away from humans and visited only by the Anunnaki.

It is also important to point out that these certain bloodlines were often referred to as demi-gods or half gods. There were pockets of this line scattered about the Earth. They became the Fairies, Elves, Rama, etc. They were able to cross breed between humans and Anunnaki without creating a hybrid. Other human lines could not intermarry with the Anunnaki without producing a hybrid giant. The offspring of the lines of Cain were larger than most people yet they were not as large as the giants that were produced by other lines. The reason giants were produced is a subject for another book altogether but had to do with the fact that Anunnaki body density was greater than that of humans since they evolved on a larger planet with greater gravity and a denser atmosphere. When inter-mating with certain races, these traits were dominant so they were passed on, however the density caused by more tightly coiled and compacted proteins, now relaxed in the offspring resulting in a very large although less dense body. Such cross breeding resulted in extreme variations in the size of offspring.

**King Gilgamesh**

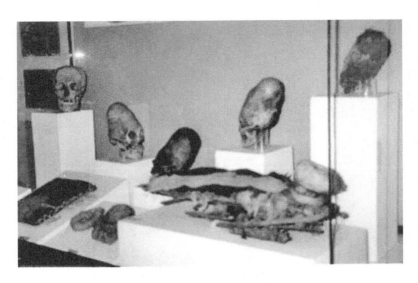

**A number of giant skulls;**
**note the obvious elongated shape of the cranium.**

**Jawbone of Gigantopithecus**
**as compared to modern human jaw.**

King Nimrod; note his obvious size advantage over the humans as
he hails the second sun Nibiru.

**Modern age Giants**

This giant, unearthed in County Antrim, Ireland, was found to be 12 ft. 2 in. high. Its girth of chest was 6 ft. 6 in., and length of arms 4 ft. 6 in. There are six toes on the right foot. This skeleton was on display in exhibitions in Dublin, Liverpool and Manchester. What later happened to the giant and its owner is unknown.

(Photo from the British Strand Magazine, Dec. 1895)

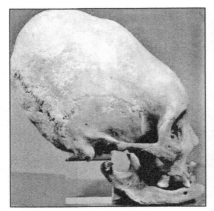
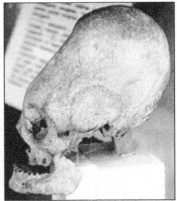
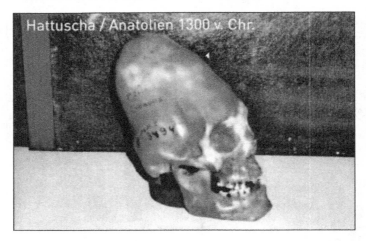

Hattuscha / Anatolien 1300 v. Chr.

**These giant cone-head skulls from Peru are probable
skulls of Anunnaki and Anunnaki/human cross.**

Here we must return to the Kings and Queens. Since it was
known by the Anunnaki and royal lines that bloodlines were
more matrilineal than patrilineal due to the fact that the
mitochondrial DNA is passed on unchanged by the female alone,
the royal bloodlines were thus carried though the female. The
fact that mitochondrial DNA exists and is passed on only
through the female has only recently been rediscovered. The
mitochondrial DNA has in recent studies been used to trace

human lines back to seven women. This work has been brought to light by the bestselling book *The Seven Daughters of Eve*.

It was known even then that longevity, health, and intelligence were passed on by the mitochondrial DNA and thus by the female. For this reason, the proper Queen had to be chosen from close kinship (or Cainship) as has been pointed out by Gardner. The Queen would nearly always be a half sister or a first cousin to the King whenever possible. This meticulous practice insured the kingly succession. It is also important to note that later Starfire Priestesses were chosen from these lines due to their Anunnaki ancestry.

### Thou Shalt Not Eat of the Blood

The King and Queen were fed starfire so that they would become perfect intermediaries. Eventually, Enlil (El Shaddi) forbade the ingestion of blood and said that earthlings from that time forward live only 120 years. It was at this time that the great scientist and alchemist Nigishzidda (Thoth) stepped in and gave Melchizedek the alchemical secrets to make a substitute for starfire from gold and other metals. This wholly alchemically derived ORMUS substance was to replace the Anunnaki starfire. Although the starfire was still consumed in many traditions even today, the potency of the Anunnaki bloodlines was eventually lost. Although these substances remain super-charged, they could not compare to that which was produced by the early flowers which were imbibed with many attributes that have now been lost.

Since the time the edict was passed down by Enlil to deny the consumption of blood, kingship turned to the use of ORMUS materials. Although the royal lines may have still used starfire, after the evacuation of the watchful eye of the Anunnaki, the starfire was never to be as great as it once was. The most powerful and vital starfire was produced by the Anunnaki Priestesses who had now vacated, and the continued practice had to be supported by the human starfire Priestesses. These Priestesses carried some of the Anunnaki DNA which was important in the production of these vital essences, however with each generation the Anunnaki blood was eventually bred out and the substances no longer possessed the same vital strength and value. However the lifestyles and practices of the Priestesses were maintained in order to insure the continued production of the starfire, and even though this rich food of the matrix was still very highly prized and valuable, it paled in the light of the original full strength Anunnaki starfire.

**Melchizedek Blessing Abraham**

# CHAPTER 8

## ORMUS for Life

Some might say, "Why do I need this stuff? I am getting along fine without it". It will soon become evident in mainstream science that all living things must have some amount of these substances in order to survive and properly function. The most important of these substances are (in order of importance) rhodium, iridium, copper and gold. Even though gold is the hardest to make into ORMUS and the most sought after, it is not as necessary for life as are the others mentioned here. The roles played by the other six platinum group metals, excluding mercury and osmium, in their ORMUS phase are not as widespread in the body as the four mentioned here and, although they have very important roles, we may be able to survive without them, albeit that we may be living with some disease born of deficiency. It may even be possible that we do not need the ORMUS gold in order to survive, however gold often has the most dramatic effect when taken as a supplement as will be explained later. Gold is among the most volatile ORMES and easily forms a gas which makes it more abundant in the upper atmosphere. It is likely that the ozone layer is partly comprised of mon- and di-atoms of the platinum group, much of which is gold. The ancient Sumerian texts explain explicitly that the Anunnaki came to Earth to mine gold which was taken back to Nibiru for the express purpose of replenishing the gold in the atmosphere. If it were not for this action, their planet would have died as the gold in their atmosphere was said to have protected their planet from the sun when passing close through the solar system and helped retain heat when the planet was far from the sun. For a thorough explanation of this information read *The Earth Chronicles* by Zechariah Sitchin.

It is undeniable that a vast majority of ancient texts speak heavily of these substances and their use by kings, priests and gods as bodily supplements. After the manufacturing methods were lost due to suppression by the Holy Roman Empire and others, humankind has been continually searching to rediscover the secrets of immortality. There were a select few who were adept enough to have probably rediscovered the secrets. Such figures included The Count de Saint Germain, Nicholas Flammel, Albertus Magnus, Father Artephious, Gibar and Orelious to name a few. A great number of alchemists throughout the ages probably were successful, however we might never know for sure if they were or were not. Those who were successful hid their success and usually faked their deaths so that they would not be targeted by religious or governmental factions.

## ORMUS: A Rebirth

In recent times, scarcely anyone had knowledge of the ORMUS. However, in the past few years more has come to light. David Hudson, the successful Phoenix farmer and entrepreneur, perhaps has done more than anyone to bring back the knowledge and reawaken the art of alchemy. Now, the reawakened interest in alchemy has budding alchemists popping up all over the world. However the world of chemistry is far behind, especially in the United States due to the arrogance of our culture.

The main stumbling block in the United States in rediscovering these substances is the fact that we do not use the correct chemical analysis methods to identify them. If we did, we would find that much of what we think is carbon is actually a form of gold and other platinum group metals; much of what we think is iron is actually another form of gold; much of what we think is silica is actually ORMUS of many platinum elements; and that all human, plant and animal tissues contain ORMUS. The issue at hand is the burn time allowed for an elemental analysis in a mass spectrophotometer and the fact that a shield gas must be utilized in the process. The normal burn time used in the United States is 15 seconds without a shield gas. The burn time necessary to completely analyze all of these substances is 300 seconds and must be performed under a shield gas.

It is due to our lifestyles that we should supplement with these substances, or at least change how we treat our foods. Since these substances repel certain frequencies and are superconductors of others, we must consider what happens to them when they come in contact with electromagnetic fields (EMF) and artificial light. Our foods are subjected to all sorts of electrical fields during cooking, storing and processing. We also subject our bodies to various forms of EMF and other forms of radiation which cause the volatilization of ORMUS, driving them off into the atmosphere. ORMUS, when in repelling mode, acts like a magnet when approached by the like pole of another magnet. When the substance is nearly as light as air in powder form, and lighter than air when a gas, the repulsion reaction is dramatic. Certain ORMUS, as described in Vedic texts and in the experimentations of David Hudson, will under certain conditions, superconduct the magnetic field of the Earth to produce a bubble of weightlessness.

I have duplicated this experiment with a glass tube and a torch. The end of a pipette (glass tube) was heated until the end melted into a glass bubble. Powder form ORMUS was placed into the tube and heated to the critical catalytic temperature of 950 degrees Fahrenheit. At this temperature ORMUS reaches its highest potential to superconduct the magnetic field of the Earth. ORMUS of copper, rhodium, mercury and others will float within the tube as the heat transfers from the glass to the ORMUS inside the tube. As long as the heat is applied to the end of the glass tube, the ORMUS will float and swirl in the tube. Mercury produces the most dramatic effect in this regard and therefore is likely the reason why it is the ORMUS most often described in the Vedic text as being used for this purpose in ancient technology. As described in Vedic texts, the vortex engine was the main engine in the *vemana* (ancient flying machines). It is important to mention that the main engine used what was described as quick silver (mercury) and might be referred to as an anti-gravity engine; however, this would be an incorrect assumption. This engine does not do anything to change the affects of gravity. The engine simply rides on the magnetic field of the Earth just as an airplane rides on the atmosphere of the Earth. This bubble of weightlessness extends outward from the engine to encompass the entire ship which produced a weightless craft which could then be easily driven in any direction by a number of other propulsion type engines that were described in the texts.

When it comes to the use of the ORMUS for supplementation, if properly made the ORMUS is completely safe. However there can be manufacturing errors which can leave the final substance very poisonous. This is why the utmost care should be taken to complete each step carefully and properly while making the proper observations. I also recommend that the maker send off at least one batch to be tested for remaining Gilchrist metals.

It is important to mention that even though metals such as mercury and osmium are very poisonous to the human body, they are not poisonous when in the ORMUS form and were used by the ancients to make supplements. They are however more dangerous to work with, and if the maker is unskilled or careless, some of the base metal could remain in the ORMUS, or the maker could become contaminated during the process of manufacture and for these reason I suggest that at least osmium and mercury not be used to make bodily supplements.

**General Effects and Functions**

Below is a list of various ORMUS materials accompanied by partial descriptions of their effects and functions within the human body. Since little is proven concerning these materials and their effects on the body, much of the information offered here is based on published experiments and theory. It does provide a firm base of knowledge however when viewed as a whole.

Rhodium is the most important of the ORMUS elements for the body and therefore is the most naturally abundant within the body. Due to these facts, and the case that more mainstream science has been performed concerning the function of rhodium within biology, the resulting information is much vaster by comparison to that of other ORMUS elements and compounds. Additionally, it must be mentioned that the greatest evidence for many of the functions of the other ORMUS compounds is gleaned from the experiences of actual users of the supplements. Lastly, there is a wealth of historical textual evidence as to the effects of these substances on the human body.

### Rhodium

Since the information on rhodium is the most expansive, and since rhodium is likely the most biologically important of all the ORMUS, it is appropriate to begin with rhodium ORMUS.

**Double Helical Field:** It is important to first acknowledge that rhodium has an uneven number of electrons (45). Since the atomic number is uneven, rhodium can only be broken down to the di-atom and not to the singular atom. The result is that rhodium possesses double helical fields as both of the atoms in the unit produce their own helical field. The fields produced are very important when considering the function of the ORMUS in biology.

**DNA:** Studies have been performed by the US Department of the Navy whereby DNA was systematically dismantled. At the end of the dismantling, a ghost effect of the helical structure remained when photographed by electron scanning imagery. The source of the helical energy field could not be identified, however it was recognized at that time that DNA actually has a template into which it is fixed. Another subsequent study performed by an unrelated party entailed the manipulation of a rhodium di-atom to the end of a DNA strand. It was supposed that the atom would increase the conduction of the DNA strand by approximate ten times. It was also thought that the manipulation of the atom to that point would be a very difficult task. However, when the rhodium complex was moved toward the DNA, it jumped onto the end of the strand all by itself as if it were attracted to it by some force. When the experiment was conducted it was found that the strand conduction had increased by some magnitude to the tenth power, far exceeding the expectations of the researchers. Further studies by various parties have shown that rhodium in its di-atomic form projects a double helical field the same as that of the ghost effect of the DNA strand. Based on these and other studies, it is supposed that the rhodium di-atom is a very important feature in DNA structure and repair and that it has a natural affinity for the DNA molecule.  Further research performed by the National Institutes of Health, with the ORMUS of rhodium that was supplied by David Hudson, showed that its effects on cancerous cells were normalizing in nature.  Tumors, when exposed to rhodium, seemed to rapidly expand and soften before they became normal healthy tissue.  While the helix is relaxed, the DNA protein tool is able to run the length of the molecule and repair the sequence per the blueprint of the ghostly ORMUS template.  The rhodium, when it newly attaches to the DNA strand, causes an uncoiling or relaxing of the DNA which allows the protein tools to more easily repair the DNA sequence.  The template offered by the rhodium also plays a role in the repair by allowing the amino acids to fall into their respective sequencing.  Exactly how this occurs is unknown.  It has been speculated by Dr. Merkl that the template for life is inherent within the ordered interference patterns of the cosmos.  It would seem here that the ORMUS template is therefore tapping into the codes hidden within the interference patterns of the universe.  Due to the ability of ORMUS to simultaneously exist in more than one dimension, it would be likely that the ORMUS could act as a tool of communication between dimensions, thus ORMUS may act as a source of coded order from other dimensional interference patterns.

The important feature here is the relaxing effect which, when it occurs, makes the entire tumor seem to expand and soften.  As the DNA strands reflex, the tissue eventually normalizes.  The mode of cure is normalization.  No cells are killed; they are simply allowed to repair damage through the rewriting of RNA instruction from repaired or restructured DNA.  It is likely that this "cure" only works for cancers that have occurred due to DNA damage or for those which are perpetuated through DNA coding and/or mutations.  When DNA naturally contains instructions for cancer, the cure then rests in the RNA instructions which are written based on environmental influences; which is to say, the internal environment of the body has called up these instructions due to cellular intoxication or emotional influences. (For further information on genetic coding and ground breaking research in cellular biology describing how thought and emotion control cellular function and health, read

Bruce Lipton's book *The Biology of Belief.*)

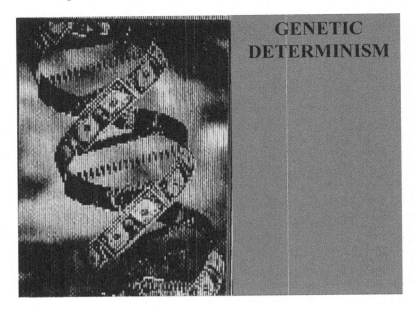

**GENETIC DETERMINISM**

Genetic determinism means big bucks for the drug companies who would like to stake claim to our genetic code and sell us our own genes. They must convince us that genes are static for their scheme to work. But the truth is, genes do change, they can repair themselves and the RNA copies carry only what is chosen from the DNA to be put into action.

More recent studies conducted at Cal Tech headed by Dr. Jacqueline Barton concern how DNA might be made into tools that can be used to cure cancer or target viruses. It has shown rhodium to be a major factor in the conduction of light frequencies through the DNA strand. When the rhodium di-atom is attached to the end of the DNA strand, it will glow when light strikes it. However, when an iridium di-atom is placed at the other end of the DNA strand, the light flows solely within the strand and does not escape so there is no glow or subsequent radiation damage to the molecule. The same research has revealed that ORMUS rhodium has some ability to help order and correct damage to the DNA strand caused by radiation. This research also indicates at least as far as DNA is concerned, that iridium can be very important by working with rhodium to reduce the damaging effects of all sorts of radiation. Further experimentation showed that if the rhodium complex was placed on the mid-section of the strand, radiation could strike the DNA without damage at the entry point. However, the radiation would move within the strand to the rhodium complex where it would then exit. The DNA would be damaged at the exit point. Yet as was earlier described, if rhodium is placed on one end and iridium on the other, no damage will occur. It is most important here to remember that the rhodium and iridium ORMUS have natural affinity to the ends of the DNA strand and will find their way to the DNA when ingested or inhaled when a gas.

**Microtubulin:** Most cells contain structures called microtubules which are constructed of smaller *microtubulin*. There are various types of *microtubule* formation within the cell and rhodium is implicated in at least one type of microtubule. When ORMUS of rhodium atoms come within a certain distance from one another, they are attracted to one another by their helical fields and they then fall into a semi-crystalline structure known as a *microcluster.* When super-charged water molecules are passed through this media, the water gets caught up in the helical field matrix which is knit together in nested spirals and, for a given time, usually only minute fractions of a second, forms a tube. These tubes are constantly being destroyed at one end while being added to at the other end in an organized quantum collapse. These tubes have been extensively studied by renowned researchers (such as Sir Roger Penrose and Dr. Stuart Hammeroff,) in order to decipher their function. Resulting theories abound, although a compilation of theories might suggest that information is transported inter-cellularly and extra-cellularly through microtubules. Microtubules are being created and destroyed constantly. It is deduced that these tubules act as switches for consciousness just like a computer uses a system of ons and offs, or ones and zeros, in computation, except that the cellular computations are occurring on a quantum level. Theories suggest that cellular communication inside the cell occurs in this fashion between organelles as well as between cells. The really amazing thing is that microtubulin extends well beyond the cell wall and in many cases even outside of the body, especially where brain cells are concerned. This gives rise to the so-called electromagnetic field that radiates from the body and can be photographed by the Kirlian method. The theory further suggests that these tubulins are actually channeling consciousness from outside the body. The microtubulin appear to be creating a quantum effect that is like that of a miniature wormhole in space suggests Penrose's colleague Dr. Stuart Hammeroff. Hammeroff further suggests that ORMUS are the magical devices in the formation of microtubules. I further suggest that different ORMUS are responsible for different types of microtubules based on the strength of their fields as well as the nature of the field, be it double or single helix. Since ORMUS are superconductors of light and the super-charged water tubes running along their helical fields act as crystalline optical pathways for light, these structures then must act just like a fiber optic, suggesting that conscious instruction is conducted by structured light waves or photons. The light waves are likely structured by interference patterns and it is likely that much of the instruction for life itself is coded in energy interference patterns as the light moves through the tubules and passes through the standing wave form that is the matrix of the universe. It is probable that much of the instruction for life itself is coded in such energy interference patterns. The US Navy also conducted cellular research in an effort to determine how light was conducted throughout the cell as a method of intra-cellular communication without success. They likely overlooked the microtubulin theory, at least at the time of that particular research study.

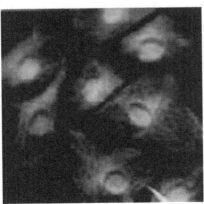

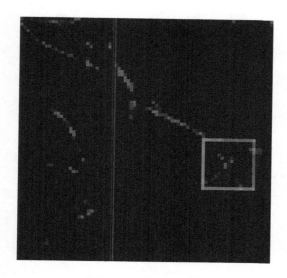

**Microtubules within the cell**

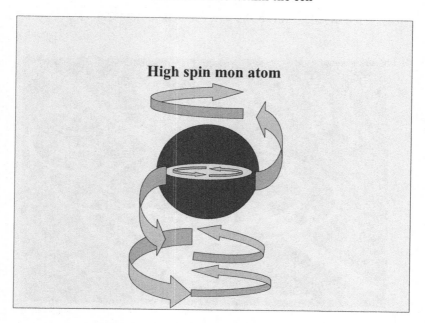

**Helical fields forming around ORMUS**

This diagram shows how the helical fields line up.

Diagram showing how spirals knit together to form
nested spirals, which result in the formation of tubes

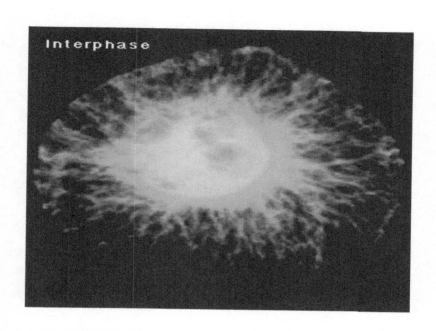

Interphase

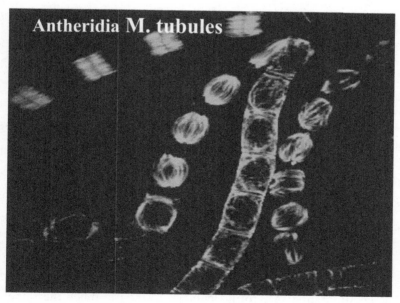

Antheridia M. tubules

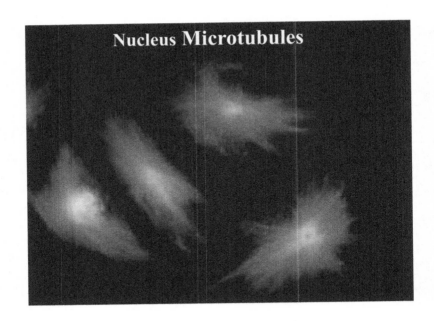

Nucleus Microtubules

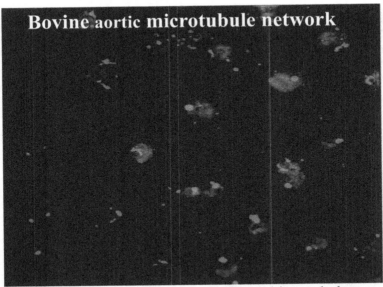

Bovine aortic microtubule network

**Microfilaments:** Microfilaments are formed in much the same fashion as microtubules except that they are trapping other molecules rather than just super-charged water. This occurs when the nested spiral fields become more compounded and firmly knit together. Molecules which are more structural than water are then trapped within forming strands. These filaments act to give structure and form for the cell. They help tie cells in place and tie organelles in position within the cell. Not all cells have these structures, as some cells are designed to be malleable or free flowing. Some cells actually form these filaments for certain tasks and then they are destructed. When microfilaments are photographed they resemble cotton within the cell. The cell must undergo a special dye method in order to capture the filaments on film however, they are much easier to photograph than are microtubules. Other similar structures are formed during mitosis. These filaments, called *actinase,* act as tracks for the genes to travel upon in an organized manner during cell division.

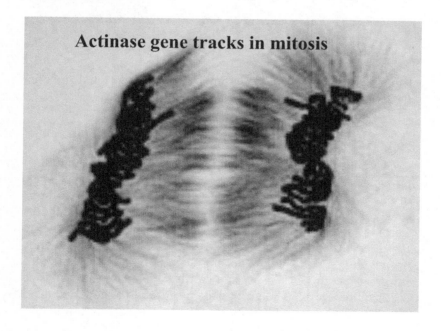

Actinase gene tracks in mitosis

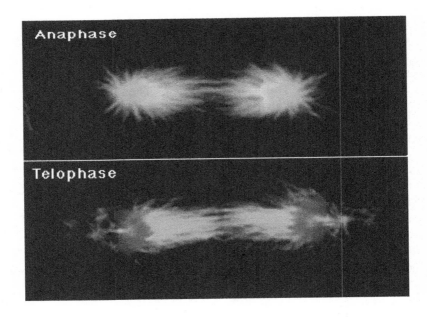

### Ruthenium

Ruthenium is involved in some microfilament and tubulin formation. It is found heavily in the cells of the body.

### Iridium

Concerning iridium, it should be noted that it is very important biologically, especially in the di-atomic form as we will soon discuss. It is especially interesting to note that all of the iridium found on Earth is from outer space. Nearly all of the iridium on Earth has been dispersed due to a few major meteoric events. It is especially interesting to me that such an element not originating on Earth should become so important to cell function. In great antiquity it was known that this element did not originate on Earth. The great alchemist *Tjehuti* (Thoth, Hermes, Nigishziddha) referred to it as the *foreign powers* suggesting that it was not of Earth and that it was in some way powerful. The name iridium comes from the word for iris meaning rainbow. The salts of iridium are highly colored giving rise to its name and it turns a beautiful lavender color during the alchemical process just before becoming totally high spin di-atomic white powder. Iridium is a hard white metal similar in color to platinum except with a slight yellowish cast. It is often recovered during the smelting process for platinum. Iridium is the most non-corrosive metal known and, for this reason, it is not attacked by aqua regia. Due to this fact, it is difficult to work with alchemically and has to be reduced by means of molten salts or brine quenches. Iridium has a very high melting point so even quenching methods are difficult. Due to its high melting point, it is often used to manufacture high temperature crucibles; and due to its hardness, it is used to harden other metals such as platinum or osmium. The standard meter rod held in France is constructed of a platinum iridium alloy so as to be durable and non-corrosive. Due to its hard, non-corrosive nature, iridium is used a great deal in the manufacture of satellite electronic components which need to withstand very harsh conditions indeed. In great antiquity, the Vedic peoples used this metal in their alloys to manufacture *vimanas* (flying machines). In modern times we have not been able to identify all of the alloys used by the early Vedic peoples. Many of these alloys would be considered greatly important to industry however, we must first learn that the alloys may contain metals that are not actually in the metallic state. These special alloys may in fact contain mon and di-atoms of certain metals locked in the metal matrix or they may contain microclusters. The introduction of microclusters or mon or di-atomic high spin materials to metals produces many effects in the host metal ranging from increased strength to increased melting point. The metals in some cases may be used as catalysts for transmutation of carbon to oxygen.

Iridium is important in metabolism and has been implicated in telomerase function. It is important in microtubulin and microfilament formation and is found heavily within brain and nerve tissue. It may also be important in DNA function, similar to rhodium. It has been shown that iridium works in conjunction with rhodium to help light flow within the DNA strand. This flow of light energizes the DNA strand so that it can transfer instructions to the RNA. DNA needs this energy for replication and repair of damage caused by radiation which is constantly occurring. When the DNA is depleted of iridium and rhodium it cannot repair itself nor duplicate and therefore the cell ages. The more the body becomes depleted of iridium and rhodium the more, and faster, the body ages.

### Gold

Gold is very instrumental in the stimulation of the pineal and pituitary glands. The pineal gland has long been deemed "the seat of the soul". Through the function of this gland we receive our intuitive nature and spiritual feelings. Through its most powerful hormone melatonin, it protects the body from oxidation by free radicals, regulates our biological clocks, and helps to time the workings of the pituitary gland. The pituitary gland is the master gland which regulates many systems and most of the other glands of the body, often with the help of the hypothalamus. So, it seems that the pineal gland is the master of the master. However the pineal gland in most people functions on a very limited basis. When the pineal is well stimulated, it produces a chemical known as dimethyltriptamine or DMT, referred to as brain sand for it manifests as tiny crystals around the base of the pineal gland. DMT, when released, produces a very deeply spiritual effect reportedly allowing the person to see visions, hear voices, remote view and foretell the future. When synthesized, DMT ingested in large doses causes what has been labeled as hallucinations. However shamans have used certain DMT-bearing plants for millennia to produce this effect as a useful oracle. So it may be that the effect is not simply hallucinogenic. We must also ask the questions: Why would the brain create something under normal conditions that produces hallucinations? What possible advantage would this lend for survival if the hallucinations were not in some way beneficial? Could it be that the effect is not simply hallucinogenic but rather something much more?

The pineal gland oddly enough is actually constructed as an eye-like structure. It is capable of sensing light even through the cranium. Interestingly, the pineal rests directly below the fontanel or the soft spot on a baby's skull which completely closes up by the time the child is two years of age. This is the reason why very young children are more open to the spiritual realm. They often see and react to things that others do not. When we were created by the Anunnaki, we were burdened with a number of defects at the order of Enlil designed to hold back our development somewhat, making us easier to control by our overlords. One of these defects was the closing of the fontanel. If one were to study the giant humanoid skulls that have been found, some of which are depicted in this book, one would notice that many have an identifiably open fontanel. However most pictures represented on the internet are taken from a side or forward angle which does not allow the fontanel area to be easily viewed. The skull of the Anunnaki has an open fontanel which allows the full stimulation of the pineal gland by light. It is uncertain, but perhaps their skulls evolved this way naturally due to their very low light environment.

The pineal gland really is the third eye. It provides us with the subtle intuitive insight of the shaman. The pineal is able to sense frequencies of light not seen by the eyes and so it is able to see the unseen energetic patterns that are all around us when properly stimulated. Gold ORMUS helps with the stimulation of the pineal. When the pineal is sufficiently stimulated it produces and excretes DMT which will make those who are not used to this a bit nauseous, just as the ingestion of DMT will produce nausea.

In great antiquity, the manna/gold ORMUS was almost always associated with the opening of the pineal gland known as the seat of the soul. There are untold depictions of priests, fish suited priests, gods such as Oanis/Lord Enki and his priests, angels, and other winged beings who carried a pail in one hand and offered a pine cone with the other. The pinecone was a representation of the pineal gland while the pail was a bucket of manna. This represented the offering of manna to stimulate and fertilize the pineal gland. This would activate a person's ability to access the soul and spiritual realms, thus open the door to enlightenment. It must be understood that the tradition was commenced by Enki who actually loved humans and wanted to see them progress spiritually.

**Anunnaki angels offering pineal fertilization by way of manna.**

**Fish-suited priests offering pineal fertilization
and enlightenment depicted on an ossuary.**

118

The staff of Adonis also sports a pine cone as does one of the staffs of the Pope. Additionally, a Vatican courtyard contains the largest sculpture of a pinecone in the world. In this regard, the pinecone represents enlightenment due to pineal stimulation.

It is important here to realize that the ORMUS transports light frequencies to the pineal so light is the primary stimulant in all cases. However, the regular use of ORMUS of gold will help to build a microtubule network within and about the pineal, making it more active and effective overall. A similar reaction occurs when a person meditates regularly, as regular meditation causes the pineal to expand and increase the neural network about the gland itself. In all cases, DMT and melatonin production is dramatically increased.

Gold is implicated in the formation of powerful microtubulin within certain cells of the brain which heightens the intuitive nature and has even been linked to certain telepathic abilities in many historical accounts. Gold helps to form the neural microtubulin which extend outside of the body and gather consciousness. An increase of this type of tubulin increases telepathy as environmental information is extracted from the photo-magnetic interference patterns of the ethereal.

### Copper

Copper is an important brain nutrient and is needed in the skin to aid in collagen production to help keep skin elastic. Copper is also useful in pigment setting, thus a copper deficiency can result in grey hair. Di-atomic copper in the high spin state is a very good healing manna. It helps the body go about mild detoxification while stimulating certain glandular activity throughout the body to help the body get going, so to speak. The effects of copper are mild and tolerable for those who have a weak constitution, or who may need a more gentle approach to stimulate health before moving on to something more radical like platinum for instance.

## Platinum

Platinum may increase the immune function and reduce allergic responses. It may cause an antabuse reaction to alcohol, as it is a radical detoxifier for the body. Platinum in its high spin monatomic form has proven to be very strong as a healing manna. However platinum may scare the user, for it causes the body to quickly and thoroughly attack any foreign microbe or any cancer or pre-cancerous tumor. One subject who received platinum suddenly realized that many of her moles became red, swollen and sore. This caused her to have the moles removed and to discontinue the platinum. If she had continued, it is likely that the moles would have sloughed off after some time. People who have taken platinum and then drank too much alcohol have often experienced an antabuse effect where they become very ill as the body violently struggles to detoxify itself. For myself, I am unable to drink too much as I begin to experience a sharp stabbing pain in the left nostril which leads up into my head as I begin to overdo it. The pain is not persistent; it only strikes with each sip of alcohol. This is sufficient to tell me that enough is enough.

## Nickel

Nickel is thought to increase learning ability as it is good for the neural network and the brain. It is also said to help increase the formation of ideas in the brain and to positively affect certain glandular function.

## Silver

ORMES silver, and silver in its colloidal form, may act as an anti-bacterial agent in the body. Di-atomic silver may also play a role in the formation of microtubules in certain cell types.

## Palladium

Palladium may help build dental enamel and maintain bone density. It is also thought to strengthen connective tissues.

## Osmium and Mercury

Since osmium and mercury are, in their metallic form, very poisonous to the body, little is known about their function in biological systems in their ORMUS state. This is likely due to the reluctance of researchers to study them in this role.

## Cellular

Under the section on rhodium ORMUS, we discussed the importance of microtubulin and microfilaments within the cell. Generally speaking, the cell needs these substances in order to communicate by way of light and to act as the template to form filaments which strengthen the cell and bind the organelles in place. Cells that are free roaming need no external filaments, however cells that are stationary use filaments to bind themselves in place while still allowing interstices for the transport of nutrients between the cells. ORMUS of iridium are likely responsible for the transport of messages across the nucleic barrier in order to write RNA instructions for cell function. Cells communicate with each other through the use of microtubules and may conduct consciousness from the dimensionless unified field through the wormhole-like microtubules. Cells may use the frequencies of various ORMUS to act as catalysts for carrying out different cellular functions. There may be important micro-transmutations that take place within the cell as a matter of course through the function and ability of the ORMUS materials to allow various nutrients to be utilized properly by the cell mitochondria and also to aid in the function of other organelles.

**Neurons**

Neurons use chemicals that conduct light in order to pass messages across the synapses. Likewise, they conduct messages within the dendrites through micro-tubule action. For this reason, the neurons of the body are loaded with iridium and rhodium in the di-atomic high spin state. When brain tissue is dried and the ORMUS is extracted after all organics are removed, 3% to 5% of the original dry weight remains as ORMUS of rhodium and iridium. This is a great indicator that the function of the brain and nervous system greatly depends on ORMUS and its superconductivity of certain light frequencies which may include the Meissner fields of the Earth and of the biological organism itself. For some time it has been held in biology that neurons converse simply by sending out neurotransmitters from neuron to neuron. These chemicals then would dock with special receptors designed to fit only one chemical like a lock and key. Each neurotransmitter seeks its own special receptor on each synapse. Recently it has been proven that the chemicals may not even dock with the neuron at all but rather go out and show themselves like a signpost while offering only their signal to the neighboring neuron or some other cell. The neuron accepts the signal and passes on the message. If it is another type of cell that receives the message, a muscle cell for example, behavior is adjusted accordingly. In this case, a contraction is performed by the muscle cell. It seems that the synapse can be likened somewhat to a spark gap on a spark plug; each chemical produces a unique frequency spark which may be transported via microtubulin from the sensory dock through the neuron eventually giving rise to the next emission of chemicals and subsequent spark. Video has actually been taken of light waves moving through neurons as they send messages. With this type of imaging one can actually see the messages traveling through the nerve tissue.

It has been shown that brain cells and other neurons produce tubulin that extend vast distances outside of the cell and in some cases outside of the confines of the body itself. This tubulin may be the actual "Genie in the bottle" which provide environmental /ethereal information gleaned from the ethereal photo interference patterns which gives rise to the quantum computations of the brain's neurons. However, this is not a one-way street. It is important to realize that the whole of the self is not encapsulated within the body. In fact, the whole of the self is not even all within this dimension. There is the higher self, if you will, that is outside of dimension. The so called higher self exists in the realm where all dimensions are unified. When all dimensions are unified, no dimension exists. This is to say that there is no before or after. There is essentially no time or space as all existence is simultaneous without beginning or end. Any point in dimensional space/time can be accessed from the dimensionless realm. This place is the place of our creation and the home of the higher self which is but a facet of the great all-consciousness *Adon*, the lord of the cosmos. As we are fed conscious input in the form of spiritual intent through the microscopic worm holes we call microtubules, we send phased interference patterns back through other microtubules. The information we send back to the higher self is coded into our one and only frequency logarithm of photo interference. This is the way our computer brain and cellular intelligence is downloaded to the operator or higher self.

### Consciousness

It is easy to get concepts like thought, consciousness, intellect and awareness all entangled and confused. We tend to use many of these words interchangeably which clouds our understanding of their true meanings. Thought is a biochemical process that happens within our brains and throughout our bodies through the transfer of electrical impulses, chemical hormones, neural peptides and other body/brain chemicals. Some of this thought is conscious, some of it is subconscious and some of it is unconscious. The hard drive for these thoughts is our brain. Our mind however is not just in our brain; it in fact extends throughout and to some degree outside of our bodies and therefore should not be confused with the brain. The mind includes the functions of the brain, our emotional being, our body communication and to some degree spiritual contact.

Thought is continuous and has a pulsing nature. Thoughts are not confined to the brain. In actuality thought pulses spread out through our entire being in all directions much like ripples in a pond, changing form as they go. The frequency of the thought pulses are determined by the frequency of the brain. Brain wave frequency is nothing more than the speed at which the various types of thought pulses occur as they originate in different regions of the brain. Between the pulses, there is space that we, for this purpose, will call the receiving mode. This space allows for the interjection of intent from spirit though the patch cord of the soul. The supplied intent or desire influences the next thought pulse. The brain operates on many frequencies at once to form a common frequency which is much like a chord in music. The frequency of this chord is the brain wave state such as beta, alpha and so on. We tend to spend most of our waking life in the beta state once we become adults. When we sleep, we go down through the levels of alpha and into the many layers of theta state. If our brain wave activity were to slow down below all the levels of theta we would be in delta which would be nearly void of brain wave activity. Many people who go into coma are in a delta state. If our brain wave activity were to speed up from beta we would be entering gamma states. The faster our brainwave frequencies become, the less space there is between the pulses for our spiritual intent to be injected. In other words, our receiving mode is compromised. Yet the computer-like brain is able to balance spiritual input with preplanned responses and functions. Some people, especially athletes, function quite well when in gamma state because they have a great deal of reflex response thought stored by the primitive portions of the brain to utilize while in this state. Quite frankly they do not need to make decisions; they have preplanned decisions which just happen automatically to certain stimuli while in the gamma state. This allows for extreme accuracy, efficiency and speed of reaction in a fight or flight situation.

On the other hand, when we slow our brainwave activity down to alpha for instance, the spaces or amount of time between pulses increases our receiving mode capability and therefore allows more easily for the injection of spiritual intent. While we are in

124

the upper levels of theta there is as much space for spirit as there is pulse or thought activity. As we get into the lower levels of theta we begin to have more spiritual activity than biochemical activity.

So, from knowing this information, one can understand that when our brainwave activity becomes too fast or, to put it into scientific terms, when the cycles per second become too high, the thought pulses of the brain become so close together that in effect they are nearly touching or overlapping. If these pulses are produced too near together, the pulsing melds into a brain storm of electrical activity without space between pulses to accommodate direction of thought. What is really happening in simplified terms is that there is not ample time for the clearing of electrochemical activity between thoughts. There is no room for the interjection of intent. When this happens, in effect the person's thoughts run together and the gray matter becomes a storm of electrochemical activity almost completely cut off from the flow of spiritual input. We often refer to this as a panic attack. In some cases such as with epileptics, the activity can increase to the point that all the signals get jumbled and the circuitry gets shorted out by the flood of activity and the person may experience a seizure. These are the biochemical frequencies of fear. When we are frightened, the pulse frequencies of our brain speed up to the point that the brain does not have enough time in the receiving mode in which to receive instructions and guidance toward the next thought. We are supposed to rely on pre-programmed responses at this point that do not require the long process of thought. But if we have few or no pre-programmed response, we freeze because we are not thinking and we are not receiving spiritual intent due to our elevated brainwave frequencies. So, in this condition our connection to the unified field is weak. This is one way that continuous fear works to sever our ties to spirit. Some people say that the forces of evil are of a lower frequency than are the forces of love which are higher frequencies. At least in the circumstances of brain function this is an incorrect assertion. The higher the brain wave frequency the greater chance one has to being cut off from spirit and being infiltrated by what is perceived as evil.
Spiritual frequencies themselves are very high as to allow for

maximum input of intent given the short injection time between thought pulses. Low frequencies, Earth bound spirits for example, do not inject intent; they merely entrain other random frequencies to their own signals decreasing freewill thought in the confused individual and then do their will through repeated suggestion. Within the biological system it is the ORMUS which offers its ability to conduct light frequencies in both visible and non-visible forms throughout the system. Efficient communication takes place via these light frequencies. As the frequencies of spiritual intent drop to lower octaves to the level of light frequencies, the spiritual intent is then able to enter the physical biological system. These instructions encoded in light interference patterns are interpreted by the brain and processed as notions, intuitions, feelings, etc.

As the microtubules formed by the ORMUS act as tiny wormholes to bring in our consciousness in this way, we are continually animated into the world and aware of self and non-self. When we are in a good receiving mode, we feel most like ourselves which is experienced often as a sense of completeness, well-being, independence and fulfillment. Outside interference from non-self, lower frequencies causes confusion, conflict, contradiction, and depression. Even if the outside force has no negative intent, the frequency is non-self and therefore will be constantly rejected by the self like a donated organ. The outside force, if not tied to its own host, will also need to feed and therefore will drain energy via the microtubulin system of the body (our auric field) by robbing light frequencies of the intra and extra cellular communication system. This cannot be thwarted with the traditional bubble of protective light as that itself is a food source and an attractant. As we will learn in later chapters, such energy can be dealt with in various ways but for the most part the self can be disguised by keeping the spirit connection strong and using that power to effectively un-create all scenarios where such robbery may occur. When a high degree of spiritual connection is maintained, the entire orchestra of bodily frequencies are thus elevated to higher octaves out of the reach of the frequencies which are bound to Earth. When we keep our frequencies elevated in this manner, there is no place for the longer wavelengths to enter. The bodily frequencies that

I am referring to are sets of frequencies which are unique to the individual and, through their own interference patterns, give rise to the individual self. These bodily frequencies are not to be confused with the brain wave frequencies that we spoke of earlier which are in effect contained within this other frequency system.

The *Shaolin* warrior-priests believed that they could reach a state of mind which would allow no arrow a place to enter, so too can we reach a state of mind and connection which will allow no lower frequency a place to enter. However as we will later learn, when we consider Inner Alchemy, the frequencies of the body and brain are governed by the mind and its many feeling states. This is why emotions can be considered as high frequency or low frequency. Love-based emotion produces low brainwave frequency and a high body or physical frequency. Fear-based emotions tend to lower the physical frequencies while elevating the brainwave frequencies. This condition reduces our ability to receive consciousness and spiritual intent. It also causes reduced efficiency in body communication. It does however increase our channeling ability with Earth bound spirits as well as opening us up to the tampering of those spirits by other living incarnates. The greatest problem with the fear-based mode is the manifestation of the very object that is feared. You get what you put your energy into. This is the Law of Attraction that we must learn to work with if we are to become a Master Alchemist. Since we are all human, we will falter. However, we must learn to become based in love more than fear if we are to become alchemists or if we are to at the least enjoy gifts of the ORMUS elements, especially the gold.

### Glandular

Since the pituitary gland is the master gland of all other glands, and since the pituitary is so heavily influenced by ORMUS, one then might say that all glands are influenced by ORMUS. There are a great number of glands that are directly influenced by ORMUS, however it is far from certain how ORMUS influences glands. ORMUS may aid in the manufacture of hormones and other glandular secretions and/or may aid in the glands' receiving of instructions. It is obvious that at least certain glands have been identified to be greatly benefited by certain ORMUS.

### Immune Function

The ORMUS of platinum, ruthenium and iridium has been observed to help immune function. It has been reported to cure allergies of many types, especially where ORMUS of platinum is concerned. Platinum and iridium are great detoxifiers and cause immediate detoxification where alcohol or drugs are concerned. One such incidence of this was relayed by David Hudson. There is one account of a group of people who took platinum ORMUS for their allergies. After a few days they all were allergy free. They decided to get together and celebrate. They proceeded to go out on the town and they all had a few too many drinks with very unpleasant results. Platinum often creates an antabuse effect in the body when the body becomes substantially intoxicated as a first line of defense against toxic substances. It happened that all of our allergy free guinea pigs got sick as dogs until the alcohol had left their systems. Other detox responses have been noted as well including profuse sweating, over-sleeping and frequent bowel movements, all followed by increased energy and feelings of well being.

It must be stressed that the ORMUS compounds do not and cannot kill microorganisms such as bacteria, flagellates, paramecia, amoeba and the like, nor can viruses be destroyed by the ingestion of ORMUS. The immune system can be strengthened by the ORMUS but there is no guarantee that the ORMUS recipient will not ever contract an infection. However, since body communication and timing is tuned by the ORMUS, the recipient will recover with short-lived symptoms as the body is quick to repair itself. The immune system can be built up over time with the proper use of ORMUS which will allow the body to more effectively fight off viruses and microbes. It should be noted here that ORMUS is at its best where genetic diseases or damage is concerned due to the ability of ORMUS of rhodium and iridium to repair genetic mistakes or damage caused by cellular invaders.

Many of the diseases suffered by humans are autoimmune in nature. Such diseases may include arthritis, asthma, cataracts, Crohn's Disease, eczema, systemic Lupus, Addison's, scleroderma, certain types of anemia, and even type one diabetes just to name a few. Some of these diseases can normalize after long term consumption of the proper ORMUS mix. The consumption of the proper ORMUS mix will help prevent immune diseases from materializing because the immune system is able to remain balanced. A balanced immune system will not attack the body and will not drop its defense against disease. The immune system remains in balance during long term consumption of the ORMUS due to the perfecting of the body's internal communication system.

So while certain immune diseases might be healed by the consumption of the proper ORMUS mix, it is certain that the consumption over time of ORMUS products in the proper mix such as that found in nature, will prevent immune dysfunction that has not already occurred.

**The Matrix**

There is one other form of ORMUS which reaches further than the subject matter of this book which I will only touch upon here concerning the work of the late Dr. Merkl. It has been discovered that the Chondriana, which create an additional immune component described as black proteins by Dr. Merkl, have actually been analyzed to be pure gold ORMUS. The technology for creating Chondriana as well as other life giving substances from ORMUS was known by the ancient Sumerians and has been well documented in their pictographs and writings as shown by Dr. Merkl. He rediscovered this wonderful and priceless information only to become another victim of the establishment. As reward for all of his dedication and genius, he was harassed by the FDA and The Patent and Trademark office, his 400+ patents were pilfered by the government even though many were patented for the government, and eventually he suffered a mysterious death. If established dogmatic organizations would only step aside and allow growth of knowledge and the dispensation of truth, there is no telling what we could accomplish. If all that has ever been known about the ORMUS were to come to light once again, we might regain the tree of life and live extended healthy lives free of illness. It is certain that if we are to attain the extended lives of our ancient forefathers, we must most definitely change our reproductive habits which so disturbed the Anunnaki in ancient times, toward those that would not overpopulate our planet. There is no way that human reproduction can morally be controlled through enforcement, this is an issue that will only solve itself via the evolution and ascension of the entire human race toward a higher consciousness and a greater understanding of the earth and its carrying capacity.

There are many ideas and concepts surrounding the notion of the matrix. As discussed earlier, Dr. Merkl was the first to ratify the theories set forth by a certain Dr. Muller of Germany who proposed that there is a standing wave form which exists throughout the universe which acts as the matrix of everything. This becomes very apparent when one studies the drawings of Dr. Merkl depicting the light interference patterns associated with the creation of Chondrianna and life crystals. The geometry is described by Dr Merkl as a six plus one configuration, a pattern resembling a flower. It is a very interesting fact that this pattern has been known throughout history as the *Flower of Life.* The Flower of Life pattern has been etched on countless church, temple and cave walls throughout history. It became quite clear to me why this pattern was so well-known through history when meditating one night. The pattern revealed itself to me in vivid red and green, and remained fixed in my line of site and remained there even upon opening my eyes. I was given a glimpse of the matrix. The reason I discovered why this pattern is so prevalent in so many cultures about the earth is that it is something that one can actually see when in the right state of mind. Possibly the ORMUS could have something to do with the ability to see the pattern, but this remains to be verified. I have now seen this pattern in all of its glory a total of three times. Each time it is as exciting as the first and so very captivating. When it happens, I attempt to hold on to the experience as long as I possibly can.

**The Flower of Life**

Now, to expand slightly on the theories of Dr Muller, he postulates that a homogenous pattern of standing waves exists throughout the universe. The standing waves are bounded by scales thus he terms the theory Global Scaling. According to Muller, these **standing/pressure waves** are always divided by three more standing waves within each standing wave. Everything has its place in this matrix residing on a node where waves cross. Since there are an infinite number of matching nodes, everything within the universe has an infinite number of counterparts. In order to find out which node one is working with, and thus all counterparts, logarithmic calculations are used to determine where the nodes are in the existing scales.

This system of Global Scaling can be used in almost any branch of science as it is used to measure the standing wave forms which are inherent homogenously throughout the universe and thus throughout all things which exist within it. This theory is constructed based on the scales of nature. It takes a crack at the explanation of gravity as well as the formation of DNA. The theory can be applied in medicine and architecture alike. It explains how teleportation is possible and how messages can be sent throughout the universe by the use of very little energy. In fact, Dr. Hartmut Muller eventually ratified his own theory by using global scaling to send messages through space. Interestingly, with global scaling, very little energy is needed as one does not have to propagate a wave; the waves rather already exist throughout nature. Normally if one were to send a message, the further the distance the more energy is necessary. An example would be that a pebble tossed into the water would send waves out a certain distance before the waves dissipated. However, if one wanted the waves to go further, one would need to toss in a bigger rock. The bigger the rock the farther the waves travel. Now if waves already exist, to send a message why not just use those waves to send it? This is precisely the method used by Dr. Muller. Instead of propagating waves which requires a lot of energy, existing waves are modulated instead which takes very little energy. One way to explain it would be to first find a node and then shake it. Simultaneously and homogenously this disturbs the entire wave and so all corresponding nodes shake with the same frequency as the one that is shaken by the sender. Interestingly, since this is a pressure wave it is a bit like pushing one end of a pole, the opposing end moves simultaneously there is no need for the ripple effect. This means that messages go to the receiver simultaneously with the time they were sent. It has been revealed to me over time that a similar method of long distance communication was utilized by the Anunnaki. The matrix which allows for this mode of communication has been rediscovered by Dr. Muller. Additionally, Dr. Merkl saw the potential for health technologies the same as those that were taught to the Sumerians by the Anunnaki thousands of years ago.

This now brings us back to the point of it all, the matrix. It occurs to me that the standing/pressure waves that exist include many levels of frequencies ranging from infra-sound to frequencies high in the ultraviolet range of light. If this is not the case, then I would postulate that at the very least light waves exist in the same fashion due to involvement with the scalar waves. For this reason, light waves were able to be utilized by Merkl to create Chondrianna and life crystals. This is one reason why the hexagon is the main crystalline structure formed in life crystals and the reason for hexagonal crystalline structures in nature. I would also further postulate that these waves are more complex than a two dimensional view would explain. They would rather be configured more like the drawings of Dr. Merkl's six plus one geometry. This is the Flower of Life pattern we are so familiar with.

Also, it is apparent how the Sephira of the Qabala, which we will discuss later in the chapter on **Inner Alchemy**, perfectly fit into the Flower of Life pattern.

**The Qabalic Tree of Life fitting into the Flower of Life**

This pattern contains a great number of **phi** or **Golden Mean** ratio expressions which is a ubiquitous ratio in nature. Global scaling also contains many expressions of this ratio. It is the inherent ORMUS which finds its way into all life that allows all beings to interface with the Flower of Life, and thus, the Unified Consciousness. The ORMUS compounds, when heated, all form a crystal lattice which is a hexagonal matrix that fits into the Flower of Life pattern. It is my opinion that all ORMUS is highly attached to the Flower of Life pattern of standing waves, which explains many of the abilities that come along with its ample usage by the **Ascension Alchemist**. To learn more about

Dr. Hartmut Muller and his work, search Google for Global Scaling.

## ORMUS and Genes

The benefits of rhodium and iridium to the DNA have been thoroughly discussed in the section on rhodium. We could say further here that the telomeres of the chromosomes contain telomerase and it is suspected that ORMUS are involved in the function of telomerase. It has been demonstrated that cancer is immortal due to its continued building of the telomeres, yet the telomeres are not the reason for the uncontrolled growth. When the telomeres run out, the cell can no longer replicate. Certain ORMUS such as ruthenium, rhodium and iridium have been connected to telomerase. Could it be that cells can go haywire in the absence of one type of ORMUS such as rhodium and yet have the ability to capture more of another such as ruthenium and iridium? If this is possible, could it then be postulated that perhaps these elements must work in balance within the body and when we become severely depleted of one type we get out of balance allowing things to run out of control? Such may be the case with some cancers. This theory has been supported by an experiment involving rhodium and iridium. Rhodium, as was mentioned earlier, has been found to cure certain cancers. It has also been established that rhodium and iridium work in tandem to protect DNA from radiation.

When experiments with iridium alone were performed on cancer cells it was found to greatly increase their growth, however rhodium alone helps cancer cells normalize. This falls in line with the fact that iridium greatly increases metabolism. However, when rhodium is administered first so that it has time to reach the DNA and iridium is added later, the cancer cells become normalized more quickly than they do with rhodium alone. This is likely due to the role iridium plays when partnering with rhodium to help light flow within the DNA strand. Additionally, the two together protect the DNA from radiation damage as they repair it. Perhaps then it is the lack of rhodium while iridium remains that allows cancer cells to exhibit such rapid reproduction and high metabolism. This could be due

135

to the fact that rhodium is the most difficult of the ORMUS to uptake into the body. Over 70% of the rhodium that we consume passes through the intestine without being taken into the blood stream. It is likely that transport and transfer of rhodium through cell walls and organelles is also more problematic than other ORMUS elements.

### Reported Health Effects

The health effects of ORMUS throughout history have, in some cases, very likely been broadly overstated while other possible benefits have been overlooked. There is a great deal of lore, conjecture, fable, and fantasy surrounding these substances and their supposed effects, however much of the information is at least rooted in reality. There is now a growing base of individuals who take ORMUS as supplementation from which to collect information. Many of these individuals are sharing their results. However, there are in my observation some reckless individuals who are taking their manufactured substances without first analyzing them for heavy metals or other toxins. Some of the techniques that exist for producing ORMUS likely produce toxins as well. I will discuss some of these techniques in the appropriate section.

### Longevity

The vast majority of alchemists who reportedly had found the Philosopher's Stone lived very long and healthy lives, most of which exceeded 100 years of age. Some of these people lived well beyond 100 while still others were never reported to have died. Some of the alchemists were thought to have faked their deaths only later to have visited or accidentally run into those they had known earlier in life. It was said that the rate of aging for the alchemist was 1/4 that of normal, or 1 year for every 4 years. Therefore, the length of life may depend more on at what point in one's life the ingestion of the ORMUS elixirs began. It should be understood that the alchemist was typically taking many substances, yet most were made from gold or electrum only.

Many biblical figures attribute their longevity to the eating of manna, mufkutz, sacred bread or show bread. Other historical names and sources for these substances also hold them in association with strength and longevity. Such substances include manna, soma, homa, ambrosia, milk of the gods, the food and/or the bread of the gods, and so forth.

The early alchemists by all accounts lived exceedingly long lives of hundreds if not thousands of years. However these life spans cannot be proven. There is a great deal of supporting evidence for some of these super life spans; however, we just do not trust the records of great antiquity. So how about records of more recent antiquity? The following is a short list of the more adept alchemists and their recorded ages. Keep in mind that alchemists often faked their deaths and would be often spotted after their recorded deaths by many who knew them. The most common age for which deaths were faked was the early to mid-eighties. This may be the reason that most alchemists seem to die around this age as can be seen in the brief list below.

➢ Avicenna (Ebu Cinna) born A.D. 980 died 1036 at only 56 years of age (so you see not all philosophers were long lived.) On the other hand...
➢ Father Artephius lived 1026 years and authored the Art of Life Extension.
➢ Bernard of Theves born 1406 died 1490 at age 84.
➢ Nicholas Flammel died in 1415 at the age of 116. This is the same alchemist who is fabled in the Harry Potter books.
➢ Sandivogius born 1550 and died in 1636 at age 86.
➢ Alain de Lisle of Flanders was born 1188 and died in 1298 at age 110.
➢ John Aurello was born in 1441 and died in 1524 at age 83.
➢ Albertus Magnus born in 1193 and lived until 1280 to the age of 87
➢ John Dee lived from 1527 to 1608 and lived 81 years
➢ Isaac Newton lived from 1642 to 1727 when he died at the age of 85

Most alchemists would rather not have their ages known as they were already a target of the authorities such as the Roman Catholic Church and monarchies of the day. This is also why they often faked their deaths. Even if their deaths were not faked, the achievement of the age of 80 in itself was an age nearly double the normal age span of the day. It does seem odd however that most of the alchemists in our list above seemed to die in their 80s. There are late-comer alchemists who were born after the age where the churches and governments held such power. Some claim to know alchemists who were of great age. One such alchemist and his wife, **Richard and Isabella Ingalese**, who themselves simply vanished sometime around the age of 80 in the early 1900s, supposedly knew several long-lived alchemists. Richard mentions in a lecture he gave in 1927 that "incredible as it may appear, I know of one alchemist more than 600 years old, and one whose age is more than 400, and another whose age is 200 and all of these look and function as do men in the prime of life at about 40 years." The Ingalese's themselves were reported to never have appeared more than the age of 40 or so.

Perhaps one of the most interesting of all alchemists is *Compte de Saint Germaine* **(Count of Saint Germaine)**. He is a shining example of one alchemist who faked his death. Saint Germaine lived during the 18th century. His birth date is not well known however he is said to have been 97 when he supposedly died. Reportedly, he went into his house and refused all but his closest friend to be with him. He announced from his second story bedroom window that he had grown tired and was going to die even though everyone who knew of him continued to marvel at his youthfulness of a man in his early forties. Some time shortly after that it was announced that he had died although his body was never produced. After his supposed death, he was seen often by friends and colleagues all over Europe. He was last seen in England in 1821. If he was born in the year 1690 when many supposed him to have been born, he may have been 131 when he was last sighted. It was reported that he still looked to be in his forties. So, if Saint Germaine did in fact fake his death, he may still be with us even today.

Since his origins were merely speculation, no one really knows the exact date he was born and some have it that he had even faked his death before. The same tradition puts his age at over 350 years. It was said by many that he had spent over 80 years in Tibet studying with the Masters. The book *The Red Lion* mentions his periodic visits to Tibet and that he thought of Tibet as his real home.

No one ever knew his name so he was called the Count of Saint Germaine named after a small town in France where he had resided for a time. He was a highly accomplished musician and violinist. It is said that one day he stated that he had learned everything that could be learned about the violin and so he put it down never to play again. St. Germaine was known to make the most marvelous gemstones which he loved to adorn himself with lavishly. Even though he greatly loved gems, he freely gave them away without consequence. Saint Germaine was said to have never eaten in public even though he spent much of his time conversing with students and intellectuals in pubs and restaurants. According to the book *The Red Lion*, his sustenance consisted entirely of a homemade gruel he made from a mixture of grains and meals. In fact no one save his helper ever saw him eat.

Saint Germaine was quite the adventurer, traveling extensively throughout Europe and the Far East. His passion seems to have been working with governments to try to help them evolve toward a higher condition. To this end, his ability to maintain status in high circles and within the aristocracies in France and throughout Europe facilitated his ability to work with governments. He notably maintained a plethora of residences throughout Europe due to his frequent travel. He is even fabled to have owned a castle in Transylvania. His Transylvania castle was said to have been the place where he would practice his magic rituals undisturbed. He is said to have worn chains of gold about his neck and a scarlet red cloak during this ritual magic. It is likely that such magic is exactly the type of thought form magic that we will discuss later in this book. This type of magic was practiced by the early Magi and was designed to carry a practitioner into higher levels of being. He supposedly practiced a form of yoga along with arduous meditation rituals that accounted for vast amounts of his time.

The Count enjoyed theater and was himself involved in acting which gave him the chance to adorn himself lavishly in the jewels which he so loved to display. Theater also gave him the chance to prove his swordsmanship in a non-violent setting as he was a master swordsman and a master of many martial arts. The Count was accomplished in so many different skills and talents that many supposed him to posses the knowledge and skills of many life times. He was fluent in many languages, all without flaw. His favorite pastime was conversing with intellectuals and students and it was said that there was never a subject that could be broached that he had not mastered.

He was never known to be without coin. It was supposed by many that he manufactured his gold by way of his advanced alchemical skills; especially since he was known to change lead to gold as a sort of parlor trick for elite guests. The transmutation entailed the immersion of a small pellet of Red Lion encased in wax into a crucible of molten lead contained within an alchemical furnace. After the feat, he would cool the specimen and allow people to inspect it. Then he would give the specimen to a lucky guest to take it and have it analyzed. The specimen would then belong to that guest.

The Count was also quite known for his soothsaying ability. He was the close confidant and advisor to many kings, queens and nobles due to this ability. It could be considered quite odd how at a time when other alchemists feared for their lives and thus had to practice their work in great secrecy, The Count of Saint Germaine freely expressed his knowledge and practice and even performed it for royalty. Perhaps his willing participation in the lives and events of royalty and the aristocracy made him indispensable to all. His ability to move about so freely at a time when all was in such turmoil was nothing short of amazing. He seemed to be untouchable.

Even though he spent the majority of his time telling futures and counseling the royals and the nobles, his real work and concern was for the common people. He never ceased to point out to rulers that to show real nobility was to ease the suffering and plight of the common people. He often manipulated Kings and Queens into acting more on behalf of the people by convincing them that they would be more loved and revered and thus more powerful.

The Compte de Saint Germaine is held in such high regard to this day that many consider him an ascended master. There would even be those who pray to him as a demigod of sorts. The name Saint Germain seems to suggest that he is an actual saint. Even though he was never actually pronounced a saint by any religious affiliation, he remains a noble and saintly figure in history and in the minds and hearts of those who would know his works.

**From left to right- Kuthumi - El Morya - Saint Germain, Madam Blavatsky (seated)**

The Comte de Saint Germaine (d.1784?) Shown here wearing a gentleman's wig.

## Biblical Ages

Did the early patriarchs actually live as long as the Bible suggests? If so, then were these biblically reported life spans average for all earthlings? Or were there particular races or groups who possessed markedly longer life spans than average people? The answer is yes, there were certain races that lived markedly longer than most people. The reason for these extreme ages was due to two factors. Firstly, the amounts of Anunnaki DNA present, and secondly, the type of supplementation ingested. There were races that lived for thousands of years and races that lived for hundreds of years and still races that lived for only tens of years. The longest lived races included the Elfin or Elvan race (*ShiningOones*), the *Tuatha De Dannon* better known as the *Fairies* or *Fair Folk*. We also have the *Nephelim* who were the giant offspring of the *Nibiruan* human mixing, and the expressly bred Kingly lines who were designed to rule humans and act as mediators to the Anunnaki (Nibiruan elite). This is just to name a few. Next, we have some other groups such as the Biblical patriarchal family line, the second and third dynasty Egyptian Kings, and the Rama of northern India, Pakistan and Tibet.

There are a plethora of ancient textual sources other than the Book of Genesis which offer information concerning life spans of various races during the biblical ages spanning back though time beyond the time of King Solomon. Many texts reference times prior to the Great Flood. Let us now take a look at a list of ages compiled from the Book of Genesis.

*And God said, "My Spirit will not contend with man forever, for he is indeed mortal and their days of life will be 120 years." (Genesis 6:3)*

Here is a compiled chronological list of biblical people who lived longer than 120 years. As you read down the list to the point where God states the "120 year rule", notice the gradual decline to the 120 years of Moses. It is interesting to see that the last biblically recorded person to live beyond 120 years was Jacob/Israel. Jacob was the father of the people of Israel.

143

- Adam = 930 years
- Seth = 912 years
- Enosh = 905 years
- Cainan = 910 years
- Mahalalel = 895 years
- Jared = 962 years
- Enoch =365 years, did not die, was translated (taken up to Heaven) at that age
- Methuselah = 969 years
- Lamech = 777 years
- Noah = 950 years, many accounts have Noah living vastly longer than the biblical account.
- God says man will only live 120 years
- Shem = 600 years, some discrepancies exist, there are accounts which have Shem living vastly longer, while there is also a possibility that Shem was killed during a takeover of Salem by the Israelites.
- Arphaxad = 438 years
- Salah = 433 years
- Eber = 464 years
- Peleg = 239 years
- Reu = 239 years
- Serug = 230 years
- Nahor = 148 years
- Terah = 205 years
- Abraham = 175 years
- Ishmael = 137 years
- Isaac = 180 years
- Jacob (Israel) = 147 years
- Joseph = 110 years
- Moses = 120 years
- Joshua = 110 years

You will not find another person in the Bible from this point on that exceeds 120 years. When referring to the **Sumerian King List** located in the appendix section, it can be seen that there were other groups that perhaps lived even longer than the biblical patriarch although they experienced the same decline in the length of their lives as is described in the Bible.

So what is actually happening here? The answer is that, at least with the patriarchal family as well as with the kingly lines of Egypt, the people were more closely associated with the Anunnaki blood lines than their surrounding counterparts. For example, it is noted in many Sumerian texts that the actual father of Noah was in fact Enki himself who as we know was Anunnaki. He was born filled with light and had the full appearance of one of the angels. For this he was granted long life genetically. Then, when kingship was again descended from heaven after the Great Flood, many of the bloodlines that were the closest to the Anunnaki were chosen as the royal lines. One such line was the biblical patriarchal family. From these lineages, kings were chosen by various Anunnaki factions to support their individual interests and to lead the peoples of their specific domains. The chosen kings were then prepared from birth to rule and were fed on the starfire supplements to improve their strength, intellect, health and to make even greater improvements to their life spans. An additional advantage to the ingestion of these supplements was to allow for the telepathic delivery of instruction to the king. In this way, the king might act as an efficient human/Anunnaki go-between without having direct contact with the Anunnaki which had been forbidden by Enlil, The El-Shaddi. This telepathy was for the most part technological rather than spiritual. The shakunah helmet worn by the Anunnaki was but one part of the technology used to send messages to the king in the form of dreams and visions.

Eventually, the allowance of the starfire was rescinded and thus the life spans would then shorten as the bloodlines were eventually bred out by the mixing with other races to the more human life span of 120 years. There were those however who continued long life. These were the privileged ones who were taught the alchemical process for the manufacture of the alchemical replacement for the starfire, the ORMUS. These alchemists were often the kings themselves in the early times. However, alchemists were eventually employed by the kings to do the alchemical work on their behalf; thus the art was lost among the kingly lines and became expressly a secret art of the Vulcans, Hermeticist, Healers and Shamans and Priests. Races such as the Tuatha De Dannon (The Elves), continued to live long lives as they abstained from mixing with other races and continued to utilize the supplements and practices once taught to them by their early forefathers Dagda (Enki) and Dannon (Di-Anu, Inanna, Mary Anna Ishtar) the Beloved of Anu.

The Fairies, as they were called after their disappearance into the inner dimensions, were a very tall and robust white skinned race with blond or reddish hair, not the little flitting winged creatures we have come to know in fairytales. Some of them who were not able to go into other dimensions became nomads and spread all over the Earth. Some came to the New World while others went to Asia. Wherever they went they were hailed as giants due to their massive stature. Their mummies can be found in Asia (as seen in the book *The Mummies of Urumchi*), in the British Isles and all throughout the North, Central and South Americas. Those who went inward, as the Fairies did, were worshipped as gods of a sort with their stories still told today.

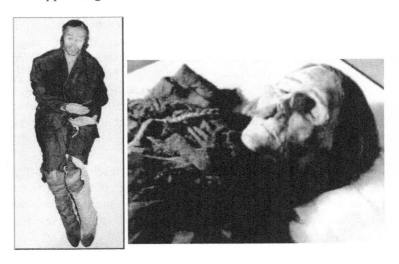

**The 3000 year old mummy with reddish brown hair known as Cherchen Man, a giant by early standards at 6' 7" tall, is now resting in Urumchi China near the place of his discovery. He was found along with a host of other very tall redheaded to blond Caucasoid mummies.**

A Peruvian red-headed mummy: apparently one of the last of the line of Viracocha, the Caucasian founders of South America

**From North America to South America, Native American lore speaks of Giants.**

*Artwork by Ernest Nelson*

**The Goddess Danna of the Tuatha De Dannan (Fairies) of Ireland and Scotland. She is depicted here with red hair.**

The Sidh, Fey,
fairies, etc. were
either opalescent
or shining

A shining Fairy princess depicted in early tapestry

Red-haired giant in Kentucky and in Canary Islands

# CHAPTER 9

### For the Health of It

The notion of cures and immaculate health comes to light even more so than longevity when dealing with the historical subject matter surrounding these ORMUS substances. The *Soma Pavamona* and the *Rig Veda* both speak extensively about how the soma juice makes the gods strong and healthy. In texts outside of the Bible, Moses sifts the alchemical white gold into the water of the Israelites to help sustain them in the desert. In many biblical stories, the sacred bread is offered to non-priests as an emergency sustenance yet it also increases their endurance and health. There are many stories of alchemists healing people with these substances, and they themselves remain looking youthful well into their old age. The white powder of rhodium, in my supposition, is the greatest overall benefit to health of all the ORMUS. The reason for this is the work it does for the DNA as well as increasing whole body communication by revving up the neural network. For this reason, biological functions become better timed and therefore the body functions more efficiently. Other benefits likely include increased sense of smell, better sleep function, regular bowel movements, and increased stamina.

Since the neural network utilizes light frequencies as part of the electrochemical message system, it stands to reason why rhodium, iridium and others would increase the flow of light through the neural network. Since all of these substances are superconductors of various light frequencies while acting as insulators to other frequencies, they lend these abilities to the system. Earlier we discussed the plausible notion that **Moses** and **Akhenaten** were actually one and the same. We are able to see through Biblical references that Moses and Aaron had extensive knowledge of the Manna. The same is true for Akhenaten. In fact, a central focus of Akhenaten's worship of Aten was to have the sun bless and charge the manna cakes with light before ingestion. Numerous depictions of Akhenaten and others of his entourage can be found of them holding up the shem shaped bread cakes to the rays of the Solar Disk. The rays are shown to extend downward with each ray terminating as a hand. The rays reach into all things in the pictorial relief. As the rays reach toward the shems held high in veneration, the terminal hands offer an ankh to the bread. This is the symbol of life and longevity. It is obvious that the sun was known to charge the manna with life giving light which could be transferred to the body upon consumption.

King Akhenaton blessing the Showbread in the light of Aten. The act of blessing the manna in the light of the sun was in fact the means of charging the manna with light before it was consumed. In the background Nefertiti can be seen blessing the showbread as well. Coming down with the hands of the sunrays one can see the ankh being offered to each representing the offering of life.

Earlier we spoke of the Soma Pavamana. This is a book found within the Rig Veda which is essentially the Hindu Bible. The Soma Pavamana is in its entirety a tribute to the God of Soma and its manufacture and consumption by the gods. It is called a "God amid the Gods" for all of the gods depend on it for strength, longevity and health. This book is laden with the secrets of the manufacture of soma and its effects on the body. Often the Soma Pavamana speaks of how the soma brings light to the body. It also associates this light with the sun. "Give us our portion in the Sun through thine own mental power and aids; and make us better than we are." states the Soma Pavamana.

The Soma Pavamana also discusses how the Soma makes the gods wise and creative. We discussed earlier how the Starfire and later the white powders of Gold were utilized to help the King reach the high level of consciousness known as the *Malku* by taking both the King and the Queen to the high plane of consciousness known as the *Plane of Sharon*. As we read on:

Vadic God holding a vessel of soma as described in the Soma Pavamana text within the Rig Veda

"Enkindled, Pavamana, Lord, sends forth his light on every side
in friendly show, the bellowing bull.
He, Pavamana, self-produced, speeds on-ward sharpening his horns:
he glitters through the firmament.
Brilliant like wealth, adorable, with splendour Pavamana shines,
Mightily with the streams of meath.
The tawny Pavamana, who strews from of old the grass with might,
is worshiped, God amid the Gods.
The golden, the celestial doors are lifted with their frames on high,
by Pavamana glorified"

Here the alchemist can see the great wealth of information concerning the *Soma* which is stored within the *Rig Veda*. However the information means little to those who know nothing of the Soma or ORMUS to begin with. But once we learn a bit about these substances, how they form, and how they are manufactured, we quickly realize to what these passages are referring. Since the soma is made from ORMUS-rich **Shilajit** mined from the rocks, it takes on a tawny appearance when processed. The tawniness is due to the lignin inherent in all plant material which is well known by anyone who practices plant alchemy. The lignin remains in the ancient shilajit detritus and tends to attach to ORMUS clusters causing a tan colored hue. The lignin can be filtered out with modern techniques. However, this was not possible using the filtration methods described in the Soma Pavamana where liquor was poured through fleece stuffed into a cylinder. The lignins carry some particular health effects and therefore were probably purposely retained to some degree. The shilajit was self-formed in ancient times as suggested by the text and carries light to those who ingest it. The shilajit moves through the rocks or firmament and extrudes each year. It was associated with gold and contained ORMUS gold. Shilajit also was formed from the grasses of ancient times ("strews from of old the grass with might") locked within the rocks under great pressure. Other descriptions of Soma from the Rig Veda follow. The second paragraph gives clues on the manufacture of Soma.

Engendering the sun in floods,
Engendering heavens lights,
Green hued, robed in the waters and the milk

By means of this eternal fleece may Surya's daughter purify
thy soma that is foaming forth
Ten sisters maids of slender form seize him
with the press and hold
him firmly on the final day

We can see from these verses that the soma is not only tawny but is greenish as well. This is due to the inherent colloidal copper, and other minerals such as silver and nickel, which had been added to the ancient detritus through percolation by the very rock which entombed it.

When one considers all that was inherent in Soma, one begins to see how great it must have been for health and why it was so prized. Soma, rich in many colloidal minerals and ORMUS, contained many surviving chemicals inherent within the ancient plant material from which it was extracted. This was the super drink of the Gods which kept them strong, healthy, vigorous, and youthful as well as helping them maintain a sharp creative intellect. It is disappointing to think that many people have come to think of soma as some sort of drug such as ephedrine. Soma was not made of the ephedra plant as is commonly thought. When the prophet Zoroaster and the rest of the Magi moved southward out of the regions where shilajit could be found they had to find a substitute. This probably led to all sorts of experimentation. Eventually, they began to use a substance known as Homa which was not the same thing as Soma. Homa probably was manufactured from the *Ephedra* plant and therefore was a drug. It is possible that some of the ancient plant based chemicals inherent in Shilajit could have created some mild drug effects, however this material likely consisted of many dozens of species of fossilized plants and therefore should not have been highly concentrated in any particular surviving phyto-chemicals in sufficient quantity to cause drug effects. Therefore, even though there may have been extremely mild drug effects produced by Soma, it was not likely that this was the focus of its use. The use and popularity of *Homa* was likely due to its drug-like qualities over and above any possible health effects.

**Intuition and Cognition**

Gold was given to the kings of Sumer and Egypt among other places in order to help the king reach a level of perception and awareness coined "*the Malkuth*". If one looks up this word the definition might be "Kingdom" yet, in its origins, it was a specific realm of kingship which would be ruled by a king who had reached a certain level of mental ability and enlightenment required by the Anunnaki. The queen also had to reach this same level known as the Plane of Sharon before they could be dynastically wed. Together they would both rule and produce an offspring fit for continued rulership. This was one reason that gold became so strongly associated with kingship. In my own experimentation, I have found that the gold ORMUS has augmented my intuition and thought process tremendously. My intuition is borderline overactive at times. I also find that my mind now soaks up and retains nearly all available information. Due to a growing hunger for knowledge, it has come to my mind of late that reading is too slow and cumbersome for putting information into the brain. So far, I have not found a way to remedy this. However, for the most part, the increased intuition and mental acuity have been a welcome change which has in many ways aided in the continuation of this, and other, work.

Gold ORMUS increases intuition by stimulating the brain in at least four ways. Firstly, and most importantly, gold stimulates the pineal gland which is "the seat of the soul" and is responsible for intuition among other things. Secondly, gold stimulates the pituitary gland which makes sure all other regions of the brain are active. These two glands, when stimulated, also help increase health to produce all sorts of important hormones such as growth hormone and melatonin to name the major two.

Thirdly, gold stimulates the amygdalae. If one is prone to anterior stimulation of the amygdalae, this can create a sense of well being as the entire brain is jump-started which dramatically increases frontal lobe activity. However, if the person is prone to posterior stimulation of the amygdalae which results in feelings of anger and depression, the gold can intensify these feelings. This will be expanded upon further in the Negative Health Effects section and in Chapter 13.

Lastly, gold can create super microtubules that extend well beyond the boundaries of the body which put the mind in touch with the external environment, other consciousness, and higher dimensional existence. In other words, psychic ability is markedly increased in certain subjects. I say in certain subjects because the gold can also have not so pleasant side effects in certain individuals. The gold ORMUS is not for everyone; this is one reason that the secret was so well hidden by the philosophers. If one was enlightened enough to join the philosophers in fruitful discourse or to read and comprehend the tractates of the philosophers, they would then find the way to make the gold on their own and, if so, then they had reached a level worthy of positive results. Persons who are depressed, negative or often confused should refrain from taking the gold as the gold has a way of supporting one's mental directions and directives.

## Senses

The sense of smell is often enhanced after taking rhodium or gold. The sense of touch is enhanced when taking these ORMUS as well. The eyesight has not been noted to improve directly unless it is poor due to nutritional deficiency and no permanent damage has occurred. Likewise, the hearing is not changed per say; however hearing and eyesight is changed through interpretation by the brain. So, in a way, these two senses are heightened although not by the enhancement of the organ itself. This may also be what is happening with the sense of smell and touch. So, through the fine tuning of the neural net and the increasing of awareness and intuition, one's senses are enhanced.

## Investigation into Validity of Claims and Historical Reference

I have verified many historical and modern claims with my own experimentation. I have reproduced many of the physical claims in the laboratory, and I can verify many health claims through my own usage and through the reports of others who have been reporting their experiences to me. To date, I have witnessed all of the above-mentioned biological effects either in myself or in others, including the negative effects mentioned by a couple of recipients. I have also recorded health effects that I have not seen in any text or heard by word of mouth.

However, my investigations into historical claims have left me to realize that many of the claims may be fantasy. Yet I must confess that there are methods of charging ORMUS substances designed to amplify strength that I have yet to discover or employ. So, at this point I am not able to say without a doubt that any one reported function of the ORMUS is not based in truth.

## Negative Health Effects

Negative health effects concerning ORMUS are primarily associated with gold. For this reason I have words of caution concerning the ingestion of gold, at least in quantities greater than can be found naturally in foods. Gold, as stated earlier, acts to jump starting the pineal gland. If the pineal gland is fairly inactive, such as in cases of seasonal effective disorder, the awakening of the gland can cause a person to become dizzy and even nauseated for a time up to a period of several hours after ingestion. The gold will act on the gland rather quickly as it is easily absorbed through the mucous membranes. This is not the case with rhodium which is very difficult to absorb. Usually after the initial ingestion, or after the first few ingestions, this feeling will no longer be noticeable. The notion that these substances will take one closer to God or cause one to become more spiritual is invalid unless the person is inclined in that way. Gold will enhance whatever direction one is going in so, if you are a crook, it will help you become a better crook. By the same token, if one is very emotionally disturbed due to a negative outlook or is stuck in fear-based thinking, then gold will emphasize that. Gold is not for that person unless they first change their outlook. If their intuition and awareness is ramped up suddenly, they may go into self-reflection overload. A depressed person usually "crashes" when they take gold while the joyful person goes into euphoria. Gold ORMUS has a way of making one take a long hard look at one's self and face all of their demons. If one is comfortable with their demons and with themselves, then they will do well with the gold. If a person fears their demons, they may find a dark chasm to jump into. People who are not willing to take a look at themselves in a true light will not be able to handle the honesty they must face. The constant reflection on your own actions sometimes causes considerable emotional discomfort. As a person works to correct the discomfort they evolve toward a higher level of consciousness and become more purified in action, deed and word.

Another effect that happens to most people is the sensitivity to other life. Some people will do well with this aspect while others will be in sensory overload. People who are too self-absorbed or who are used to ignoring the pain they cause others my find the sensation unpleasant. Yet if a person has no conscience and is truly unable to care about others, then they will use the intuition toward their pursuits and may not let it bother them. The latter is rarer than one might think. Most people have some sense of a conscience whether they follow that inner guidance or not and so will find themselves wrestling with the angel upon consuming ORMUS on a regular basis.

## Other Effects

Over the past few years I have been ingesting the various ORMUS substances with great success. During this time I have made notes of all results and effects. Here I shall list these effects and note corroborating statements by other ORMUS takers.

**Reverse healing** - When I first started taking the ORMUS made from mined ores that contained, in various amounts, all of the ORMUS substances, I experienced a curious effect that lasted for approximately 2 ½ weeks. It started with a feeling of very warm water flowing down my lower back and then down my left leg. This happened several times per day and was so intense that I actually checked my back and my leg on many occasions for water. After this subsided, I had a pain in my shoulder for a couple of days. Then I experienced a pain in my foot and this continued for other parts of the body. It came to mind that these sensations were occurring in exact reverse order in which I had received injuries in these areas. According to David Hudson, the body goes through a sort of healing crisis whereby all old injuries and damage that may not have healed completely re-heal in reverse order in which they occurred.

**Increased sense of smell** - One of the first experiences that I noticed was the increased sense of smell. Even though there was nothing wrong with my sense of smell, it still markedly increased.

**Increased regularity** - Over the course of my entire life I have always become constipated when on a trip away from home. Soon after beginning the usage of these substances this problem ceased and has never returned.

**Increased intuition** - This effect slowly increases over the years and starts about 10 to 12 months after beginning ingestion. Increased intuition takes many forms and I believe it may differ from person to person depending on their own latent skills or propensities. With me, it mainly enhanced my sense of how other people and animals felt, not only emotionally, but sometimes included what they might be thinking. This empathy and/or telepathy may manifest either in the presence of another or remotely by mentally focusing on them. These abilities take many forms and tend to increase and evolve over time.

**Mental retention** - Perhaps the most obvious effect that I have noticed is the increased ability to retain information. My mind has become a steel trap for information and I have a ravenous appetite for new facts and information. Now in my early 50's, I can think circles around the person I was when I was in college. I now understand why all alchemists are considered philosophers and why figures like Comte De Saint Germaine were thought to possess the knowledge of many lifetimes.

**Nada** - After about 10 to 15 months of ingesting the ORMUS, one begins to hear a sound. This sound is often called the nada. The nada is also sometimes called the Hu. The human is the man who can hear the hu. The hu or nada is a sound that is historically associated with enlightenment as it always accompanies the state of Malkuth or the Plane of Sharon. It was said in some cultures that the hu was the sound of God and in other societies the hu or nada was said to be the sound of life energy or life force. This sound is likely the biological interface with the energetic matrix via the heightened ORMUS connection.

The sound seems to be outside the head. It is loud when intuition is spiked and often quiet when one is mentally resting.

The sound is like a ringing in the ears but is not bothersome like tinnitus. The sound sometime changes pitch as if something is tuning and can also become a rushing sound like that of water rushing through a channel. On occasion it gets very loud when one is connected consciously with another person. I had a friend who for a while was also taking ORMUS call me by phone when I was thinking intently about him and said "What are you doing to me, man? This sound is out of the roof!"

**Telepathic link** - People who take ORMUS often become linked when they are taking the same ORMUS mix and think about one another frequently. I have become linked in varying degrees to all with whom I have provided ORMUS. This means that when we think of one another, especially when there is significant emotion involved, the one who is thought of is most often aware of it. This has been demonstrated many times. For instance, I think of the person and they will call within a few minutes to ask me what I want or tell me that they were aware of my thoughts. Additionally, anyone who is prone to skills like channeling will, after about twelve months of ingesting gold ORMUS, find that the ability has markedly increased. This holds true for other abilities such as remote viewing or remote sensing, especially between individuals who are taking the same mixture of gold ORMUS.

**Visual nada** - I call this visual nada only because I do not know what else to call it. The first time I saw this, I thought that it was something in the night sky but it turned out to be some aspect of my visual cortex. This illusion appears as an extremely bright pinpoint of light that seems to be shining into my eyes from elsewhere as if there suddenly were a hole in a curtain with a bright light on the other side. The effect lasts anywhere from a few seconds to several minutes. It is rarely in the same place. The interesting part is that it is not an art effect nor is it in any way an aspect of the function of the eye, for even though it appears to be out in front of me, it is fixed in its own space and does not move with the movement of the eyes. Even though it may stay in my conscious sight, I can turn my head far enough that it can leave my field of vision, yet it is still noticeable, and often, as if by choice, it will move back to my field of vision after a few moments. This happens in darkness or light. It also appears in my dreams. The light is also visible when my eyes are closed. The little bright light appears most often when I am having a great insight of some sort or when I am having one of those quintessential "Ah ha" moments during a conversation. It is as if it is telling me that there is something important coming down the old mental pipeline. I know of only one other person at present who has reported this effect and I have not read of anyone else having this effect. As more people use these substances, more evidence of this may come to light…no pun intended.

## Assumptions and Implications

Many assumptions can be made concerning the ORMUS and related materials. For instance, it can easily be assumed that since all living things have these substances within them, they are indeed essential to life. It might also be assumed that as we learn more and more about the roles of different ORMUS in nature and biology, we will begin to discover a great deal about biology that we did not previously have the means to learn. It might also be assumed based on our previous discussion that certain ORMUS help to form not only our DNA template but in many ways form the template for our entire being. For instance, it has been surmised that our aura is in part or entirely the template of our being. When a leaf is cut in half or when a finger is cut off, for a given period of time, the aura of the missing portion still shows up in Kirlian photography as a ghost image. So, the template remains as part of the whole even when the matter that filled the template has been removed. It has been supposed that ORMUS plays some role in this template structure.

Due to analytical problems associated with ORMUS materials, it is not known how much of the body's silica, calcium or even carbon for that matter may actually be ORMUS materials. We may need to reevaluate the chemical makeup of the body based on this new knowledge, and for that matter, we may need to reevaluate our nutrition as well.

## Implications in Homeopathic Method

It has been implied that the homeopathic method of treatment is connected to ORMUS. Homeopathy is "to treat like with like" and to dilute the medicaments down to contain only the very essence of that which the treatment originally contained. The dilution then is basically carrying only the signature or frequency of the original substance and may in fact contain in actuality none of the chemical structure of the original compound or element. What then holds on to the signature or the essence of the original through so many dilutions? It is true that all things can be entrained by consistent frequencies no matter how weak they may be in order to create an overall signature of the one consistent background frequency; however this explains homeopathy only in part. Certainly water is a very good medium for entrainment and water is easily able to be entrained and to carry frequencies. For this reason, so called "new water", or water that has been stripped of frequencies, is the best water to use for homeopathic dilutions. However, what is it that gives water this uncanny ability to carry frequencies, especially those of light? It has been suggested that ORMUS, well dispersed in water, aids in this ability. In varying degrees, ORMUS can be trapped from almost any water found on Earth. It is the highly aligned water molecules that are used by the ORMUS of rhodium and others to create microtubules that conduct the signals by which our cells communicate. It is the template of the double helical fields of the high spin di-atom that captures the water molecules long enough for this to occur. The water in the tubule then becomes a fiber optic that channels the frequencies that the di-atom emits or superconducts. This happens only with a given range of frequencies. Frequencies that fall outside of the given range will be insulated against by the ORMUS. At this time, this seems to play against the previously proposed theory since homeopathic remedies could then only be made of substances which had signatures that fell within a certain range. Yet there may be some sort of transference going on that is not well understood. For instance, when a cell is fed the frequency of iron without an actual iron molecule being present, the cell gates which have receptors for iron still open to receive the iron even though no actual elemental iron has been presented. At first glance this seems cruel to the cell as the cell is being tricked into thinking that it has received its needed nourishment. But under further inspection, it becomes apparent that the cell actually receives the same nourishment from the frequency of iron as it would have for the iron molecule itself. How is this possible? And if communications between the cells are conducted by microtubules, and these communications handle the cellular processes, it might be assumed that the cells would ignore frequencies outside of the range that were conducted by the ORMUS. But this is not the case. So it may be assumed that the ORMUS are at least able to conduct the frequencies of light which are in themselves reflections of compounds and elements. This brings us to quantum mechanics which suggests that everything is made up of some form of light. At this time it remains a mystery. Yet one thing seems apparent, and that is that somehow the ORMUS are integral to the process.

## Health Implications

There are many health implications associated with ORMUS. Many bodily supplements can be made of the ORMUS in various combinations which can be ingested for the relief of many ailments or to enhance health. Partial ORMUS can also be brought into the picture to further expand on the plethora of different applications. Further, ORMUS can be mixed with other elements and compounds to create remedies and enhancements for the mind and body. And if ancient texts are correct, these are the only supplements that can feed the light body. So, in this respect, they can aid the mind, body *and* spirit. In the ancient texts of Sumer and of Egypt, these elements were used in conjunction with a concentrated ray to recharge the body of a recently deceased person, effectively resurrecting the person from death. One such Sumerian text explains how Enki sprinkled the water of life on the lifeless body of Inanna seven times while he focused a beaming device over her until she was resurrected. Pictures of this process appear to show a body lying prostrate on what appears to be an operating table with a large lamp-like structure above with depictions of wavy lines coming down to and penetrating the body. The lamp looks somewhat like a modern light fixture. This process was taught by Enki to his son Ningishziddha (Thoth) which made his first son Marduk (Amman Ra) jealous and angry that Enki did not teach him these secrets as well. Whether or not depictions such as these represent actual events, they do suggest that the role of light within the body and of the ORMUS was known well into antiquity. It was common knowledge that the body consisted of two parts, the Ka body of light and the physical body. It was also well known that in order to remain healthy one had to feed both bodies.

## Health Applications

We have been taking advantage of the health benefits of ORMUS for millennia, perhaps without being aware of it, by using certain curative plants and by bathing in certain healing springs and hot springs. When we take mud baths in special healing earth we may be bathing in soil of high ORMUS content. Clay masks used as beauty aids for centuries often contain high amounts of certain ORMUS. Sea salts, especially concentrated inland sea salts such as those found around the Dead Sea, contain high amounts of ORMUS. These salts have been used well into antiquity for their curative effects to the skin and their beauty enhancing qualities. Some peoples touted for their extreme longevity have been found to practice an age old method of dietary mineral supplementation which entails the daily drinking of tea made with a chunk of special inland sea rock salt in each cup. Another such society, the Hunzas of eastern Pakistan live on an average of 120 to 140 years of age. They live high in the mountains and drink glacier melt. They also water their gardens and fruits with this water which is extremely high in minerals and would likely be very high in ORMUS as well. Their foods therefore are likely high in bio-available chelated minerals as well as concentrated ORMUS. The peoples of old Soviet Georgia who have been known to have similar life spans to that of the Hunzas are known to produce and consume large quantities of red grape wine. They also raise and eat chestnuts and pomegranates as staples, all of which are high in ORMUS. In fact, pomegranates have been known for this purpose far into antiquity and thus have been associated with alchemy, fertility, longevity, kingship, and star fire.

It is likely that if we as a species could live a nurturing life full of the proper balance of exercise, nutrition, positive thinking, and minimal physical, emotional, or dietary abuse, we could easily exceed our current average life spans. If we were to add ORMUS to this routine so that our light bodies could be properly nourished, we should easily live as long as the oldest of the Hunzas. Further, if we were to unlock the secrets to the proper use of the ORMUS materials we might find that our life spans could reach biblical proportions.

### Product Applications

There are all sorts of product applications that could utilize ORMUS. The fact is that these substances have had applications as far back as recorded time and likely beyond. Any use that we employ could be a rediscovery of some lost information just as the ORMUS elements themselves are a rediscovery. Nonetheless, the applications for ORMUS await us to find them and employ in our day to day health.

### Manufactured Supplements
The first application that comes to mind is the use of ORMUS supplements to feed the light body, which is integrally intertwined with the physical body. As explained earlier, there are twelve ORMUS which can be used separately or in various mixes of each other. They can also be used wet or as powder. Then there are the twelve partial ORMUS elements (ORMUS that contain ions or a colloidal version of the parent element) which can also be used in order to enhance bio-transport. There are also other methods of charging and enhancing ORMUS that are too complex to broach that could also be employed in the production of supplements. To add to the possible mixtures, there are other complimentary compounds and elements that could be mixed with the ORMUS in order to create specific remedies and health enhancers.

### Skin Care
Many skin care products could be manufactured containing

ORMUS of copper as collagen supporters and with ORMUS of rhodium and iridium to rebuild skin DNA where age or sun damage has occurred or to repair scar tissue. Such applications are already being employed likely without the knowledge of those using them. A product called "Wound Care" used in hospitals makes use of a patented process of freeze dried aloe that has been independently tested and found to contain very high amounts of ORMUS rhodium. This substance is working wonders in many healing applications. If we begin to understand what is really occurring in such remedies, we can create enhanced remedies using the ORMUS and other complimentary compounds.

**Rhodium Rich Aloe Vera**

### Disease Care
An injectable extract of the same product discussed above has been used by a number of veterinarians to cure feline leukemia. This substance is called "Acemannan" and is produced by Carrington labs and has been analyzed and discovered to contain 90% ORMUS rhodium. It is prudent to state that these substances are naturally occurring and do not act as chemicals in the body and therefore, unless they are compounded with other chemicals, they cannot be called drugs. For this reason, the drug industry will likely avoid the study of the ORMUS for potential drug manufacture.

Di-atomic rhodium has been found to cure various cancers. This may be one great use for ORMUS of rhodium. Rhodium and iridium are essential in the structure and function of neurons and for this reason they may prove to be very effective in the treatment of neurological diseases and disorders. Rhodium might also be supplemented as a means of increasing one's mental capacity and retention.

ORMUS of copper might be employed for brain function where low copper is a problem. Copper may also be used in the treatment of arthritis and skin conditions. Copper can also be used to support collagen production in the skin as a beauty aid and anti-aging ointment.

ORMUS of gold might be used to stimulate the pituitary, and pineal glands as well as the amygdala. It is important to stimulate the anterior rather than the posterior active amygdala or fear and aggression may result. The gold is not determinant as to which it stimulates, therefore it is up to the recipient to make sure the stimulation is in fact anterior rather than posterior. This ability is taught in ancient inner alchemy and is necessary with taking gold ORMUS and is reflected in the foremost rule of alchemy (As above, so below).

ORMUS made from ores which contain a wide naturally occurring mix of all twelve elements can be used to support basic health and longevity. This type of mix is often the most pleasant in its effects. This mix is most suited to be used as a basic ORMUS supplement. The ORMUS mixed in its naturally occurring percentages is likely the best mixture to support basic health.

**Other Products**
There are many other products that can be made utilizing the ORMUS materials. These products can include topical arthritis and joint care products, liniments and creams, tooth care products, and spiritual and healing devices made of the philosopher's stone. There might also be hair care products made of ORMUS materials. I have certainly used ORMUS in the manufacture of such things with great success. Pet supplements can be made of ORMUS as well as ORMUS plant foods. Hydroponic additives might add high amounts of ORMUS to hydroponically produced fruits and vegetables which would in effect allow us to grow supercharged foods that make minerals and elements more bio-available in our diets.

## Products and Substances That May Not Be Safe

Certain products that advertise that they include monotonic elements may not be safe. Many of these products can contain high levels of heavy Gilchrest metals. When ores are taken as they are naturally found, they may contain high levels of chromium and other heavy metals. Products that have been made with the use of magnetic or vortex water traps may contain heavy metals as well as other concentrated toxins. I have found that magnetic and vortex traps can capture and concentrate colloids. Levels of toxicity and specific metals captured would depend on the source water. Consider the fact that even though non-ferrous metals are not attracted to magnetic fields, they are affected by them. For instance, when a magnet is dropped through a copper pipe it falls very slowly as if it is lighter than a feather. The same is true when a chunk of copper is dropped through a magnetic pipe. In effect the magnetic trap works to force the ORMUS into a tight space as it is repelled by the magnets. Theoretically colloids will be slowed by the magnetic field and follow the path of least resistance into the trap along with the ORMUS. Water can be tested to see if it contains any undesirable substances but I have yet to hear of anyone who has tested their tap water except for myself. If the water is clean then you should be able to use it without further testing unless you change your source. It is not recommended to use municipal water for this purpose. Well water or spring water where the source is monitored and clean is the safest. Ocean water will produce good results but is likely to have concentrated metals and therefore may need to be run through the alchemical process. But why use ocean water when one could run concentrated sea salt through the process with better results?

Manufacturing techniques that have not completely transformed all of the metal into ORMUS may not be safe since there would be a remaining heavy metal content. Products that are not properly washed or that have employed the usage of unclean chemicals or that have been stored incorrectly may also be unsafe.

The rule of thumb is to do your homework. Study what these substances can contain. If you make your own or if you purchase them, send a sample to the lab and tell them what to look for. Make sure that there are none, or at least very low levels, of the things that you don't want to find in your food such as lead, mercury, trivalent chromium, arsenic, etc. Remember, the sample may seem to contain aluminum but this is likely a false positive if the ORMUS is indeed present. It is my opinion that even some vitamin and mineral supplements are unsafe and contain coal tars or heavy metals in a form that may not be agreeable with the human body. So the advice "do your homework" applies to all supplements, not just the ORMUS. It is up to the consumer to decide what is toxic and what is not. For instance, certain heavy metals in the metallic form or as oxides may be very toxic to the body while they may be considered nutrients in another form such as a salt, a chelate, a citrate, or a malate. Oxides however may be very toxic. Or metal compounds such as bromides or arsenides which can be very toxic may be present. Yet we are always learning that even those things that are considered poisonous have their benefits in the correct dose or proportions. One such metal is arsenic which has long been thought to be lethal. It has been recently revealed as a cancer treatment and preventative when found in things like certain seeds and nuts. The same holds true for cyanide compounds found in certain seeds such as cherry, apricot, and peach pits and, to a very small degree, in almonds. These substances have been found to be very beneficial in the control and treatment of parasites, cancers, and as an overall body purifier of undesirable bacteria and fungi.

So, do your homework and if you manufacture your own supplements, run an analysis on them and make sure you know what is in them. Just remember that the ORMUS will show up as alumina silica, silica and calcium. The analysis may show one or any combination of all of these. If you know that there is no reason for these elements to be present in such quantity, then you know that the ORMUS is there. It is also important to be sure the laboratory does not store the sample in electrical fields. Make sure the bottle remains shielded with aluminum foil throughout the shipment and analytical process. Unscrupulous dealers that sell supposed ORMUS may in fact add these substances to fool anyone who would have them analyzed, but these substances will not produce the same effects as those I have discussed in this report, so do your own experiments to see how the substance behaves and then make your decision based on your informed intuition. This is all that can be done. We must go with either trust or intuition when we take supplements. If we guide our intuition with logic and research, we ultimately are making a more healthy choice.

## Cautions

I would here like to leave you with some final words of caution. I have seen it written often and have often heard it said that if the ORMUS is fused to a glass it can be ground back to a fine powder which is again what it was before it was made into glass. It is also said that this powder can be ingested the same way as the original substance. Although it is true that the glass of ORMUS can be ground down to a fine powder, it is not like it was before it was made into a glass. The ORMUS after grinding might appear as fine as it was before it was made into a glass but the tight glass matrices bond still exists. If this substance is ingested it will be as if you have ingested ground glass. Further, the powder cannot be transported throughout the body as it is still in chunks of atomic matrices. If one were to look at this under a microscope, one would see shards of microscopic glass. This would do the same thing to the intestinal tract that eating any other form of ground glass would. Ground glass has actually been used throughout history as a form of poisoning which causes death by internal hemorrhage. I have seen these statements passed on even by well known authors, which proves that they know little of chemistry and have not performed this act themselves. This is not to say that if one did this it would kill them. That would depend on the amount and frequency of the ingestion, but it most certainly would have no positive effects as the substance would be unable to be transported properly to the cells throughout the body and definitely could not enter the cell through the cell gates. The only way to get the substance back to the original mon and di atomic structure is to run it back through an alchemical process which breaks down the crystal lattice that was created by the intense vitrification process. This happens when the energetic fields that have become tightly knit during vitrification have been relaxed due to the drop in the energetic spin state and then at least partially re-knit in the process. The annealing stage of the alchemical process restores the strong high spin state without going as far as to vitrify the ORMUS to glass. For this reason, be careful in your annealing process not to, as the alchemists say, "scorch your stone", as it will have bits of microscopic glass in it although without sharp edges like ground glass. The Philosophers used to say to gently heat the stone like a hen sits on her eggs. This is not to say that one would only utilize a heat equaling the body temperature of a hen, rather it alludes to the careful, vigilant nature of which the annealing process is performed.

So, my final words here are 'be careful and don't eat glass!'

# CHAPTER 10

## New Alchemy

In this section all known methods of manufacture and collection/isolation will be discussed. However, due to proprietary reasons and for the purposes of safety, there will not be detailed information supplied that will allow exact duplication of this work. It is far better for students to learn to make these substances safely in a classroom environment and to simultaneously learn how to use them. Persons wishing to take Alchemy classes may contact me through my website templeofmelchizedek.com and inquire about joining an alchemical class where all of these methods are taught as well as the necessary inner alchemy. Yet if one is savvy in chemistry, they will quickly see how to apply the methods I am about to discuss without instruction. There is a method of gold ORMUS manufacture which has been patented by David Hudson. I do not use his methods nor do I believe that the patented method is efficient for my use. Since his patented method is more cumbersome and painstaking than my own method, I have no reason to use his method. For those who are interested, David Hudson's method of ORMES manufacture can be found on the internet. However, I will later in the section **Voices Across The Void** provide an ancient formula granted by Tjehuti, which, if followed properly, will produce the ORMUS in good quantity for the practitioner and need not utilize strong acids; although the use of such acids do speed up the process during the pH balancing stage.

**Alchemy Lab**

## Methods of Collection and Manufacture

The following is a list of health, psychological and spiritual effects of taking ORMUS found in historical accounts.

**Extraction** - ORMUS naturally exist about the Earth in many places and forms. They are found in ores, ancient plant deposits such as detritus clays, the ash of certain volcanic eruptions, almost all water to varying degrees, the atmosphere, and in all living things. There are methods by which these materials can be first dissolved to release all minerals and then put through a process by which most of the organic and inorganic matter falls out of solution leaving the ORMUS still suspended. The remaining liquid can be drawn off meticulously, vacuum filtered to remove any remaining Gilchrest metals, and then further pH adjusted to cause the ORMUS to precipitate out of the solution and microcluster in the adjustment vessel. The whole of the remaining water and precipitate is then placed in a settlement container for a period sufficient to allow the ORMUS to settle and release all ORMUS that are volatile gases. Once the volatiles have released the milky clusters and the precipitate is allowed to fall bright, the washing process begins. The washing process removes pH adjustment chemicals, salts and anything else unwanted leaving nearly pure ORMUS and water. The washing process takes about one week. At this point, the resulting elixir can be charged and ingested as is or it can be desiccated and evaporated to a fine white powder. There are many ways to charge the elixir. Essentially the elixir should be charged with the very frequency of light that one wishes to flow through the body which most safely would be sunlight. The elixir can be charged with sunlight by simply rotating it in bright morning sunlight for about 15 to 20 minutes. The elixir can also be charged with other forms of energy such as torsion waves and certain forms of magnetism. Additionally, ORMUS can be charged with another substance that can act as a transport agent throughout the body. These substances are things such as salts or partial ORMUS materials.

It is essential that no electrical fields are present in the vicinity of the extraction process or the ORMUS will all become volatile and will be lost into the air. The entire extraction process, from prima materia to dried usable ORMUS powder, can take three weeks to one month when properly performed. However, there are short cuts that can reduce the time. It should be noted here that some of the old alchemical techniques took twelve months.

**Transforming** - Transforming metals to ORMUS can be performed in a similar way as the extraction process. The metals are usually worked with individually. If the extraction process is modified to involve more cooking and sintering, then not only can naturally occurring ORMUS be removed from ores and organic matter, but platinum group colloids can be transformed into ORMUS during the same process. In the transforming process, the goal is to divide molecules into smaller and smaller molecules until they reach a critical number, which varies from metal to metal, at which point the molecule blows apart on its own resulting in di- or mon-atoms. The nuclei then go into a high spin state so that the atoms cannot re-bond into molecules. If the spin state drops, the atoms will re-bond and some colloids will be formed. The spin state can be increased further after manufacture in order to increase stability by an annealing process. The above process can be performed by many methods of wet or dry chemistry with varying degrees of safety and difficulty.

**Trapping** - There are various forms of magnetic traps that can be placed on water systems or can be used during the filtration of sea water. The result is highly charged ORMUS water which possesses very strange qualities and appearance. The resulting water however, in my opinion, is not safe to drink as is without putting it through the extraction and washing process. The reason for this is that the trap can capture and concentrate many other impurities such as metals and radon gas. People who have used trapped water for ingestion report negative effects such as headache.

**Fire Methods** - Many of the oldest alchemical methods utilize a forge or furnace to heat the ores or metals under various conditions for long durations in order to produce white annealed powders which are pure and usable. However, the process, although not complicated, is long, hot, and arduous. There are modern methods using dry heat which are much less time consuming. One such method utilizes a sodium boat and torch and is called the sodium burn. There are other methods whereby a plasma torch or a monatomic oxygen/hydrogen torch is used to create heat that is in excess of 5,500 degrees Fahrenheit. Some high temperature methods produce a very different quality product than other methods and the substance is cooked into a glass while all other compounds are burned off, resulting in a greenish glass. This glass can then be crushed into a fine powder, dissolved and extracted. ORMUS that has been made in this way, or which has been reprocessed in this way, produces products with strong effects due to its very high spin state. When plasma is used to melt ORMUS, a shield gas should be used in order to stabilize the material, otherwise it will fly away due to the strong electric fields. The plasma method can cause fusion of the anode under certain conditions and therefore should be conducted with care. This method can utilize a plasma or heliarc/tig torch with argon shield gas.

Another fire method utilizes an acetylene torch and a sodium boat. The sodium burns in the process which produces the heat and provides the proper placement of heat. This method quickly produces a white powder that can then be washed as mentioned earlier.

**Quench/Re-quench Method** - This method requires the use of a forge or torch with which to heat the desired material to a cherry red. The metal is then quenched in a special pickle solution. This is repeated until the solution is heavily laden with metallic salts. The solution is then dried to crystals. The crystals are then reduced in muriatic acid and the transformation method is then performed. This is a very ancient method and is described fully in the section **Voices Across the Void.** This method happens to be the best for the reduction of metals like iridium and rhodium which are extremely incorruptible.

**My most frequent method** - The method that I created and use the most was mainly gleaned from ancient textual information, including the texts attributed to Miriam of the Israelites. After studying countless texts and weeding through all of the sophism, I was able to achieve satisfactory results which I have refined and expanded to my needs and equipment. My methods vary depending on the *prima materia* or "first matter" used. The modern term for this is primer. Metals are treated in different ways depending on the metal and are not handled the same as other primers. When plant matter is the primer for vegetable/plant alchemy, I first burn the material to a clean white ash in controlled conditions in order to concentrate the natural mon- and di-atoms as well as the colloids. I then use a wet/dry chemistry combination transformation and extraction method to produce ORMUS. This method is the one that I teach to students since it can be achieved with the use of mostly common materials and equipment.

When detritus clays are used as a primer, they are treated in the same manner as ashes in plant alchemy. When ores are used, they are treated similarly to a metal by first dissolving them in the **Secret Fire** (aqua regia) and then making a series of pH shifts and boiling and performing wet chemistry to transform and extract ORMUS.

177

Animal tissue, such as brains, used in animal alchemy is handled the same way as plant material except that the sintering is done by (Our Liquor or muriatic acid) HCl rather than by fire or by secret fire.

Sea salts are also good primers and are handled like ores by both extraction and transformation. Sea salts are often high in gold, and silver, but particularly gold. The first attempt by the Anunnaki to mine our planet for gold was performed by filtering it out of sea water. However, this proved to be very laborious so further efforts were made toward terrestrial mining of various sorts.

Once the goals of the various steps of alchemy are understood, the process can be tweaked and changed often with positive results. It is important to think of alchemy as more similar to cooking or making wine and less like chemistry, since exact calculations do not often produce the exact same result twice. The reason for this is that many other forces are coming into play in alchemy that are ignored in chemistry. For instance, the position of the moon is most important in order to achieve favorable results. If the moon is in the wrong place, less ORMUS will be made or it can be lost in the process. The most important clue to this in the old texts is described by the naked queen making love to the naked king. And later they are married and clothed. Partially, this refers to the moon and sun which must be conjoined in the sky during a particular portion of the process in order for the forces to be married together in the philosopher's stone. When one makes wine, the chemistry is not the greatest matter, because the wine is controlled by living yeast, the forces of nature and other factors like altitude, barometric pressure and season. Everything can be done correctly according to the chemistry or formulation, yet it can still turn bad seemingly without explanation or it might turn out to be the most exquisite batch that can never be replicated. This is the way of alchemy. Alchemy is more about observation and less about exact measurements. Of course, exact measurements can be used but they are for the most part unnecessary and are more for the purposes of quantifying results in order to possibly produce some sort of reconciliation of materials through the various stages in order to determine changes throughout the process. The only real measurements that must be performed precisely throughout the wet chemistry method are pH readings. However, all observations must be keen and decisions must be timely or the whole process will be fruitless, deriving no ORMUS. Yet even pH readings were not used by the ancient alchemists as they relied on precise observations of changes in the character of the broth as they made their adjustments. This takes great practice and diligence.

Finally, it is necessary for the alchemist to be in the right state of mind when performing alchemy. This sounds ludicrous, but it is the reason why alchemy was considered to be sacred. The alchemists were the philosophers because they were alchemists and not the other way around. They were all enamored with how the ORMUS reacted and came about. From this sense of wonder, philosophy was born. For this reason they felt that the ORMUS was no less than the spiritual essence of all things captured in solid form. Alchemy almost appears to be a religion when one notices that many different philosophers from many different religions all applied their religious beliefs to the alchemy as a way to maintain its sacred nature. They all worked together to solve problems and to develop a language that was universal to philosophers alone.

### Substances Found to Contain ORMUS

The substances found to contain ORMUS basically include just about everything to varying degrees. Organic materials and special ores are those things that contain the highest amount of natural ORMUS. Metals contain no naturally occurring ORMUS, rather they must be converted to ORMUS.

Below is a list of sources found to be high in the ORMUS materials.

- SALT- DEAD SEA AND OTHER NATURAL SEA SALT
- WATER- SPRINGS, GROUND WATER, RIVERS, HEALING SPRINGS, HOT SPRINGS AND OCEANS

179

(Hot springs and oceans usually contain the highest amounts)
- AIR- OUTSIDE AND AWAY FROM ELECTRIC FIELDS
- ORES- VOLCANIC, IGNEOUS, METAMORPHIC, SEDIMENTARY, METEORITIC.
- SHILAJIT (fossilized compressed plant material)
- PYCNOGENOL (maritime pine bark extract)
- GRAPE SEED AND JUICE CONCENTRATES (Seneca brand has been tested and found to contain high levels of rhodium ORMUS)
- BLUE GREEN ALGAE
- BRAINS (highest percentages of 2% to 5%)
- VITALI TEA
- CERTAIN OCEAN FISHES
- PURPLE, ORANGE AND RED VEGETABLES (carrots, beets, red or purple cabbage, etc.)
- ORANGE AND PURPLE FRUITS
- SHELLFISH OF ALL KINDS
- CERTAIN MUSHROOMS
- NUTS AND SEEDS
- SEA SILVER PRODUCT
- CARRINGTON LABS ACEMANNAN PRODUCT
- SHARK CARTILAGE
- ESSEAC TEA- FOUR HERBS
- BILBERRY JUICE
- ALOE (especially purple tinted varieties)

**Personal Observations**

In the first two years of taking the ORMUS materials I made note of many physical, biological, mental and spiritual changes. Below is a partial list of my personal observations. The list includes most of the significant effects that I have experienced.

**Physical and biological observations include:**
- Reverse re-healing
- Regularity of the system such as bowel movements and sleep patterns
- Greater endurance even when I have not been working

out regularly
- Rejection of certain toxins when they are at toxic levels such as alcohol when I have reached a certain limit. This occurs as a stabbing pain in the left nostril and frontal lobe or temple.
- Fewer aches and pains
- Beginning arthritis in phalangeal joints completely gone
- Increased sense of smell
- Muscle tone maintenance with less exercise
- Regular detox through skin, fecal and urinary excretion
- Increased ability to heal after injury
- Decreased injury to joints, muscles, or tendons
- High sense of bodily well being
- Relief and healing of skin irritations, such as poison ivy, with ORMUS of wood in gel form
- Feeling of youthfulness
- Sense of strength

## Mental, emotional, and spiritual observations
- Extreme increase in the ability to absorb and retain information. This has been the most profound result of taking these substances
- Escalating desire to learn and absorb information
- High sense of mental well-being 95% of the time
- Lessening of frustration
- Higher sense of inner peace
- Higher sense of compassion and empathy
- Greater ability to empathize with others and other animals without feeling overwhelmed by foreign thoughts
- Increased psychic abilities including remote sensing of all types, channeling information, feeling the emotions and thoughts of others, and remote linking with other people even those not of Earth
- Increased ability to detect lies, deceit, game playing, or coercion
- Increased mental clarity
- Feeling of mental and spiritual evolution
- Increased desire to create and to invent
- Increased desire to work through hang-ups and problems

and to evolve toward a higher condition and to help other interested persons do the same

➢ Increased desire to teach what I am learning during my own process

➢ Deja vu is perhaps the most interesting and very profound effect. The sense that you have experienced things before becomes extremely commonplace and will usually happen from one to several times per day.

➢ The nada is an effect that has been with me for some time and for me it is a sound that comes in through the ears. Sometimes it is loud and sometimes it is quiet but it is always present. It does not interfere with hearing and is not aggravating. In fact, I used to have tinnitus very badly due to an infection that destroyed nerves in the ear, now the tinnitus, although it is still somewhat there, is overshadowed by the nada which seems to act as white noise and nullifies the tinnitus as an opposing wave form. The nada also seems to get very loud when I am in the psychic receiving mode or when something is very inspiring such a wonderful music or elegant words.

➢ The visual nada, as discussed earlier, happens frequently from three to more than a dozen times per day. This effect seems to always point to a profound thought or statement or will almost always accompany an epiphany. This intense dot of light is not distracting nor does it interfere with sight in the least. It rather is quite exciting and feels like awareness pouring in from elsewhere.

## Experimentation

Over the years I have conducted many experiments with these substances. Most of the lab experiments have to do with industrial applications including catalytic, anti-gravitation, conductivity, resistivity, light absorption and optical qualities. Used as a catalyst, certain ORMUS will transform carbon to oxygen. This is likely a transmutation and not a catalytic reaction as discussed earlier. I have witnessed or performed many experiments of this nature and have proved this effect in many applications.

It is reported by David Hudson that certain ORMUS will ride the magnetic fields of the Earth when heated to particular temperatures. I have witnessed ORMUS floating in a glass tube when heated and often it will swirl like a whirlwind within the tube. This is not a result of moisture or of gasses evolving during the heating process. I have not been able to reproduce this effect with any other material.

I have found ORMUS to be extremely resistive to heat. In its microcluster form, it will resist thousands of degrees. For this reason it could be used as a heat shield material or as an additive to products that must be fireproofed. ORMUS is also a perfect electrical insulator to frequencies which it does not conduct.

ORMUS has also been found to be a great conductor of certain frequencies which are light frequencies, such as magnetism, and visible and non-visible light. When ORMUS is not quite at its prime superconductive temperature, it can be made to absorb so much light that it becomes luminescent or glows in the dark. This happens after certain methods of annealing have been performed. A friend of mine who is a glass artist used some of the ORMUS that I gave him to fuse into glass tiles and these tiles glow bright blue in the dark. Philosopher's stones also often glow. The Knights Templar employed alchemists to produce the glass for the Notre Dame Cathedral utilizing a material known as Spiritus Mundi (The Spirit of The World) which is glass made of gold ORMUS. This glass has a very strange luminescence.

Gold glass as stated earlier has a very long history as it has been used to make shems and yads for temples, umphalus stones, and even crystal balls. Gold ORMUS glass becomes a beacon, a receiver, and a transmitter of certain frequencies which are expressed by the earth, sun and moon as well as the person who has taken the gold ORMUS/ manna. Remember in the preface of this book we read from Revelation 21:21: "and the street of the city was pure gold as it were transparent glass" which speaks to the knowledge of the glass made of gold in biblical times. A jewel made of ORMUS must only be worn by a person who has fed upon the gold ORMUS for some time or it will cause noticeable discomfort. In ancient times, temples where adorned atop by the shem in order to fill the temple with the frequencies conducted by the shem and to transmit on high the frequencies projected by the priests. The use of gold glass in the windows of the early cathedrals of France was intended to produce just the same effect as the shem or yad upon the early temples. The difference here is that the temple space now becomes surrounded by ORMUS with priests and attendees fully encompassed by ORMUS and its effects as they view the wonderful luminescence of the stained glass windows all about them while the entire space is bathed in sacred light altered by the spirit of the glass. No one can deny the consciousness altering effects of the stained glass within the ancient cathedrals of France. It is true however that entering a cathedral would be a much more powerful experience for one who has fed upon the manna.

**The craftsman/alchemists used *Spiritus Mundi* in the manufacture of the beautiful luminescent stained glass of the cathedrals of France. Here we see some of the Notre Dame cathedral glass. The oldest portions are the upper rose window sections.**

**This old lithograph depicts two alchemists working to make ORMUS to be used in glass making.**

ORMUS will also ride on magnetic frequencies at room temperature when certain frequencies are used. I am in the primary stages of building an electromagnet that attracts all metallic metals, including nonferrous metals. This device attracts platinum group metals well. This could yield some very interesting experimentation and could be used to help give the ORMUS a charge that would boost its strength or change its qualities.

Superfluidity has been found to be a common effect when dealing with ORMUS. It has been noted to climb the sides of a container.

**Three stages of copper as it is transformed into ORMUS: Note the bottle to the right containing ORMUS in its final stages as it exhibits the cone effect of super-fluidity.**

It will tend to flow away from a container lip when pouring. It flows and swirls easily in powder form and even more so if heated. It will not flow through the separation/titration funnel petcock; it tries to flow away instead. This has been a problem as a titration funnel cannot be employed in the manufacturing process. Even when the opening is large and there are 5,000 mls of liquid above the opening, the ORMUS will not let a drop go through. This quality may not sound like something that is *super fluid*, but the *super fluid* nature of ORMUS somehow resists the flow direction of liquids in which it is suspended. When powder ORMUS is heated to about 950 degrees, it will flow anywhere one wants it to go just like a liquid. Most people do not realize that ORMUS can also be made into a liquid. If ORMUS could be made purely in its liquid form and kept in that state, there is no telling how incredible its *super fluid* qualities would be.

Tunneling is an effect that I have often witnessed in the lab. Only certain types of glass can be used as vessels to work with the ORMUS. Stainless steel quickly splits as if it is sliced into ribbons. Some glass will explode as if under extreme pressure and all glass will eventually crack during the boiling process. Glass jars used during the washing process become wavy and wiggly-looking, just like antique glass and sometimes the bottoms fall out. The reason for this is that the gas of ORMUS passes through the glass. Sometimes, as the atoms pass through the glass, they drop to a lower spin state at which point they lose energy and become solid. As more and more atoms get caught in the glass or other material and the pressure builds, this eventually distorts the glass or even fractures it.

Certain microcluster formations I have witnessed seemingly burn when in a vacuum. This occurs without significant heat. At first glance, this appeared to be some sort of oxygen reduction reaction, but there really was no material capable of sustaining combustion. Later, I theorized that the vacuum caused a metered release of light energy stored by the ORMUS within the microcluster material matrices. This may be likened to the flash capability of the rhodium ORMUS discussed by Hudson and others. These reports describe rhodium ORMUS under certain conditions to flash out of existence in a blast of light without causing shock waves. I have not reproduced this effect, however, the two may be related.

The newly formed precipitate of ORMUS which forms near the end of the alchemical process just prior to the washing phase, off gasses ORMUS as tiny, nearly indiscernible bubbles that can be best viewed in sunlight. This effect can be drastically elevated by desiccation. During the desiccation process one can get the absolute purest and most powerful and immediate intake of ORMUS by breathing the vacuum exhaust from the desiccator. Often I have come up from my basement lab with an ORMUS influence by breathing the gas while working. It actually is somewhat of a buzz although not judgment altering, nor does it impair any function of the body or mind. Rather, it causes a feeling that is not easily described but might be seen as light-headedness, openness, or expandedness.

There are many other experiments that I have performed, however they are likely of little interest to anyone not involved in the science aspects of this subject and most of them do not apply to health related issues. There are also many experiments performed by others that I have yet to reproduce in my own lab. One prominent experiment that I have yet to reproduce has shown certain ORMUS to disappear and reappear by the application of heat under certain conditions.

### Analytical Technique

It is important that anyone experimenting with the ingestion of ORMUS periodically have their products analyzed to make sure that there are no Gilchrist metals remaining within the product. It is also important to know what to look for in the analysis that will indicate that ORMUS are indeed present, for as we will soon discuss, the ORMUS themselves cannot be identified by standard analytical techniques used in the United States. However, ORMUS are identified as other substances in the analysis. If these substances are present in the analytical results and they should not be present in the sample, this is an indication that the sample contains ORMUS even though the method could not correctly detect the ORMUS substances.

### Difficulties of Analysis

The ORMUS cannot be analyzed by common techniques used in the United States. Our common technique for analysis of such solids is accomplished by burning the sample in an arc furnace at 5,500 degrees Fahrenheit. The burn lasts only 15 seconds and the resulting color spectrum is recorded and analyzed by the computer. This technique is called spectroscopy. The problem however is that ORMUS do not burn within 15 seconds since they resist extreme amounts of heat. This was known even in the old days and alchemists referred to it as "the phoenix and the fire stone which could rise from the ashes more white and beautiful than before". The alchemist knew that the "fire-stone" (Philosopher's Stone) was unable to be consumed by fire and they denoted this characteristic by the salamander that was fabled to be so cold-blooded that it was thought to resist even the hottest of fires.

However, there is a spectroscopy technique used by David Hudson that was devised by the *Soviet Academy of Science* that requires the use of a shield gas of argon and a burn time of 300 seconds. Analytical techniques used in the United States miss a great deal or incorrectly analyze a great number of compounds and elements. I would have to agree that David Hudson proved this. He put gold through his method of transformation into ORMUS. When the process had come to the point that the gold turned black, one half of the sample was sent off for analysis (in the United States) and the results identified the sample as carbon, yet it was gold. This is the substance referred to as the Ashes of the Phoenix. The retained portion was continued though the process until it turned red (the alchemists called this substance when refined, The Red Lion). Hudson again divided the sample in half and sent it off for analysis. This sample was identified in the analysis as just what Red Lion looks like, iron oxide, yet it was still pure gold. The final step of the process turned the sample to white powder which was analyzed and was reported to be just what it looks like, silica, alumina silica and calcium. Again, the sample was pure gold. In my research I have experienced the very same results.

Hudson finally realized that in order to correctly analyze these substances, he had to purchase his own arc furnace and test with a 300 second burn under an argon shield as specified by the *Soviet Academy of Science* spectroscopy methodology. When applying these methods, he found the samples were identified correctly as gold at all stages. All twelve of the platinum group ORMUS elements respond to analysis in the same manner.

I have found that the white powder of any of the twelve ORMUS types will analyze the same way and will be identified as silica, alumina silica, and calcium by mainstream methods of analysis used in the United States. This would be seemingly impossible yet this is what happens. Therefore, if one is making ORMUS, the sample analyzed should identify these compounds in the results in order to know that one has ORMUS, unless of course the sample is sent to a lab that has made the appropriate adjustments as recommended by the *Soviet Academy of Science*.

The main thing that one should be attempting to do by analyzing a sample is to confirm that no harmful material remains in the resulting product. The problem is that it takes a lot of work to make a small amount of ORMUS and the lab requires a fairly large sample. So if ORMUS is shipped to a laboratory for analysis, ask for the remainder to be shipped back and give explicit instructions as to handling so that the sample will not be compromised by electrical fields or mal-illumination.

### Observational Analysis

If you know what you are looking for during the manufacture of ORMUS, there is no need for analysis in order to identify it. Alchemy is 90% observation. During the process one should look for the correct color, consistency and pH changes. When the ORMUS reveals itself, it comes into view as a cottony precipitate that will collect tiny bubbles of gaseous ORMUS that will make the cotton-looking material float. This will continue for one hour to two days before the precipitate will stop moving and sink. It is at this time that the washing process can begin.

During the washing process you should observe that the color is as it should be and when the process is complete, the liquid should be tested by taste. If any salty taste remains then it is possible that other metals could remain. Washing should resume until no salty taste remains. In fact the ORMUS water should have no taste.

The ORMUS precipitate can vary in color depending on the primer used if the intent is to take the element only to the semi-high spin state. For instance, copper and nickel can be sky blue, rhodium can be tan to pink, iridium can be the most beautiful shade of lavender, while silver is silvery and gold is grayish. The ORMUS from wood or detritus is always tan to brown. All of these elements can also be varying shades of white when they reach the full high-spin state. They are so white in fact that one cannot nearly see the different shades unless different ORMUS elements are sitting next to one another for comparison. Wood and detritus need to be filtered to a greater degree before pH adjustments are made in order to remove all of the lignin which produces the brown color. Once all of the lignin is removed, the ORMUS made from wood can be snow white. However, it should be noted that the lignin have their own curative properties and it may be desirable to retain some of this for topical applications.

Once one learns the colors, consistencies, changes and characteristics, then analysis is not necessary for identification. There are also the characteristics of the product such as its strange luminescence, its super-fluidity and its anti-gravity tricks that help to identify it.

Before pH adjustments are made, one needs to filter the liquor a number of times to remove all Gilchrest metals and other impurities that can be filtered out at this point in the process. If the liquor is heavily laden with ORMUS it may not be visible, however the liquid will exhibit some strange characteristics. The liquor will have a strange luminescence about it and will be watery yet move as if highly viscous. The substance will be difficult to filter and may defy the use of vacuum during filtration. When acid is introduced during the pH adjustments, there may be localized precipitate which shows up and then disappears. The milky, cottony precipitate will fully reveal itself once the pH has been lowered to 8.5. This is, to an alchemist, the most beautiful sight. The adjusted liquor is then placed into a large settling vessel. However, it does not settle at first. As the Emerald Tablet states, it first ascends to heaven before falling back to Earth. Observation of this stage may convince one that the ORMUS is alive as it will rise and descend and rise again in a slow rolling fashion. This is due to the tiny bubbles of volatile ORMUS which try energetically to attract the more solid state ORMUS just as the solid state ORMUS itself bonds together to form the precipitate. The bubbles will eventually slip away or change to a solid and the precipitate will settle out. The tiny bubbles may have one baffled as they are so small you have to hold the jar in just the right light in order to see them. There are certain conditions which will make the ORMUS rapidly volatilize whereby all of the solid precipitate will turn to bubbles and rise out of the container into the atmosphere. Ordinarily this is not what you want to happen however, when it does occur, it is quite beautiful indeed. It is prudent here to mention that when making ORMUS it is at the point just after pH adjustment that the maker can get the greatest and most pure dose of ORMUS by inhalation of the volatile ORMUS. Gaseous ORMUS is also the most active and high spin phase of ORMUS and will rapidly go throughout the body to where it is needed. For this reason the Alchemist almost always reaches a higher state of transformation than one would through regular ingestion alone. I routinely spend time during this phase of production taking nice deep breaths after the acid fumes have been removed and sometimes I conduct a procedure to cause the ORMUS to become volatile for the purpose of breathing the ORMUS gases.

### Identifying ORMUS in Nature

I do have one very interesting method for identifying ORMUS which has formed in natural compounds and substances. This would include soils, salts, organic materials, and ashes. This technique involves the use of a laser pointer. Before I divulge how this is done I would first like to explain my theory on why and how it works. You may use your own hand to demonstrate this theory. For this experiment you will need a strong red laser with a focusing aperture and a dark room. If you were to shine a laser at the flesh of your finger you would be able to see three main things occur. First, the light would penetrate your finger and illuminate the flesh itself. Secondly, a red aura would form around the area where the light is penetrating the finger which would extend well out from the finger. This would be more pronounced in the dark of course. Thirdly, you would witness a very interesting phenomenon that I have yet to hear anyone discuss. There would be tiny dots of light that would be in constant movement both within your finger and in the resulting aura. If one were to shine the laser at a dead object such as a table or wall, you would see little to no penetrating luminescence; there would be very little aura and there would be mostly dots of stationary light rather than dots that are moving as if alive.

All things are like holograms of varying densities. The holograms are produced by the interference patterns of various energetic frequencies. When the laser is shined at an object, the particle beams/waves intersect with these interference patterns. This produces tiny localized dot reflections within a wash of more defused wave-like light. The result is a red spot of light with stronger red dots within the red spot. When this occurs with a living object such as your finger, the interference patterns are more active due to a greater amount of inherent light, internal motion and the emitted light frequencies of the human aura. The result is a higher degree of movement in the reflections. The living material gives off non-visible light which is in movement and which also reflects the laser off of its interference patterns. Living things possess movement due to the internal activity of the blood, cells, fluids, etc., but they also possess ORMUS compounds which help to transport light throughout and create an aura as well. For this reason when one shines a laser at soil for instance, which contains a large amount of ORMUS, it produces an aura and moving dots. The greater the aura and the more dot movement there is, the greater the amount of ORMUS there is inherent in the material.

So, for this reason you can use a pocket laser pointer to identify good primer material. The use of the laser takes some practice with comparisons of different materials but works quite well once you get the hang of it. The trick is to find a substance that makes the light do the same thing as it does when you shine it on your finger or even better. As said earlier, the best type of laser to use is one that can be focused. The slightly defused out of focus beam works best in this application.

I have one other thing to mention concerning this matrix of interference patterns inherent in all things. Once one has taken the ORMUS for a sufficient amount of time and once one has practiced seeing with the subtle inner eye, one then begins to discover that sight is an aspect of awareness and interpretation rather than a simple photograph of the environment taken by the eye in conjunction with the brain. When you get to this point, you will find that you are able to see many things in nature that others do not see. The thing you thought you needed the laser to see begins to become apparent to you simply by looking with a calm mind. We will discuss this further in the Chapter concerning Inner Alchemy.

## Ashes

If one has ever burned a large amount of wood such as in a wood stove or wood furnace over a course of weeks or months, certain characteristics of **superfluidity** can be seen in the ashes at certain times once the ashes have become very concentrated and hot. This is most apparent when cleaning out the ashes from a furnace where the ashes are above 950 degrees Fahrenheit. The ashes, when hot and completely burned to a nice grey soft powder, will act like liquid in this state. When you shovel them up they easily pour over the side of the shovel and when placed in a bucket they can be stirred and will continue to move for a time even after the stirrer is removed. I am often amazed at how liquid-like hot ashes are; how they can be poured and sloshed around. This characteristic abruptly resolves once the ashes cool below the point of 950 degrees as they become stiff and dense. This phenomenon is due to the weight defying aspects of the concentrated ORMUS at its prime catalytic temperature. The greater this characteristic, the more ORMUS can be collected from the ash. When performing plant alchemy one must chose the proper plants to obtain the greatest amount and type of ORMUS. Also it is sure that different plants concentrate different ORMUS elements in varying mixes. The type of plant chosen would determine the ORMUS mix. In India and Tibet, Yogis and other masters produce a substance called **vibuti**. This is sacred ash. I have tested **vibuti** and have found it to be high in ORMUS elements. This practice no doubt stems from an ancient alchemical practice. I do not know if all vibuti is high in ORMUS however, Vedic alchemical texts give formulae on how **vibuti** is produced and it is clear that the goal here is to produce ash high in ORMUS. So if it is produced properly it will be laden with ORMUS. However, the Vibuti is still ash and may be impure and therefore not likely fit for ingestion on a regular basis.

## Past Methods

In the past, there was never an analytical technique that was used to identify ORMUS. Rather there were only methods of observation and tests used to make sure that the Philosopher's Stone had been achieved. One of the most well known tests that was employed became a joke over time. People thought that the alchemists were trying desperately to change lead to gold so that they could get rich. In fact, many of the alchemists quite regularly performed this seemingly magical feat, but not for the reasons we think. The method of seemingly transforming lead to gold was no more than a test used to make sure that a high quality ORMUS had been created, as the true elixir has the power of transmutation and can tinge other base metals or transform them entirely under certain circumstances seemingly into a different base metal. Since the stone and its resulting elixir was far more valuable than gold, it would make no sense to the alchemist to use up his elixir in such frivolity as to use it solely to make gold. Occasionally throughout history, the trick was taken outside of the alchemist circles and performed for kings and noblemen in order to gain their attention or favor.

In recent times, a controversial discovery of a platinum cannon associated with an old Spanish shipwreck off the coast of Abaco Bahamas generated some debate. No one had ever seen such a thing. At first there was quite a bit of speculation as to why a cannon would be made of platinum. The main theory that arose was that the treasure that the ship was carrying must have been hidden in plain sight as a platinum cannon and related platinum items, especially since no other treasure was found. Eventually during some cleaning operations, the surface of the cannon was fractured in a couple of locations and small chunks of metal fell away. It was then discovered that under the few millimeters thick platinum layer, there was iron. This created confusion and undermined the best theory to that date. Why was an iron cannon overlain with platinum and other platinum group elements? Further probes into the shipwreck revealed that the cannon had been found next to some barrels of gray limestone-like substance with a probable dry weight of some 40,000 pounds. What were these barrels? Speculation has it that the barrels were themselves the true treasure which may have been wooden vats of platinum group ORMUS, since when samples were analyzed, platinum group elements were identified. This indeed would have been most valuable. Tests revealed that ORMUS, under certain conditions, will transmute base metal as well as other elements. The iron cannon left to lay for 200 hundred years next to and within the spilled platinum ORMUS submerged in a salt water bath may have performed a gradual natural alchemical transmutation of the surface iron into platinum and other platinum group elements.

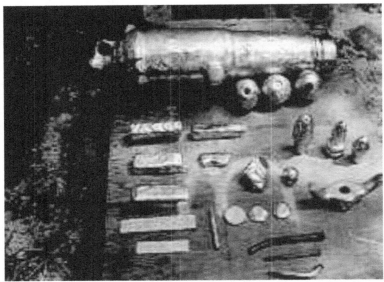

**Platinum cannon: For more information Google "Platinum Cannon Shipwreck"**

**Limestone-like substance thought to have transmuted the surface of the cannons to precious metal.**

Another very old test used to demonstrate that the ORMUS was in fact ready to ingest is found in the Vedic texts. This entailed the transformation of mercury ORMUS into gold and then back to a white powder of gold or gold ORMUS. In this test, metallic mercury was virtually made into ORMUS and then transmuted to gold metal and then made to change into ORMUS of gold to insure that no elemental mercury remained. When this was performed, the substance was ready to ingest. However, I do not recommend working with mercury for the purposes of ingestion as the Vedics once did simply for the reason that one cannot be too careful. If metallic mercury is left remaining in the product, "it's all over but the crying" as my dad use to say.

The Elixir of the Philosophers was also touted as having the ability to perfect certain gemstones by interacting with their inherent elements to produce perfect color and clarity. These stones logically would be those which were composed of elemental metallic compounds. Possibly, the ORMUS could have some sort of effect on such materials under certain conditions. Saint Germaine was one who supposedly had perfected such techniques and was noted always to possess the most huge and wonderful gems which he freely gave away to those who were gracious.

Many other tests and observations were employed by ancient peoples in order to prove their products either to themselves or to others. It is also interesting to note that these same observations and tests were used as a metaphor in the transformation of the spirit from the mundane (lead) to the noble (gold). Gold was held to be of great nobility while lead was said to be mundane. Gold was the representation of the end of the work when one had reached a great height of nobility while lead was used to represent the beginning of the work and lead was associated with the Earth while gold was associated with the sun.

One of the oldest premises of the alchemist, found on the Emerald Tablet of Hermes, begins with the words "As above, so below..." It denotes that that which happens in spirit, also happens in matter, and that which happens in heaven also happens on Earth. Therefore it is easy to see that the spiritual

197

transformation from the mundane to the noble was the same process as the physical transmutation of lead to gold. And so the age old test of the alchemists became a metaphor for spiritual transformation from the lowly to the noble, or from the ignorant to the adept.

**Hieros Gamos Ritual of the Moon.**
**Compliments of the Grand Lodge of Ath-Ka-Ptah.**

# CHAPTER 11

## Voices Across the Void

I have heard stories about people who, after taking the manna for some time, have ascended as far as to make love to angels. Although this sounds very intriguing to me, it has not been my experience. I do however have a wonderful teacher who is an ascended master. In fact, I have more than one teacher who are in the spiritual realm. My teachers seem to have expertise in different areas. They are very thorough and persistent in their methodology. One of the most surprising things that one finds after taking the ORMUS elements for some time is that communication with angelic frequencies does become possible and may be frequent especially if one is predisposed to such communions. But that is not all; one finds that it becomes possible to mentally communicate with other incarnate beings as well. Some of these beings might be on Earth while others might be elsewhere. All it takes to accomplish this is to be able to tune into someone else's frequency. Or in some way you might naturally be on the same wave length so to speak, or the same node of the matrix, however you might look at it. However this is not channeling in the basic sense of the word, for often channeling can be dangerous as one surrenders one's own consciousness and/or changes one's own base frequency. This is not necessary and not advisable as I have been taught by my teachers. In short, I have been taught a method of channeling which is always purified through the higher self. This is performed from higher self to higher self when communing with other incarnates and masters, while all angelic frequencies (if in fact that is what they are) will always come in through the filter of the higher self. In other words, leave the ghosts, demons, and astral projections alone if possible for they may corrupt you. This is also something that I have rarely discussed as it is a very private subject for me, however I feel it is prudent here to let the reader know what to expect and how to deal with the things that could be faced if the manna is consumed on a regular basis and in the proper regimen. Although communion is most often a choice, occasionally it will flood in for those who are prone to it.

So be aware that this may occur. The next chapter **Inner Alchemy** will hopefully help the reader in dealing with such things.

Now with this much said I would like to introduce to you a formula that was recounted to me by one of my teachers. Before I give the formula I might first explain who gave it to me and why. I should also explain why it is written in the manner that I will present it to you. The formula that I shall relate to you was given to me by none other than *Master Tjehuti*. He will introduce himself more thoroughly at the beginning of his work as he always does. This formula describes a method used thousands of years ago. The master was prompted to grant me this formula as a result of my questioning concerning past methodologies in comparison to methods used in more modern times. I had inquired about how people were able to use heat to make manna without the convenience of strong acids and powerful bases. He related to me that there were several methods but that he would pass one that is very efficient and easy for one person alone to perform. I should also say that the text that I will grant here to the reader is written in an old form of English. The Master speaks dozens of antiquated languages and often mixes them. The most modern form of English he will speak is akin to that which is found in the Bible. He seems not to be interested in vulgar English as he terms it although he will mix in modern words and terms. He also speaks Old English but to me this sounds nothing like English and is too difficult for me to speak and translate. The form of channeled communication we use is different from that which is the norm and which I use with all others with whom I communicate. Tjehuti sends me the actual words, whereas when I communicate with others I receive pure understanding through the filter of the higher self which acts as a sort of universal translator and purifier. It has taken great amounts of practice to perfect the method which Master Tjehuti and I utilize and requires a great deal of concentration within an altered state. The Master does not believe in taking control of anyone during this procedure and so the whole thing comes to me as prompts. It has been proven to me time and again that it is the manna and other ORMUS that strengthens this form of communication and allows one, with practice, to become adept at it. I would like to make it clear that I neither communicate with nor pay any service to earthbound spirits or, as they are more commonly known, ghosts, except to occasionally help them on their way when they are bothering me or someone who is plagued by such a spirit. But this is a whole other subject. The form we use here is rather a regular form of mental communication utilized in many societies throughout our galaxy. It is prudent to say that the master is not a ghost nor an angel but rather an incarnate who has lived many thousands of our years. We will learn more of him in later Chapters.

It is also appropriate to say that this formula, if used, does not insure that you will make a clean usable substance. For this reason one should have any substance produced by this or any method analyzed for heavy metals before ingestion or topical use. Keep in mind that although this is a food, there are many foods that can be poisonous if improperly prepared, some of which we eat on a regular basis. One example might be green beans. When they are frozen without being blanched, they may produce a toxin. There are also many seafoods that are very poisonous when improperly prepared. The ORMUS is no different. Great care must be taken in order to remove all Gilchrest metals from the final product in order to insure the substance is safe.

Now with that said, I will present you with the formula given by Master Tjehuti in his own words.

> I Tjehuti Apin, who art Ningish of my Sir Ninsimon, hath come to thee upon this day bearing tidings. And tis with great aunju (*heart space*) I do bestow unto thee that which thou hath charged. Now ere I bequeath to thee what thou hath commissioned of me, shall I testify unto thee of mine honor. For verily do I attest to thee, and lo doth I bespeak these things that thou wouldst arrest all what thou seekst. To thee I Tjehuti bequest no ill, for tis with honor for thee I serve. Thou hath quested of mine own favor a

manner in which yon kindred in days of yore wouldst prepare the stone. Though these times agone art buried in earth and obscured by sophists spells, I wilt bestow unto thee this honor by my breath to thy inner ear. So too shalt thou behold my favor with the inner eye of thine, such that illustrious visages shalt come within, of what sayst I unto thee. Now ere I unfold to thee, that which thou hath sought with a greatness of craeftmead *(skill or ability)*, shall I faran *(advance)* forth and first most by a reminder of mine own spells. For tis with great acceptation that mine spells hath been received. Remember thee, as above, so below. I Tjehuti art the great grinder *(tutor or teacher)* to baltu (*student Translates as My Splendor*). All who seek art to me, baltu (*he calls his students, My Splendor*). Nether thou wert, should I find thee and bestow unto thee the rich food (*refers to the food of the matrix*). So say I, anon whilt I belay and bewray this one thing to thee.

First thou wouldst find within thy self the powers which art in lack. Turn thou to thy guide, or to thy master, or to thy Adon *(Lord)* or to thy Adon of Rightful Justice (*Michael*). Find within thee powers which thou lackst or haveth not. This unto thee shouldst be the threshing floor and doorstep. Whence thou hath come to this, the choice thou hath made wouldst reveal the element to seek. Shouldeth thou be weak of heart or blood or sinew or bone, then take for thy self the cupric amon *(The Secret of Copper).* Shouldeth thou be weak of mind take for thy self the foreign powers which resideth in all the annu above yet sleepeth in all the Earth below (*iridium*) and as well choose for thy admixture the incorruptible lunar essence (*rhodium*). But sayeth I, choose not the electrum (*natural gold admixture*) lest thou wert of solid mind and aunju, that thou wert in the three fold philosophical mind of Aunju, Antu and conjo conjoined *(joined heart, emotions and cognition,)*. Then to thy self shouldst thou behold, for what is this *(Manna)*. Even so that thou wouldst by fire and vulcan craeftmead and spagyric *(Purify and reunite)* works prepare up thy auride *(PureGold),* this for weak minds or quibbling hearts wouldst wreak tumult upon thee.

Now list thy ear, for this I say art most true and noble. Tell thee I this in veril manner with no sophistic intent. This be plain and simple such as bakers work. Follow thee this and wilt thou behold the stone. As above take thee thy vaporous stone *(salt)* or pickling thereof and with pure water prepare unto thee a brine of one omer *(about 4 liters)*. In affectation prepare thy picking until saturation is beheld, and lo, such thickening shouldst occur. Put thou this aside to rest, save the next day whenst thou wouldst bestir the brine to thickening. Also thou must need prepare for time of late, the strong alkali. This may thou prepare from alkali earth or prepare thee of ash. If thou hath chosen ash then percolate thou this ash with purest of water and retain thou thy lye, and for this evaporate to dryness. Grind thou this to dust and lay thou this aside. *(This step can be supplanted by the purchase of pure sodium hydroxide crystals)* Prepare thou anon alchemical fire to the heat which cherry the ferris *(iron)*. This fire adequate is for the elements spoken ere, but not so for the platos *(I think he means platinum)* nor for so much as the Foreign powers. This by different means must be rent to dust or by the most intense burning whence enclosed. Need thou now an ferris ladle. Heed well my compass *(direction)* and place for the heating our element within.  Place thee now aperched our flame which burneth still.  Keep thou this upon our flame until such time of calcination.  Now most quickly quench our element within our prepared pickling to whit our pickling hath begun.  Bestead this operation and so repeat time and again.  Do thus until thou observest the pickling color to change.  Shouldst thou hath chosen auride, then thy pickling wilt beget the power and color of sol.  Shouldst thou hath chosen the incorruptible lunar essence, then so wilt thou beget the powers and color of pomegranate.  Shouldst thou choose for thy self cupric or salice de mundi (*copper or nickel*), then shalt thou beget deep azure which doth behold the powers of sapphire. And so if thou hath chosen electrum the color varyeth, wilt they not?  For electrum may unto its self containeth many elements. So to reckon thou wouldst, that such colors art charioted in the belly of auride, the powers of which vary.  For this thou wouldst behold a deep violet such as the powers of amethyst of thy brine or pickle. This be lest thou faction a sol and beget the powers of citrine.

Whence our water hath turned and begot a dark and clear color, tis of time for thee to lay to rest our water until whence our queen hath come to our king in Annu.  Thence hath they conjoined, then so commence our next operation, for thou hath begotten the mercurous menstruum (*spirit laden solvent*). Ere our next operation, beget thee a cooking tureen of glass or unglazed stone. This must needs be not of metal nor glazed pottery, nor stone which harboreth metals. (*The best thing available is amber Pyrex without Teflon. If you use Teflon it will poison you as it will break down during this process and corrupt your liquor.*)  Thou also wouldst procure thyself an covering for to retain thy boiling, that waste not occur. This of glass again needst be. Now lay to boil our water pure, upon a fire so soft. Take thou care to boil at day whence the king and queen art one. Mild boiling we provoke until our water is nil. See thou these crystals cometh from above. Yet takest thou care not to lose all of our water in what thou doest, for in this operation, wish we not to scintillate, nor to scorch. Then add thee pure water whence again our salt hath cooled, the amount to fill thy hat. And mix thee now with industry our salt thus returned to solution. Now unto this sift thou into our water that which thou hath prepared from ash, our alkali. Aptly to our water to whitlow so that to touch this wouldst thou beget so burned (*get as close to 13 pH as possible*). So guard thou this such that thou wouldst not touch for loss of flesh. Mix with assiduity the two to one. Now whence again the queen and king unite, boiling thou wouldst resume. Boiling now our water in a closed house (*A closed gas grill may be used or a gas oven, but not indoors*) retaining our heat about. Boil this now the breadth of the day till liquid remaineth not. Observe thou thy earth prevailing within thy vessel. Whence it hath given up all moisture, an oil doth now succeed. Gently with glass rod touch thou this and move about the oil. Thou wouldst now see mite sparks there glimmering. If thou observe not the flickerings then moisture remaineth and thou shalt continue so even heat. Also I say to thee, observe now thy color. Auride showeth tawny, now cupric show thee kale, still the foreign powers and incorruptible lunar showeth to thee black. Whence all liquid art liberated, continue thy heat for a period of nearly one fourth of a track of the sol about the sky above thee. Lay thou this to cool within the house thou builded for to remove to air would fracture thy vessel and rent it to many parts. Whence the vessel hath given up all heat thou mightst remove it to thy work place. Now thy oil wilt be as stone and affixed about thy tureen. Dislodge thy crystals upon the cover and place within thy tureen. Now draw thou more alkali water into thy tureen. Cover thy stony earth a measure of two or three fingers. Now leave this rest for one full solar round. Upon returning, gently with great attention crush the weakend earth and mix our waters gently. Thou mightst for this befain *(enjoy or have)* a pestle or a rod of incorruptible iron, unglazed stone, pottery or glass. Now leave this to rest in fermentation whence our powers become solute and our vial earth dissolute. Now leave this for five full rounds of sol. If thou wish the most profit of return, then leave this for one lunar cycle till the queen cometh once again to the glory of the King. The advanced affect of all who seek the stone, be to perform the next operation whence the queen hath stepped before the king in utter embrace darkening the king's light yet exalting his powers. Conjointly in their nakedness, they embrace lending much power to that which is below. Yet this occasion is a rarity indeed, and so we must need bare the norm which cometh by the common circuit of our queen.

Now thou hath retained thy mercury and whilst thou acknowledge near completion, lose thee not thy attention for here thou must portend thy result. Begin now the work of the fleece. Thy sleeve compact with this to act in filtration, do thy work in earnest. With gentle pouring above, direct thy flow through thy apparatus thus. Receive thy mercurous *(containing spirit)* waters in thy basin below. Do this time and again and change thy fleece thrice whilst in operation. *(Tjehuti his relating to me how this could have been done in great antiquity so a fleece is used for filtration (thus the "Golden Fleece"). We however may use a Buchner filtration funnel and filter paper or coffee filters and a non-metallic screen strainer. If coffee filters are used, the liquor should be filtered at least four times with a fresh filter each time.)* Care now, thou must take in such to requite *(repay)* thou thy dead head, yet for thy self thou must needs retainest this for a time thence, whence thou wouldst revisit such works. There art a surety to remove such from thy succor lest a poison thou makest.

Behold, whence thou hath completed filtration and thy dead head art left alone, thou then mayest take observation. Our mercurous waters art strong and thick and hath glimmer and slight showing in color. Be thou then proud without hauteur, for thou hath begot the strong menstruum which containeth the powers of the whole world and hope of the one thing. Prepare now the strongest of vinegar, such that could burn thy flesh *(use hydrochloric or very strong acetic acid)*. Add thee this to thy water drop by drop again. For this there wert frothing and vulgar seething, so take thee care in this that thou wouldst not be scorched nor loose thine eye. Do this whilst fanning away all vaporous vulgarities lest thou singe thy nose and breath and eye. Persist until thou behold a milk to form within. Whence the milk be strong, now conclude. *(Without the observational skills of the accomplished alchemist, a lay person cannot accomplish this task of pH balancing without the use of a ph meter. The pH should be brought down to 8.5 where it will continue to adjust toward 7 during the washing operation to come.)* Draw now this draft into a tall vessel of glass such as that of mine own name sake *(Hermetic flask). (A half gallon jar works fine but as Tjehuti suggests, a hermetic flask is best due to the bulbous bottom section and slender neck.)* Now watch thee this in sunlight for tis a most beautiful spectacle of fermentation indeed, whence the powers rise above and fall below all the while trading estates. This with the mitest of faren *(advancing)* bubbles up to great acceptation whereto the word art emblazoned on high. Breathe thou this mine Baltu, for this be the vaporous stone in most pure form and most efficacious in essence. Thence now the marvel lost, allow all to settle complete in congealation.

Gently now with great care draw off thy waters above and fill our vessel, pure water therewith, and stir up our congealation into suspension. Thence allow to congealate in so that the pleroma so doth return. Do this time and again. Tip thou thy finger with these waters to test the presence of salt by taste. Whence all salt hath been cleansed, so to hath all ill things in thy alchemy, I well bid thee. So for this say I Tjehuti, our art hath begotten a strong elixir and so thou mayst partake of this, for twas the cooking beyond the aridity which vested such power. *(Cooking the stone to cintilation charges the stone even before it is extracted from the dead head.)*

Yet thou mightst do greater than this and receive yet more from shem. This I now bequeath as well that thou wouldst behold the brightest of the one thing and translate the honor and breadth of the Great Arcanum. Then so place thy elixir within a clean crucible or slight basin. Gently heat thou the hatching egg in evaporation to aridity complete. Boil thee not this, for loss would befall thee. Whence thou hath completed this, a fractured shem remaineth. Now place thou this into a crucible of iron or fine baked white earth *(high temperature porcelain)*. Place thou this on constant flame for this art the whitening of the stone indeed. Endure this now for a quarter of the track of sol above. Do this until whiteness in total hath been achieved. Take thou care in so, thou hath not the flame to neither impress nor singe thy prize nor doth thou loose thy stone to the winds of thy flame. With succession doth thou retort *(return to the flame)* thrice or more. Heat thou this not to calc nor to stone that thy food be lost, lest for the shem or yad shouldst thou seek only, which for all glory doth hordeth light by day and sown glimmer by night. Great the qualities art of the shem stone yet thy ka shouldst go in hunger for sustenance or succor. *(Here Tjehuti tells us that if we heat the stone too strongly, that it will be singed and may start to vitrify. Should this happen you have lost your food or medicine. If you do singe the material you can take it to a higher heat to completely vitrify it into a solid shem which retains light and gives off a noticeable glimmer. If properly accomplished with an exceedingly high heat, proper procedure and additives to perturb the light retention powers of the stone, the shem can actually glow a beautiful shade of blue.)*

Once complete, now then cool and behold thy prize. Situate then our stone to the mortar and with pestle and so mill thy prize to fine flour and hear thine own refrain. What is this!! *(Manna)* doth I behold? Now behold thine own achievement. This thou hath made, tis the glory of the world. This fine stone affectioned to many great blessings art indeed. For thy elixir sift to pure water or wine. For thy succor drink thou this. For thy vitality and thy fortitude drink or consume as dust. For thy zounds *(wounds)* or thy afflictions consume thou this. Make thou this thy succorer *(doctor)* for twill aid thee in all thy life. What is this!! Now comprehend thy own heart and the alchemy therein for thy self origins reign herein. Use thy prize in wizened ways and cultivate thy aunju (*heart space*). Learn thou thy proper progression of the stone thou must need obey that thou doth not hamper thy senses and ascension. Seek thee pure wisdom of the stone and of the use of it, lest thou move staggeredly in thy advance. Suffer thou not the mitest things, for these wilt thwart thee in thy craeftmead *(skillfull work or ability)*. Seek thou equally philosophy whilst seeking thy stone for tis love for sophia that doth beget the one thing. Behold thou then ere my leave, all that I hath bid, for verily these things I bespeak art on thine own behalf. And list thou, the ear of thine ear to all I hath spelled unto thee. For where mightst thou overturn spells so champaign or ardent. (*Here he uses the word "champaign" meaning an open level ground to illustrate that he is eagerly giving us this information openly and on the level*). Render these I doth to thee thou Philomath, that thou wouldst consume this favor for thine own philosophy. What is this I Tjehuti hath bequeathed? Oh what is this *(manna)*? For thy favor, what is this, for thy love and wizened shem? Oh what is this of brilliance *(shem manna)*? What is this above and below, within and without? What is this that hath brung the light of Adon unto the world. What is this that hath filled all daath with light and sophia *(wisdom)* of thy imperishable mind? What is this that hath lain in the wind and rested among the world, and sojourned thy annu *(Heavens)*. Tis the gate of Adon *(lord)*, the light and the fancy of sophia. Tis the one thing and the conductor to the oneness. Tis the solid light of Adon who art the cosmic mind of all, come to terra as clay. Now then, thou hath the light and the way. I hath bid this unto thee. Pray thou doth as fair will *(good intentions)* wouldst have it, for the token is great indeed. Work thy will in nobility, even as the stone, and faulty thy treadings wilt be not, and all would impart perforce in salubrious works. Goodspeed to thee in this work. For thy accomplishments, I call after thee, Baltu! *(My Splendor; his name for a student)* For thy proficiency I say behold, thou art the Magister. Now thy solar work is accomplished. As it is above, so below.

Now I would like to pass on a word of wisdom and warning from the Master. This warning has to do with the Red Lion which he has referred to below as the Dragon, "that noble serpent of tawny scarlet". It is no doubt that if one learns to make the ORMUS of gold he too will learn eventually the manufacture of the Red Lion. While it is true that the Red Lion is valuable in many ways, it is to be used with great care. Further information concerning its use and misuse can be found in Chapter 13 on Inner Alchemy.

"To thee mine Baltu, should I upon thee bestow yet a caution indeed. Tis the dragon I bring up to thee. That noble serpent of tawny scarlet winged and wizened yet savage in its ways. Tis she who guardeth the cave that would be the hoard of the life arcana. Tis she who wouldeth ignite the breath of passion to consume all who dare enter save the purest of heart. Even so in stealth she bareth up to the world, a thing so great and awesome as she, to remaineth hid for our sake. Tis she who even so lureth us to our own consumption. Yet to the pure of heart she scorcheth the eye of our eye to granteth thus but a glimpse of the all in her light. Those who wouldst befriend her even so shouldst take head,

for with her thou mayst run, and aft so rest with
her, yet slumber not to closely with her for the
breath of our noble beast is searing and in her
nature she hath no regard. Even so in repose she
with her scorching breath wouldst consume thee.
And shouldst thou meet her acquaintance and
take for granted thine own knowings about her,
then run not with her for upon thee wouldst she
tread. And even so shouldst thou contract the
successful friendship of her, it would be so in
vigilance that thou behold such, lest thou
become trapped in the bowels of the cave by her
greatness whilst she turneth her attention to the
mouth and guardeth even thee as a treasure
within. So to the purest of heart sayeth I, run
with her oft if thou must, and get to know her,
but live with her not, for the wilderness within
her art more than thou couldst know. And if it
wert for thy attention to fail, yet for just a
pittance, then so, thou wouldst be vanquished
even by a friend, for her natures art deep and
powerful and untamable. And so she oft resteth
alone, and she remaineth hid for the sake of all."

# CHAPTER 12

## The Emerald Tablet of Hermes

The Emerald Tablet arguably has been the most reproduced text on Earth. It is a time honored document which has been either adopted into or has become the primes of countless religions, spiritual and scientific traditions. It has been touted as possessing the inherent power to captivate and enlighten the reader. The Emerald Tablet is also one of our most mysterious relics and is likely the only philosophically based text that has been transferred throughout time from culture to culture without significant changes to its meaning for the fulfillment of any agenda. The wisdom of the tablet appears to be incorruptible; through translation after translation it has retained its integrity.

The Emerald Tablet is fabled to have been around since well before the great flood and has been said to have been passed down throughout history having been hidden in various places for safe keeping at different times. It has been described throughout history by those who have seen it and it is always described as a single leaf tablet of molded emerald green crystal with characters written in bas relief. It is described as being of the most exquisite craftsmanship. Said to have been molded out of a single piece of green crystal, or emerald which is a green beryl (a silicate of beryllium and aluminum), the Emerald Tablet carries a prophetic message full of hidden meaning. Although its true origin is lost in conflicting legends that go back over 10,000 years, the wondrous artifact was translated into Greek by Alexandrian scholars and actually put on display in Egypt in 330 BC by **Alexander The Great** after his conquest of Egypt. During the display of the Tablet in Alexandria, scores of scholars, philosophers and alchemists journeyed from far and wide to get a look at the marvelous pre-flood relic that had until that time been hidden away from all public sight. For this reason the Emerald tablet became one of the most copied texts of the ancient world and was translated into many different languages.

Before that time perhaps the last person to hide it away was Moses/Akhenaten.

Lore has it that it was passed down to Miriam who brought its wisdom to the Israelites. Miriam, who was the Miri Kya, was of great royal descent and likely gained title of the tablet for this reason. And as we have discussed, Miriam was a great Alchemist in her own right. Miriam, being the sister-wife of Moses, likely granted it to him when he was Pharaoh. Moses was said to have hidden the tablet away for safe keeping in a cave. To attest to this possibility, there can be seen a monumental early fresco in the Borgia section of the Vatican which depicts Hermes, the supposed creator of the Emerald Tablet, walking with Moses and clad in alchemical symbolism. There are many legends of those who have possessed the tablet down through history. The most succinct and probable trail of decent would likely end with a Syrian boy named **Balinas** who supposedly found the tablet in a cave in Cappadocia. **Balinas** was said to have been most wise and was able to translate and eventually understand the tablet and its truths. After great study of the tablet, Balinas became adept at its understanding and introduced its teachings once again. He became known for his gift to the world and was dubbed **Apollonius** for his great work. The epithet he gained referred to Apollo, as Apollo/Ra was the brother of Hermes/Thoth who had supposedly authored the great Emerald Tablet. Hermes describes himself in the tablet as "thrice great". Many people have taken this to mean that Hermes was incarnated three times. This has led some to believe that Apollonius was the third Hermes. Yet why would he have been termed the brother of Hermes had this been the case? Later we will discuss the actual meaning of "thrice great". After Apollonius obtained the text, it has been said that Aristotle may have inherited it, however there is no real evidence of this outside of his teachings. The Greek philosophers Pythagoras (570-500 BC) and Plato (429-347 BC) before him drew heavily on the wisdom of the teachings of Thoth. It is likely that they had either access to the Emerald Tablet or its words along with other teachings of Thoth/Hermes. Aristotle drew heavily on the teachings of these two philosophers and therefore on the teachings of Thoth making it seem as if he had possible access to the tablet.

Before Apollonius, the Emerald Tablet was held as we have discussed by Alexander The Great who hid it away only to have Apollonius/Balinas find it in the cave where it had been hidden. However, after the time of Apollonius, the tablet's whereabouts has been kept secret. Before Alexander there are legends that it was given to Miriam the Daughter of Moses by Hermes. Other legends have it given to Miriam the half sister of Moses. Either way, Moses would have had access to it. Before Moses it is said that it had been owned by Solomon and before him by Melchizedek. Some traditions have it going back to Lamech, then Enoch and eventually to Cain while still other traditions have the tablet passing from Adam to Seth and then to the Enoch of Seth's line. It is important here to explain that there were many agendas to fulfill during the compilation of the Old Testament narrative. The utmost agenda was to hide the line of Cain and its importance from the El Shaddi/Enlil. The motivation here was not because Cain had killed Abel. This has been shown by Sir Lawrence Gardener in his works to have been a mistranslation. The real reason was simply that the El Shaddi thought ill of Cain due to his parentage by Eva and Enki. As stated in Genesis, the Lord was the father of Cain and in those days, the Lord was Enki the brother of Enlil. So not only was Cain considered an abomination, he was also defiant and unmanageable due to his high level of Anunnaki genetics and resulting intellect. Cain was what Enlil had feared. The Man has become as one of us. Enoch was even more Anunnaki than his father, as his mother was full Anunnaki. She was a full bred Anunnaki priestess known as Luluva, who was the daughter of Lilith who had originally been paired with Adam and who spurned him. Even though the stories concerning who owned the Emerald Tablet and how it had been preserved throughout time are varied and often conflicting, these things hold constant concerning the tablet. Firstly, it has always been said to have been written by Thoth. It has always been said to have been created before the great flood. It has always been described as an emerald green tablet in bas or raised relief and lastly, its wisdom message varies little over the course of millennia.

Now that we know a little about the history and stories surrounding the Emerald Tablet, we should learn a little more concerning its author and how he came to be known as Hermes Trismegistus. It is generally reckoned that Hermes and Thoth are one in the same. The Greek pronunciation for the Egyptian Tjehuti, Djehuthi or Thothi, became Thoth. The sound in English does not apply to the beginning of the word. Rather the sound is pronounced like a T sound with an h sound after it like the name Thomas. In ancient Egyptian the word Tjehuti starts with a TJ sound or a DJ sound Djehuti Tjehuti both apply. Thoth is most often represented as wearing the mask of an Ibis head which is associated with the moon. The Ibis bird has a long and curved beak which resembles the crescent moon. Thoth is considered to be a Moon God and often has the crescent moon motif displayed on his head. The Ibis bird was also a representation of the weighing of the heart which was one of Thoth's duties as a *Netjer* or *Netter* (high archetype). It was the Duty of Thoth to judge the Pharaoh and his past deeds before he could pass on to Thoth's wife *Maat* who would weigh the Pharaoh's heart against a feather. If all went well, the Pharaoh would be able to cross the River Styx and on to *Kirt Netter* (the After Life ).

**The weighing of the heart: Compliments of the Grand Lodge of Ath-Ka-Ptah.**

Thoth is an Anunnaki who came to Egypt according to Egyptian tales around 12,000 years ago. Thoth was vested with the duty of starting all of the world's major civilizations at one time or another. He brought languages, scribal techniques and music. Thoth taught humans math, poetry, art and sciences. As the son of Enki the Egyptian *Ptah*, he inherited all of his father's science. Thoth was often considered the scribe of the Gods as he wrote everything down concerning the Gods and their actions. He was of low rank even though he was the brother of Ra/Amon/Apollo to the Greeks, and the son of Enki. However, Enki gave him the sciences that he dared not entrust with Thoth's elder brother Ra. Thoth was never one to get in the middle of squabbles and always remained on everyone's good side. He was the one all the gods turned toward to settle moral, theological and scientific issues. Perhaps Thoth was best known for the designing and aligning of pyramids and temples and calendar hinges. It seemed that no temple of ancient times was attempted without at least his consultation.

This brings us to the name Hermes. Thoth not only built temples but all sorts of stone monuments like time keeping and computation devices such as those found in the British Isles, south and central America, the Middle East among other places. For this reason he was associated with stacking or piling rocks. The word Hermes means *He of the Cairn* or stone heap. This seems at second glance to be an appropriate epithet for one who has built more out of stone on Earth than any other.

### The Triune Philosophy

Now let us examine the second part of the name *Hermes Trismegistus*. Most people have assumed that *trismeigistus,* or thrice great, refers to reincarnation. Most have supposed that Hermes has returned three times to teach man. This notion has led to scores of postulations as to who the other two Hermes characters are after Thoth. These assumptions are all over the map beginning with either Seth or Cain, then including both Enochs, going on to Moses/Akhennaten then including Balinas/Apollonious, and finally Aristotle. There are scores of other assertions not mentioned here.

As we dissect the word *Trismegistus* we first see the *Tris* which means thrice or three times. The root word is *megistus* which translates as magnificent or exceedingly great. So in short, the epithet at first glance seems to say that Hermes is thrice magnificent or thrice great. We can also make note here that this Thrice Great epithet is a translation from some more Egyptian-like original. We can find that this same epithet shows up on the *Rosetta* stone in ancient Egyptian as *Au Au Ur* which means *Great Great Greatest*. But we wonder, greatest what? We also find the original Trismegistus epithet translated as *Megistos Kai, Megistos Theo, Megistos Hermes* which means *Greatest indeed or, Greatest divine, Great Hermes*. Shortened, this would be stated *Greatest and Devine Hermes.*

The word *Megistus/Magistos* is translated to mean exceedingly great or magnificent. From this word we derive the English word *magister* which means superior one. The word *magistrate* also derives from the Greek *magistos* and means much the same thing as magister. We also find that the word *Magus* which is a title often associated with adept alchemists, is derived from the same root and means virtuous authority, high importance or excellence. The word magus is also associated with the word *Mage/Mag* or the plural form which is *Magi* meaning wise ones. From the word Magi comes the words *magic* and *magician.* Our common modern definition for the word *magic* is trickery or illusion however the original translation of magician describes one who practices the art of positive change using the mystery of the natural and supernatural forces. To the magi, this positive change was most often effected within the self which would externalize into the environment. In other words, to change the world, change the self.

From all this we can see the rich in-depth meaning woven into the *Trismegistus* epithet. This epithet describes an exceedingly great, virtuous, authority of something. The word *tris* or *thrice* however implies that this exceedingly great, virtuous, authority is three fold. To realize the nature of the *Thrice Great* epithet, we need look no further than the Emerald Tablet itself. The answer is plainly stated in the twelfth line of the work **"Therefore, I am called Hermes Trismegistus, having three parts of the philosophy of the whole world."** In this verse Hermes tells us of the threefold or three part philosophy. This was a most important concept in the ancient world especially to the Celtic peoples and the Gnostic societies alike. The number three had great significance due to the three part philosophy. All things could be divided into three in the way stated in the

Emerald Tablet such as *mind, body, spirit*, and *earth, water, fire* and *heaven, astral and earth*, or *thought, emotion and soul* and *Animal, vegetable, mineral* and *sub-conscious, conscious, super-conscious* and so on. Each and every thing can be broken down into three parts and each of those three parts can be further broken down into three. *Qabala* is broken down into *bina, hockma, kether* while the teachings of the ancient goddess temples were broken down into three stages of life known as the *virgin, mother*, and *crone*. In many forms of Christianity the trinity is normally expressed as the *Father, Son and the Holy Ghost*, while the Nazarene trinity was actually *Father, Mother and child*. The processes of chemistry and early alchemy are also three fold and are known as *anabolic, metabolic, catabolic*. Even our experience of time itself is three fold breaking down to *past, present, and future*. This is indeed the philosophy of the whole world. The Celts took this philosophy to the extreme believing all things came in threes. And there was a correct and fervent belief that whatever one puts out comes back three fold as we learn in Chapter 13 Inner Alchemy.

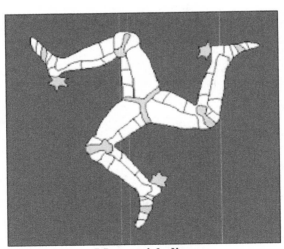

**Manx triskelion**

**Sicilian triskelion**

The Manx running man is a wheel of three legs in apparent running motion. This insignia and national Manx symbol appears as three legs shrouded in armor emanating equally from a central point and configured in an apparent clockwise running motion. It was originally a symbol of the Sun, the seat of power and life and symbolized the three part philosophy. In ancient times, the emblem was particularly connected with the island of Sicily but the Sicilian "legs" were always naked, more stylized and generally displayed Medusa's head at the central point. A rather similar device was popular among the Celts and Norsemen in northwest Europe. Similarities may be seen in the appearance of the Celtic devices such as the 'triskele', and triquort (triple knot) or simplified "Three Legs" emblem often found on coins of the tenth century Norse King, Anlaf Cuaran, whose dominion included Dublin and the Isle of Man. Many of the Celtic sun and life symbols were depictions of three whether it was three knots, three swirls, three legs, three bird heads or other zoomorphic heads. These were the symbols that were the embodiment of the "three part philosophy" and "the operation of the sun" in Inner Alchemy. In fact, the whole of the Celtic spiritual tradition was entirely based on the Celtic concept of spiritual wholeness which is defined by three conditions: *Crabhadh* (pronounced cravah) the trust of the soul and its devout observance, *Creideamh*

221

(pronounced creejeev), the consent of the heart or its belief, and *Iris* (pronounced eerish) the mind's pledge.

**Basic triskel, triquerta or triple knot**

This is the Celtic version of heart, mind and soul described in the Emerald Tablet. In Celtic wisdom, when these three concepts are experienced as one or as the One Thing as it is explained in the Emerald Tablet, then the soul shrine (*coich anama*) is strong and powerful. This is to say that life force, or chi as it is called in eastern traditions, is strong. Additionally, one of the main principles of ancient magic/divine manifestation among the Celts was the law of three. It was believed that whatever one projected emotionally or in action would come back to the person three fold. This is a principle we will surely learn applies to inner alchemy and the manifestation of reality through thought and action. This is a principle of three that one must become intimately acquainted with in order to become an alchemist or when taking the ORMUS substances. But what does modern science teach us in this regard? It is unfortunate that most of our scientific understanding is based in an understanding of a binary code. This is in great part due to the nature of the modern computer which works by computing ones and zeros. But as humans, we also often tend to see things in binary or dualistic fashion. For instance we tend to experience many things as polar opposites such as dark and light, dead and alive, good and evil, pass and fail, male and female, north and south and so forth. Even in politics we tend to leave out all but two major parties which are perceived as polar opposites in ideology even though they often have the same issues and goals. This type of thinking is unfortunate for it is just thinking and is real only because we deem it so. In fact nature and the universe is not binary at all. It is just as Hermes tells us. The universe is ternary, triune or trinary in nature. Recent discoveries in physics have revealed a code of sorts that pervades the universe in the form of scalar waves. These scales are standing waveforms that are ternary in nature. Leading the way in this work is Dr. Hartmut Muller of Germany. His work has been ratified by other great scientists such as Dr. Merkl whom we introduced in earlier Chapters.

It has been shown that a blueprint for all that exists is coded in the scalar standing waves just as Hermes tells us. Even the genetic code is coded into the nodes of these standing waves. As this new science unfolds, we begin to see that there are other explanations for things like evolution and that communication of information can take place over great or even infinite distances with only small amounts of energy needed to modulate the already existing waves. This means that waves do not need to be propagated in order to send messages since the scalar waves already exist homogeneously throughout the universe. This type of communication has been tested and shown to work, thus helping to prove the scalar wave theory and its triune nature. The triune nature of the universe is something that we must learn to understand and master in order to bring about resonance with what we wish to attract in our lives as the laws of attraction are based in this notion. The laws of attraction are in fact no doubt the way consciousness modulates the frequencies of the universal code to cause the manifestations of events within the specified event horizon. Thus, cutting edge science teaches us an age old concept of the three part philosophy stressing the need to do away with our polarized, binary way of thinking.

Much of polarized thinking is applied to things that are imaginary or manufactured opposites, such as the concepts of light and dark, or good and evil. Dark for instance does not actually exist as a thing. Darkness is simply the absence of light. It becomes darker as light is reduced; therefore, there is only one thing: light. The same philosophy holds true for good and evil. Evil is not a thing; rather it is the absence of good. As one becomes more evil, they are becoming less good. Einstein argued that good was love and love was the mind of God, so evil was a reduced connection to God; therefore, evil in itself did not exist. He compared this concept to hot and cold; cold does not exist but is simply the absence of heat. These seeming polar opposites are really not dualities; they are the presence or absence of one thing.

Another example is Yin and Yang which is classically represented as shapes intertwined within a circle. It seems to break down as opposites of male/female at first glance, until one perceives the entire symbol blending the forces into one (hermaphrodite). Black and white, again perceived as opposites, really is the singularity of light (white) moving toward the absence of light (black). Big and small are just comparative concepts of size. Most "opposites" are actually a spectrum of the movement within a singular concept.

Another way to look at "opposites" is to view things as complements. A relationship is the perfect example. Often we hear that "opposites attract" regarding relationships. When thinking of two individuals, they can never be truly opposite in all ways. What occurs in a relationship is two independent personalities complement each other to form something new, something greater than each individual. Complements, not opposites, attract and the relationship created by the complementary behaviors becomes the trinity.

It is true that polarized thinking has caused the majority of the conflicts and ills associated with our existence on this planet and we become more and more polarized with the passage of time. Due to polarized thinking, we find much of our lives in grid lock unable to travel in cycles like the Running Man motif of the Isle of Man. The teaching of the Three Fold philosophy is no doubt important to our survival as a species, yet such notions have become foreign to us. All we must do to learn these important concepts is to open up to them and see nature as it really is. We can find these concepts in most ancient traditions for the teachings of Hermes/Thoth turn up everywhere as he was charged with the responsibility of starting civilizations all around the world.

### The Many Names of Hermes

According to the Ebers Papyrus, a 68-foot-long alchemical scroll which has been determined to be the oldest paper book in the world, "Man's guide is Thoth, who bestows on him the gifts of speech, who makes the books, and illumines those who are learned therein, and the physicians who follow him, that they may work their cures". Hermetic concepts are drawn on or even touted in hundreds of spiritual, religious, scientific, life style systems about the world. One example of this might be found in the Hindu sacred book *Mahanirvanatantra* which states that Hermes was the same person as Buddha, while both Buddha and Hermes are referred to as the "Son of the Moon" in other Hindu religious texts. Master Thoth perhaps had more names than just about any other archon due to his omnipresence. In Rome he was *Mercury* the messenger God, while in Greece he was known as Hermes or Thoth which derived from the Greek pronunciation of the Egyptian *Tjehuti*. In Egypt he was the lunar god of writing, math, geometry, calendars and alchemy among many other attributes. In ancient Sumer he was the great *Ningish-*

*Ziddha*. The symbol associated with all of these names was the double entwined serpent the *caduceus*. To the Celts he was *Ogmius* and was likened to the Roman Mercury with his winged feet. *Ogmius* was often depicted as flying through the air with chains attached to his tongue leading back to the ears of his followers denoting his eloquent speech which would captivate the listener. He brought an alphabet to the Celts which they named *Ogham* after his name. In the Americas he was known as *Viracocha, Quetzalcoatal* as well as by other names, and was the God of the sun and moon who promised to one day return. It was the mistaken identification of Cortez that led to the destruction of the Aztecs and others in their impatience for his return. Quetzalcoatal even prophesied this event saying that one day a man who looked like him being tall, light skinned and bearded would destroy the Aztecs as he would be mistaken for the returning Quetzalcoatl. In all cases, Thoth is associated with a feathered, plumed or winged serpent. In fact, Quetzalcoatl means just this, *Feathered Serpent*. This serpent motif has to do with wisdom and rejuvenation. His father also was associated with the serpent as the serpent of wisdom in the tree of life. The serpent motif goes even deeper than this as it symbolized the DNA double helix in ancient times.

**Upper left shows the entwined serpents of Ningish Ziddha The upper right shows the double helix of Enki and Nimma. Note the serpents have a ladder-like structure between them to equate them with DNA. There is also the Ankh symbol to represent life. At the bottom we see the workers manipulating the DNA sequence.**

## Thoth: the Master Alchemist

Above all that Thoth brought to humans was the teachings of Alchemy and the understanding of the One Thing, the Lord of the Cosmos, Adon. Through Alchemy, Thoth taught us how to ascend spiritually, rejuvenate physically, and be whole psychologically in accordance with his "three Part Philosophy". After Hermes, the alchemical arts were dubbed the *Hermetic* arts. Many of the early Philosophers summarized his works which eventually became known as the *Corpus Hermeticum* which was in part inspired by the Emerald Tablet. Certain scientific procedures invented by Hermes are still named for him today such as the procedure for the sealing of a glass vial which is termed hermetically sealed. This term also denotes something that is well sealed against corruption of any kind. Also, the very typical long necked flask associated with chemistry is often called a hermetic flask after Hermes. Master Thoth was said to have written all the books in the world. Hundreds of books have been said to have been written by Thoth in his own finger. Among these are the Book of Breathing and the Papyrus Ani. Many of his books are hidden while many were destroyed along with countless other ancient and invaluable texts when the library at Alexandria was burned by an angry zealous Christian mob in 391 AD. But even though most of his works have been destroyed or are hidden away, so much of his wisdom is ingrained in so many different traditions we need not look far to find it once we know how to recognize his words. And even though the Emerald Tablet is hidden away, it seems to pop up from time to time throughout recorded history, so it is possible that some day when we are ready, we will see it yet again.

## The Tablet

Now that we have learned about the autho,r we should discuss the physical makeup of the Tablet before going on to discuss its content. Many people have assumed that the Tablet is made of either emerald or green crystal made molten and then poured into a mold. First, I think we can easily rule out crystal. This simply would not have stood up to the test of time. Emerald, although it is much harder and more indestructible than crystal, it too may not have been quite noble enough to withstand the test of so many years of existence being passed around from person to person. We must remember that the tablet was made before the flood which theoretically makes it more than 12,000 years old. During that time this object had to withstand floods, earthquakes, storms, wars, fires, travel, and handling. What could withstand such rigors and then amazingly been readable when put on display in Alexandria, much the less have been as beautiful as it was described by those who pilgrimage to see it. There are some clues to be found in the description of the pillar it was hidden in to protect it from the great flood along with other things which needed to survive. It was said that two great pillars were constructed to withstand the flood. One of these pillars could not drown and the other could not be consumed by fire. One of the pillars was itself an emerald green and was said to glow in the dark. This is our clue, for emerald is certainly green but does not glow in the dark. It is said that the content of the stone from which the pillar was made was recorded in the Emerald Tablet. Perhaps it was that they were made of the same substance. So, what is emerald green, has the ability to glow, and can withstand the test of the millennia? In the Libyan Desert there is found a special green glass known as desert glass.

Samples of Libyan Desert Glass

There are also other places about the world where such glass is found. It is now common knowledge within scientific circles that such glass cannot often occur naturally. In fact the only natural way that it can possibly occur is by a perfect lightening strike. However, this is only speculation for it has never been documented that lightning has cause a green colored thunder egg. When lightning strikes the ground, it most often produces grey or brown colored cinders of fused silica compounds. When something like silica beach sand or desert sand is vitrified by lightening, a clear glob of glass can be formed. There is one way however that green glass is most always produced and this is caused by nuclear fission or fusion explosion. Beautiful green glass can be found anywhere nuclear testing is performed. But this is no ordinary silica glass. The qualities are quite different than if the same sand were vitrified to mere crystal. This glass is stronger, denser, and harder.

Uranium used to be used to produce a type of yellowish green art glass known as Vaseline Glass. The manufacture of this type of glass is now prohibited as the product is mildly radioactive. The color and quality of this type of glass distinctly reminds one of the Libyan Desert glass shown above.

Now you think, 'how would there have been atomic activity in ancient times?'. There in fact is quite a great deal of evidence to support that there were atomic wars and other weapons that utilized the power of the atom or its temperature equivalent. There are partially, as well as totally, vitrified stone forts all over the world where rock has been melted turning the entire structure to glass. Many of these places are radioactive. One well known site is **Mohenjo-Daro** in India. There are many melted forts in Scotland such as the famous and first discovered, Tap O' Noth.

**The Mohenjo-Daro remains. Research done for David Davenport by the CNR Rome (National Research Council) in 1970 indicated that the vitrified (melted) portions of the walls were subjected to a temperature greater than 1500 degrees.**

Experiments have been performed to try to vitrify even a small section of wall by burning many trailer loads of wood piled over and around the wall, with little success of vitrification. There are many ancient texts that described weapons of mass destruction; so well in fact that the reader is left little doubt of what is being described. To learn more on this read *The Earth Chronicles* by Zechariah Sitchin and *Technology of the Gods* by David Hatcher Childress.

So now we know that extreme heat produces emerald green glass, but will it glow? The answer is: not necessarily. Might there be another substance other than silica that works this way? There is, and it is the subject of this book. ORMUS, if heated to temperatures exceeding 6000 degrees Fahrenheit under controlled conditions, can produce beautiful green glass that may glow if made properly and is very durable. One may ask, 'How can manna be heated to such high temperatures'? There are two ways to achieve this other than nuclear energy. One could use a heliarch/tig torch with a tungsten stinger rod and an argon shield gas. But this will only produce a very small chunk of glass. As we read on, we see there is another way.

## The Vapor of Life

As soon as you thought that there could be no other amazing substance like ORMUS, I bring to you yet another one that was likely known by the ancients. In the 1960s a man named Yule Brown invented a new form of electrolysis. This form of electrolysis was found to produce hydrogen and oxygen, both in the mon-atomic form, from splitting the water molecule $H_2O$. When burned, this blend of oxygen and hydrogen free atoms produces some very amazing effects. This gas mix is every bit as amazing as ORMUS elements. When burned through a torch, the flame is cool, hardly exceeding 200 degrees F. It can be played over the bare arm without burning the flesh as long as it is not held still. This cool flame is long and laser-like, as these burning gases produce a vacuum or implosion flame. The flame has the uncanny ability to release the electrical potential of the burning atoms of hydrogen and oxygen into anything upon which the flame is focused. This light and clear looking cool flame will create the temperature necessary to ionize the subject material up to and beyond an astounding temperature of 6000 degrees F. while even the very tip of the torch remains cool to the touch. This flame is an electrical flame which dispenses stored electrical potential. Even substances that are insulators can be totally ionized by this flame and in fact, the more insulating the substance is, the faster it will heat up and the hotter it will become. For this reason, the torch will drill a hole through firebrick, stone, and all metals. It will even drill holes though wood without consuming the wood material by fire, especially if the wood is damp. And it does so without smoke as the implosion flame takes in the smoke and consumes it. This flame will do all this but will not boil water.

This gas, known as **Browns Gas,** has a range of uses from hydrating the body to nuclear isotope neutralization. One very interesting ability of the flame produced by this gas is its ability to render iron non-corrosive. This is one of our major connections to ancient history. It seems the ancients had a means to treat large iron objects in such a fashion that they would be protected from oxidation and therefore they would not rust. As Gardner has said in his books, an age old tradition

231

found in the King's Chamber of the Great Pyramid relates what the builders had placed in the Pyramid "Instruments of iron, Arms which rust not, glass which may be bended and not broken and strange spells."

This day in time if one wishes to build a sword that "rusts not", one would need to use stainless steel. These items however were made before the time of any sort of steel. It is reasonable to assume that if the ancients could build an electrolyzer, they could also as easily make stainless steel. This is true, but there are other examples of iron objects manufactured in ancient times which do not rust. These are not steel, which is an alloy containing iron; these are rather pure elemental iron. Pure elemental iron is among the most corruptible of metals. Any object made of pure iron would not survive long when subjected to the elements and therefore even large structures would not survive the test of time and would be rendered to a brown red dust in relatively little time.

The Pillar of Delhi India is but one example of a large iron object that does not rust. It has stood naked to the elements for over 1600 years without surrendering to oxidation. Even the simple fact that the ancients of this time were not supposed to have the capability to cast such a colossal object in iron is perplexing enough beside the fact that it does not rust. Scientists have analyzed this iron and have found it to be quite simply 98% elemental iron with no detectable additives or treatments. So, the Pillar of Delhi is not an alloy of steel and is nothing more than elemental iron with a minute amount of impurities such as sulfur which might even be more of a hazard as far as rust is concerned. But iron rusts! So what did the ancients do to the iron to protect it? When a flame of monatomic oxygen and monatomic hydrogen mixed in the proper proportions is played over the surface of iron, it changes the molecular structure of the surface iron so that it will no longer rust. The reason this happens, just like the reason some ancient iron structures will not rust, is at this time unknown.

There are also other indications that the ancients had an understanding of electrolysis, electroplating, and were able to split the water molecule. There are numerous examples of ancient batteries that have been found that could have been used for plating precious metals. One example of this is the Bagdad Battery.

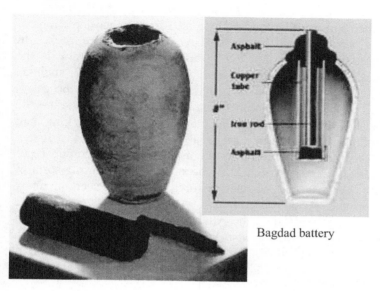

Bagdad battery

Iron Pillar-New Delhi
6 tons and 7.5 meters tall

Additionally, gold and silver plating were very common in ancient times although the techniques that were used are not well understood today. There are countless examples of gold plated artifacts from all over the world that date back to the annals of recorded time and beyond. There are also ancient depictions of special torches used in the carving and mining of rock. In modern times, one such torch capable of carving rock is the plasma torch. Certain types of metamorphic rock such as granite, which contains trapped water molecules, can be easily carved by any high temperature torch. This is due to the expansion of water molecules and subsequent cracking and exploding away of the surface as it is heated by the flame. However, this technique only seems to work with certain types of stone. Mining would have been undertaken in all sorts of stone. An example of such a torch would be seen in many Mayan and Aztec deceptions. Also, there are great stone statuesque pillars called the Atlante which stand atop the Aztec **Pyramid of The Moon** also known as **Quetzalcoatl Pyramid**. These great god-like figures all carry a special holstered torch-like nozzle on their right hip with corresponding fuel storage back pack

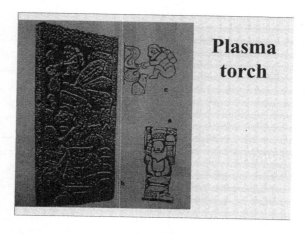

# Plasma torch

**Atlante plasma torch**

This same setup can be seen in many depictions, with the gods using the nozzles to produce stylized flames to cut and carve stone. This has been proposed to be some sort of an ancient plasma torch, however there is another clue to consider before this theory is accepted.

Over the past twenty years, a number of crystal skulls, thirteen authenticated in all, have been found all about the world. Among these skulls was the Skull of Doom, otherwise known as the Mitchell Hedges skull. The skull was determined to have been from great antiquity yet, when the surface of the clear crystal was examined under a microscope, there were absolutely no work or tool marks observed. I vaguely remember a television show called *In Search Of* which many years ago aired an experiment where this skull was loaned to a world renowned crystal manufacturer to see if they could reproduce the object. At first glance, the skull that was produced appeared to be a perfect replica. However, under microscopic examination, the reproduction revealed gross tool marks and sanding striations. What then could smooth the surface of a large crystal object so much so that even under powerful microscopic inspection the surface would still appear perfectly smooth yet not heat the internal quartz resulting in a fracture? Our current understanding of the working of crystal would actually require hundreds of years of man hours to attain such smoothness. So, what technology could have been used? This could have been effected by the use of monatomic oxygen and hydrogen. In fact, a flame fueled by these gases has proven to be substantially better for working crystal than any other torch gas. This gas can melt, weld, polish, and ionize crystal as well as other materials. Some other stones can be easily and effectively drilled using these gases, as the localized explosion and or ionization creates a perfect hole through the stone media. A more defused flame can literally strip away layers of any rock. Since the rock matrix itself is more resistant to heat than any inherent metals sought by the miner, the rock would be stripped away faster than the metals. Remember that the more something resists heat, the faster it is heated where these gases are concerned. In my experience, when colloids of gold or other metals reside in rock which is heated by this torch, the rock either melts and ionizes leaving beads of metal behind, or the rock explodes into dust as soon as the flame touches the surface, depending on the nature of the stone that is being worked. When the stone is exploded to powder by the torch, the resulting dust can easily be collected and the metals separated out, effectively doing away with the arduous milling process associated with hard rock mining. Also there are examples of ancient stone machining that defy modern explanation and appear to have been carved by erosion or melting of some form. Volumes could be written on this subject alone but we are here to show how the Emerald Tablet could have been made.

It has long been rumored among the alchemists that the Emerald Tablet was molded of an alchemical substance which defies all weathering and is extremely durable. And as we have mentioned, rumor also has it that it was hidden in one of the Pillars of Enoch constructed before the flood in which certain items were preserved. It is said that the tablet was a transcription of the stone's content which was made by Hermes. It is easily seen that the Tablet does not list items hidden within the pillar. It may however record the very formula of the substance from which the Pillar, as well as the Tablet itself, was constructed. This is in fact the case. As alchemists have always known, the Emerald Tablet encodes the formula for creating the

Philosopher's Stone this is most true and even obvious to those who have worked very much with alchemy. The final step which makes the stone turn emerald green remains obscure within the formula of the Tablet or is not included. So it may be that this step was considered beyond human capability and unnecessary to divulge. The true objective of the physical alchemical formula, as opposed to the inner alchemical formula coded within the Tablet, was to teach man to create the manna or Philosopher's Stone. Hermes/Thoth likely did not feel the need to take the formula further than this. However, there may be something that I have missed and the final step to forming the emerald stone may still yet be hidden within the text. If it is there, it may be interpreted from the last line; *"This, that I have called the solar Work, is complete"*. Even though the meaning of this statement is obvious, it contains multiple meanings. Perhaps the simple mentioning of the Sun also relates to the temperature of the sun which is required to turn the Philosopher's Stone to a greenish, indestructible, hard substance. This would be the ultimate end to the physical work as well as for the spiritual work when one has elevated the soul to a level of such beauty and indestructibility.

**Emerald Tablet redrawn from Sigismund Bacstrom's
original alchemical manuscripts**

### The Words

Now that we know what the Emerald Tablet was likely made of
and who made it, we must now go further to see what the words
of the tablet actually tell us. Before we broach this subject
however I will say that multiple volumes could and have been
written on what has been gleaned from these few scant passages
of the Emerald Tablet. Likely there have been few works in
history that have packed as much meaning in so few words. So
for the sake of our work we will only briefly discuss the
meanings of each line of the Emerald Tablet. It should be noted

before we continue that the Alchemists went to great lengths to obscure the meaning of their work. The sophist would obscure meanings by the use of special language and by corrupting the order of the formulae seemingly given in plain words. But the Emerald Tablet is plain and in order. For this reason, all alchemists kept a copy of the Tablet's words on the wall upon which to refer when attempting to decipher the sophisticated writings of other philosophers. Below we have but one translation of the Emerald Tablet which we will discuss between the lines with a little help from **Master Tjehuti**.

*It is true without untruth, certain and most true.* This work is the truth and the light and the proclamation of that which is inherent in the one thing. Hermes tells us that the tractate is all truth and there is no sophism within it. He assures us that we can be certain of its truth.

*That which is below is like that which is above, and that which is above is like that which is below; by these things are made the miracles of one thing.* Heaven and Earth are but mirrors of one another. That which exists in matter also exists in consciousness; as that which happens on Earth happens in the heavenly realm. So, transformation on a physical level also occurs in mind and in heaven. The one thing is the all consciousness which resides within all things and encompasses all. The stone of the philosopher is the earthly representative of the one thing as it, to some degree, resides in all, encompasses all, and is necessary for all life just as is the spirit of the all. Here we also begin to see the three part philosophy as the material, mental and spiritual.

*And as all things are, and come from One, by the mediation of One, So all things are born from this unique thing by adaptation.* All matter is born from one first matter and is created as individual by the negotiation of the one thing. Likewise, all matter is manifested by the one overall thing. For instance, reality is a product of consciousness. Universal consciousness is the one thing or the mind of God. So, through the alteration of consciousness all things are born. As such, all things contain spiritual essence which is what the alchemist wishes to extract and retain in the stone. The alchemists of old called this the Mercury.

*The Sun is the father and the Moon the mother.* In alchemy, the sun and the moon represent many things. The sun is the gold and is the masculine energies that must be inherent in the work. The sun also can represent the end of the alchemical work, or success, due to its noble nature and gold color. The moon is the feminine aspect and is represented by silver. In material alchemy, the forces of the sun and moon must be properly in position before there can be any substantial yield. The trinity here is the Sun, Moon and Earth. Here it states that the sun and moon are the parents which represent the conjoining of these forces. In alchemy, the sun and moon (represented by the naked King and naked Queen) respectfully must be married and come together to give birth to the Stone. This not only represents the conjoining of the forces but the actual need for the sun and moon to be in their proper places during certain alchemical operations. On the spiritual level, the Inner Alchemist must seek to conjoin these forces within. The Earth is the grounding force and the marriage of the inner Queen and King represents the alchemist's necessity to balance the masculine and feminine self to become the hermaphrodite within. This is likened to a quote found in the Gospel of Thomas 22. Jesus saw some babies nursing. He said to his disciples, "These nursing babies are like those who enter the kingdom." They said to him, "Then shall we enter the kingdom as babies?" Jesus said to them, "When you make the two into one, and when you make the inner like the outer and the outer like the inner, and the upper like the lower, and when you make male and female into a single one, so that the male will not be male nor the female be female, when you make eyes in place of an eye, a hand in place of a hand, a foot in place of a foot, an image in place of an image, then you will enter [the kingdom]."

*The wind carries it in its stomach. The Earth is its nurse and its receptacle.* It is likely that this verse has been partially misunderstood. Due to a more modern understanding of chemistry and physics, this verse can now be better interpreted than it could in the past two millennia. Firstly, we have learned of the volatile nature of the ORMUS and its ability to become a gas.  The peoples of Nibiru came here to mine gold so that it could be made into a gas that could be released into their atmosphere in order to protect their world from the harsh consequences of their highly elliptical orbit.  Here on Earth, the ORMUS is most definitely carried in the wind and, as it is lighter than air, it seeks the highest level in the atmosphere where it helps to comprise the ozone layer.  We have also learned that when ORMUS is manifested within the Earth from the heat and pressure exerted on transition elements, it is often held within the matrix of the earth as microclusters or found mingling within ores.  It is spewed into the air by volcanic activity and carried about by winds and dispersed as fine powder everywhere.  In material alchemy the substance which contains the ORMUS must be located and separation must commence in order to capture the stone.  While the stone rests in the earth, the earth nurtures, protects and strengthens the mercury of the stone as it nurse.

*It is the Father of all perfection throughout the world.* The ORMUS is considered to be the embodiment of perfection and the solid nature of the one thing.  The Philosopher's Stone has always represented the perfection and purification of the mind and spirit.  The material process here is to perfect, and purify the first matter (*prima materia*) to give rise to the next level.  In material work, this is often commenced by dissolution or dissolving so that the mercury spirit can better be concentrated.

*Its force, or power, remains entire if it is converted into Earth.* When the first matter matrix is dissolved, its mercury/spirit remains intact without corruption.  At this point, the ORMUS remains mixed with all sorts of material.  The alchemical term **putrefaction** refers to the next step which is a reduction of the dissolved menstruum (especially that made from metals) into a muddy, dark, clay-like material described as earth in alchemy.  At this point, the mercury is ready to be released or separated because the matrix has now been broken down.  Here, the forces of the ORMUS begin to be noticeable to the learned observer.  On a mental level, the inner alchemist has released the essence of the stone from its original rigid matrix and is now ready to remove all of the non-essential, mundane and negative mental

241

forces. When this stage comes about in nature, the ORMUS newly created from one or more of the transition elements can actually mix with other elements of the earth and eventually take its place within the earth matrices. These substances may form microclusters. As said before, these matrices must be located and broken down as stated above in order to release the ORMUS. Interestingly, the preparation for separation is the same performed by nature to instill the ORMUS in the rock matrices of the earth. In all cases, the powers of the ORMUS remain intact.

***You separate the Earth from the fire, the subtle from the gross, gently with great industry.*** This is the separation stage where the ORMUS is removed from all other material or earth. This operation is performed with constant and long enduring heat. Other operations can be added to help speed up the process such as pH shifting. During the long boiling process, the ORMUS is liberated. If the work is performed utilizing actual metal such as gold as the first matter, this process becomes firstly a corruption of the gold creating a black ash and then a red powder as it is slowly perfected. The earth is separated from the fire as all things have inherent fire and the potential for fire must be retained after separation. Here the fire represents the potential, active nature and ability for transformation which has been kindled during the last stage of calcination. The subtle nature of the ORMUS at this stage is removed from the grosser dense material. This also includes filtration. The steps represented in this passage must, as the passage says, be done with care and great industry. These are the most important steps which will determine success or failure. Also during these operations it is most important that the sun and moon take their rightful places. The mental operations here suggest the removal of old baggage and the separation of the subtle qualities of mind from the gross and dense day to day negative build up which has made up the mental matrix. This subtle nature within the mind is also the mind's fire which retains the archetypal ability for transformation.

***It ascends from the Earth and descends from heaven, and receives the force of things superior and things inferior***. After the ORMUS has been successfully separated from the gross, it appears alive. This is the most exciting step: when the pH adjustments are made and the ORMUS begins to show up, for all the world appearing like fluffy white clouds in a pure blue sky. The ORMUS then poured into a beaker or jar begins to rise as it attaches to very tiny bubbles that cause it to ascend. The bubbles are so small they can only be seen in the right light and at just the right angle. These bubbles are ORMUS which ascends to heaven and resides in the belly of the wind. Some of the tiny bubbles get trapped in the glass as they pass through and cause the glass to eventually appear wavy. The fluffy white groupings of ORMUS rise and fall, apparently full of life. The action of the liquor must be allowed to continue until it becomes still, at which point it will stratify, forming layers of clouds separated by clear water. This to me is most beautiful. This stage is considered to be fermentation as it must be allowed to sit undisturbed and the rolling of the liquid appears very much like the yeast fermentation of mash when making alcohol. If anyone has ever seen mash or still bear as it is often called, as it is working by fermentation, it can at times appear to be alive, which in fact it is, and rolls in the container as a whitish milky bubbly substance.

The rising and falling represents the gathering and conjoining of the forces of the above and the below, or earth and heaven. This is also symbolized by the father and mother, or masculine and feminine. The earth represents creation and the heaven represents the idea and intent for creation. Mentally, this is what we must do to be complete. For if a person is spirit alone, they cannot stay anchored and thus tend to slip away. If one has not the power of spirit, they are dense and gross and are unable to ascend. We therefore need the powers of the above and below in order to experience wholeness. Likewise, we need the masculine and feminine forces to conjoin within the whole and, by this way of the three part philosophy of the world, we are made whole.

Picture showing a wash jar full of ORMUS of gold just after pH adjustment and suspension in clear water. Note how it has begun to seek layering.

*You will have by this way, the glory of the world and all obscurity will flee from you.* By these methods, or this way, we have created a very wondrous thing which is the glory of the world. It is at this point that the washing or cleaning begins. Once the ORMUS has been allowed to *fall bright*, it is washed or cleansed. The result is a thick, milky, white liquid which is the glory of the world. During this stage of distillation, the ORMUS coagulates into a thick, completely white and clean milky substance. There is nothing left to obscure its magnificent light. When the mental process reaches the cleansing stage, everything becomes clear and darkness is no more. This also is the glory of the world, for from this state of clear mind are all good things born.

*It is the power strong with all power, for it will master every subtle thing and penetrate every solid thing.* The ORMUS is the power strong with the light and consciousness of the all. It is the great antenna, the conduit for the flow of light to all that lives. The ORMUS can penetrate any substance when in its

244

gaseous form and masters all that is imperceptible. The ORMUS takes over and penetrates all material existence and is in this way omnipresent yet remains imperceptible. The mental work of the inner alchemist follows the same path. Once the consciousness has been perfected, it can penetrate all physicality and all astral space. The mind is then subtly omnipresent doing its work in mystery, mastering all subtle reality. The mind as the Philosopher's Stone becomes the power that is strong with all power or, should we say, the all mind. Hermes also tells us in the Hermeticum that, if we were to receive but one ray of the light of Adon, which is to say if we were to gain just the slightest understanding of the all consciousness, we would be free from the laws of nature. With such enlightenment and subsequent ability and insight, we can master every little thing we wish, or project our consciousness into anything.

*In this way the world was created.* This passage is what it is. This is no doubt the way the world was created. The process described thus far created the world on a material level, and the world on a mental level. And, the All Consciousness self-manifested as the one thing in this same fashion. Here again the three part philosophy becomes apparent.

*From it are born wonderful adaptations, of which the way here is given.* Hermes states here that he has granted a means to create wonderful changes and transformations, just as the Philosopher's Stone is able to transmute base metals into noble metals. So too can the mundane person be transformed into nobility. This method grants us a way to adapt to whatever we wish in the world. Without pain and heartache, we simply change to meet the challenges of the environment if and when we wish.

*That is why I have been called Hermes Trismegistus, having the three parts of the universal philosophy.* And here Hermes states that within this work are the principles of the three part universal philosophy that we discussed earlier. He tells us here that this is why he is called *Hermes Trismegistus* because he has the three parts to the universal philosophy, not because he has incarnated three times. And from this we can see Hermes

Trismegistus is not a name, but rather a title denoting Hermes as one who possesses the understanding of the trinary or triune universe.

**An Emerald Tablet diagram**

**Some of the stages of gold as it is transformed to ORMUS**

**ORMUS of gold**

***This, that I have called the solar Work, is complete.*** The solar
work is that which has been called the ***Operations of the Sun*** by
the early alchemists. The sun, as we have said, represents the
end of the work and the achievement of the stone. Of course the
achievement of the stone in mental work means the purification,
transformation and perfection of the mind, body and spirit.
Though in alchemy as well as in inner alchemy or psychology
there are many variations to the formula and as many different
techniques and steps that can be employed, the basic philosophy
is stated here in the words of Thoth, Hermes Trismegistus.
Perhaps also the notion of the sun as the end of the operation is
the achievement of communion with God, the Aton or Adon, the
great Lord of the Cosmos which was venerated by the solar disk.
Since man was first taught about the great Lord of the Cosmos
by Hermes/Thoth himself, and since the Emerald Tablet formula
is a method to achieve both spiritual and physical excellence,
why then would he have left out the very notion of the cosmic
Lord of which he so often taught. To me it is obvious that the
solar work is synonymous with the solar disk of Aton Lord of the
Cosmos, the one God of the Egyptian Israelites. It was as if

Thoth himself was the chief angel of the Aton/Adon teaching all peoples about the one high God and how one might achieve access to its light. Access to the Adon is rooted in the triune philosophy on all levels as taught by Thoth. There is the calculating brain (Conjo), the emotions (Antu), and the deep mind of the heart space (Aunju), all together working in the human mind. When all is balanced, one can through Aunju achieve pure communion with Adon. The Adon itself above is composed of the same three part blueprint as humans below. The triune philosophy runs deep into the matrices of nature. We see that Adon is masculine, feminine and hermaphrodite. Humans seek the same qualities in order to be whole. The cosmos is an inseparable collage of matter, energy, and consciousness as is all within it including ourselves. Interestingly, each depends on the other for existence just as an art collage is composed of a foundation, pictures and glue; if any component is removed the collage cannot exist. As we have discussed, the triune philosophy of the universe resides deep within the universal blueprint. When we learn to see this philosophy in all things, then we more closely understand the thoughts of Adon. When we seek this truth in nature, we seek the all truth and cease to be polar, binary thinkers of offs and ons. When we see the trinary truth in nature we begin to see that all things are possible through consciousness, that life never ends and that nothing is truly dead, that there are no opposites, just compliments, and that Adon stands at one corner of the triplex across from us pleased that we do our part in the trinity.

**Recapping the Formula**

The basic alchemical operational methodology discussed in the tablet in alchemical terminology would be as follows. Calcination, Dissolution, Separation, Conjunction, Fermentation, Distillation, Coagulation and Purification. It is obvious that there are many other steps within the basic operations of the tablet and that those steps can differ depending on the individual preference and technique. Yet the basic alchemical seven step operational method, followed by purification, should remain intact in order to achieve success. And so here we have a basic overview of the Emerald Tablet story. Surely tons have been written about it and even more writings have been inspired by it. The tablet has been the inspiration for many spiritual systems and has found its place within many established ideologies and spiritual, religious, scientific and even therapeutic modalities. This one succinct and noble tractate has delivered more to the world over the longest time than any other writing. May it someday return to us intact, that we might once again read its passages and translate its meaning for our own time. The 3500 year old Papyrus Ani offers to us a blessing by which we might take solace, "May Thoth write to you each day".

**A scene from Papyrus Ani**
**(Image in the public domain)**

# CHAPTER 13

## Inner Alchemy and Ascension

It is often said concerning the stone of the philosopher's that it can be the strongest medicine or the most potent poison. There is in fact nothing in these substances that is poison if they are made properly without impurities. So, to what could this often used statement be referring? The platinum ORMUS has a wonderful way of causing the body to quickly and severely reject everything that is a disease state or poison within the body which can often bring on a harsh healing crisis or high level immune response to cancers or precancerous moles or warts. This can scare some people into believing that the ORMUS is making them sick and they usually discontinue its use. However, if they had been properly prepared by the use of other ORMUS elements in the proper ratios over time, the platinum reaction would have been more gentle. One thing Inner Alchemy teaches us is how the ORMUS elements are to be used in order to gain maximum and safe effects. But these reactions are not what were referred to when the statement was made concerning the ORMUS as a potent poison. Earlier in this book, a certain book titled *The Red Lion* was discussed. This book describes what can happen to someone who is either not ready to receive the ORMUS or who achieves it with ill intention. Certain ORMUS elements, such as gold, tend to open the inner eye of subtle insight. This gives one a very sharp image of one's self. Many people cannot face their imperfections or emotional and spiritual flaws. But once the gold is consumed for a time, we have no choice but to face ourselves. We also become more sensitive to those things that we are prone to be effected by. The amygdalae (Latin: corpus amygdaloideum) are an almond shaped set of neurons located deep in the brain's medial frontal lobe, one in each hemisphere, shown to play a key role in the processing of emotions. The amygdalae form part of the limbic system. In humans and

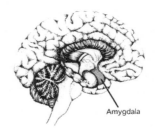
Amygdala

other animals, this sub-cortical brain structure is linked to both fear responses and pleasure. Conditions such as anxiety, autism, depression, post-traumatic stress disorder and phobias are suspected of being linked to abnormal functioning of the amygdalae due to damage, developmental problems or neurotransmitter imbalance. The gold ORMUS recipient must learn how to make sure that the amygdalae of the brain, which are stimulated along with the pineal gland, are anteriorly stimulated rather than posteriorly stimulated. The anterior stimulated amygdalae, as we have discussed earlier in this book, will prompt frontal lobe development and subsequent expansion of paradigms. Yet the posterior stimulation of the amygdalae will bring about anger and aggression.

In the 1960's and 1970's a man named T. D. Lingo established and ran a research clinic called the dormant brain lab where he taught techniques designed to awaken dormant areas of the frontal lobes of the brain. These techniques primarily focused on teaching the participants daily stimulation of the anterior amygdalae. The techniques used were simple visualizations, such as imagining flicking the amygdalae forward as if they were a pair of light switches. Another method included visualizing their almond shapes as a pair of almonds being tickled at the pointed front (anterior) end by a feather.

This technique can be perfected to switch between the right and left hemispheres of the frontal lobe. This can increase right or left brain activity as desired. I find the tickle technique to be quite effective and a most wonderful daily technique to add to one's inner alchemy regime. Lingo found that such techniques created a great sense of expansion that substantially increased frontal lobe activity in the form of joyous creativity. Consider using gold ORMUS once these techniques have been practiced for a time with success. The gold ORMUS will then enhance the process many fold. For more information on awakening the dormant brain, perform an internet search for T. D. Lingo and the dormant brain project.

In ancient times, there must have also been a system devised to help the ORMUS recipient deal with the changes that would occur during consumption of these substances and methods teaching the recipients how to use these substances and how to channel their transformations in a positive and healthy direction. In fact there was a system. These methods were taught in the great Mystery Schools of old. The methods were revealed to people like Moses and Aaron. Of these traditions, the most well known today is *Cabbalah*, spelled many different ways. And although *Cabbalah* as it is taught today is little more than a shadow of what it once was, it remains an important tool of Inner Alchemy. Inner Alchemy is a dynamic system which includes various traditions, techniques, modalities and sciences ranging from early forms of psychotherapy to cabalistic meditation techniques. It includes physics and metaphysics as well as hypnosis and mind expansion techniques. Inner Alchemy is essential to the evolution of the consciousness toward a higher state of being whether or not one has consumed the manna. In the Dead Sea scrolls discovered in Qumran there were teachings attributed to the Biblical Moses. The Essenes, who were the inhabitants of Qumran, followed these teachings faithfully. The disciplines they followed were imbued with a schedule of contemplations, communions, meditations, confessions, blessings and thanksgivings for each day of the week and various times of each day. The Qumran Essenes followed works such as "The Manual of Discipline", "Thanks Giving Psalms" and "The Book of Hymns" among many others which describe the Lord God as the "Law". This reference to the "Law" is in accordance with our current understanding of natural law. In my opinion, Moses must have been a wonderful observer of natural law and an adept student of the earth sciences in his time. The teachings describe how the natural laws affect all things as well as us humans and that all natural laws fall within the One Law. Most certainly if one were to evolve one's awareness to a higher state of being, one must understand and even sense these laws and thus the One Law on a deeper level. Thoth also teaches us these concepts concerning Adon, Aton, Aten, Atun or Atumn. We learn in hermetic tradition that the Lord of the cosmos is natural law. We as humans are subject to these laws and the workings of the cosmos. These laws cannot be usurped. However, if we receive but a single ray of the light of Adon, we may exceed the law. According to Thoth there is a way of bringing the law within in order to exceed it. And, should we exceed the laws of the Cosmos, we are released from the cycles of the cosmos. We may be released from the confines and restraints of the cycles of time, birth and rebirth. We may even choose to physically ascend, thus overcoming the force of gravity and the need for sustenance. We may even choose to walk in higher worlds or dimensions taking sojourns to Earth as we desire. The purely hermetic knowledge passed on by Moses makes it quite clear that he was a student of Thoth.

## Alchemical Teachings in Religion

The Teachings of Thoth were passed to the Israelites just as they were to Melchizedek and his people. Miriam the prophetess played a major role in Israelite culture and educated the people concerning the hermetic arts and the understanding of Adon well before the exodus. Master Thoth teaches us in his Emerald Tablet an all important message of inner alchemy. This lesson resides within the very first passage; "That which is above is as that which is below". This preaches volumes. It tells us firstly that heaven and Earth are but mirrors of one another. It tells us that the alchemical formula for the creation of the "One Thing" is but a mirror image of what the inner-self must experience during the alchemical evolution of the consciousness, body and spirit. It also tells us that the kingdom of Earth is a mirror image of that which is in heaven. This passage explains to us that there are always compliments, locked in a constant embrace ever mingling with one another. This is likened to the ever popular Asian concept of yin and yang. *Yeshua* (Jesus), most often in texts outside of the Bible, speaks in very ardent alchemical terms. He refers to himself as the Bride and the Groom, the Son and the Daughter, the Mother and the Father, and so on. The Adon (Adoni = my Lord in Aramaic and Adonai in Hebrew) in hermetic teaching is a hermaphrodite encompassing all masculine and feminine energies. Yeshua again reveals this outside of the Bible by referring to the Lord at one instance as Mother and at another as Father while still at other times as Parent or All Parent. Many texts containing the teachings of Yeshua profess the Holy Spirit to be the feminine aspect of the Law/Adon while the masculine aspect is referred to as the

Father. There remains only a smattering of hermetic teaching within the Bible itself as these passages were edited out by the male dominated Catholic Church during the authorization of the texts which would eventually make up the Biblical cannon. The early male dominated church just could not allow itself to accept femininity as equally important much less agree that any male should nurture the inner feminine. Yeshua often speaks in highly hermetic and alchemical terms by making statements such as "That which is above is as that which is below; I am seated at the right hand of the father and the right is to the left as the left is to the right and that which is before is as that which is after and the inner is to the outer as the outer is to the inner, the masculine is to the feminine as the feminine is to the masculine" and so on. These types of statements leave little room for doubt that Yeshua was himself a student of alchemy. If we delve further into the Nazarean Essene culture we find that the kings were well prepared by the mystery school located at the Essene Kingdom of Heaven monastery. Since Yeshua was to be the David (the king from the Davidic line), he was so prepared by the Essene community as a Malchuth (Enlightened King or foundation) and through the inner alchemy and Cabalistic traditions he would have become Tzedeque (a teacher of righteousness). After becoming King (Melech) he was ordained to continue forever as a priest after the Order of Melchizedek (Melechi Tzedique) bound to such practice and bid sacrifice with bread (Shemmannah) and wine after the way of Melchizedek. He would have been trained in the physical alchemy as well, as were the ancient kings and artificers.

**Typical artistic portrayal of Yeshua and stone with Aramaic renering of "Yeshua".**

So, Yeshua would have been not only familiar with the Hermetic arts, he himself would have been a full alchemist. The bread offered at the last supper would have been the real deal. The actual manna or shem-manna as it was called in the days of Melchizedek. The massive amounts of manna consumed as a twelfth of a manna cake would have been sufficient to bring the apostles to a higher state of being. Subsequent consumption on a regular basis would have brought the apostles to a level equal to that of Jesus. The apostles had been sufficiently taught by

Yeshua concerning inner alchemy so that when they consumed the bread it would not disturb them, but rather, they were able to begin working miracles of their own. The Essenes, Nazarenes and the Theraputae were all students of Alchemy and Cabbalah which seems to have been in part based on our modern notions of quantum mechanics and metaphysics. This at first sounds crazy, how could they have known of such things at that time? But as we study the teachings of the Magi and the Essenes among others we begin to see that they were, on at least some level, aware of such things. They knew that reality is influenced by thought, action and emotion. They knew that a person must become aware of this fact and then learn how to positively influence the world so that our co-creations would be valuable instead of **Beliel** (worthlessness).

Here it is prudent to mention that the word **Beliel** which is found in the Bible is most often assumed to be a name for Satan. However, what it means is worthlessness. When we make worthless actions, have worthless thoughts and experience worthless negative emotion, we create worthlessness in our lives. Since all that we do and think causes effects on the entire cosmos, we are always creating reality through the influence of events on the quantum level which manifests in the tangible reality in which we exist. When one consumes the ORMUS compounds, this power that we all possess is amplified.

If we then go back to our original question concerning why the Stone of the Philosopher's could be considered a potent poison, we can easily see that if we base our lives in worthless action and worthless thought and negative emotion, we will then create for ourselves more of the same. Moreover, when we have made ample consumption of the ORMUS, this effect is amplified so greatly that our lives could become a quagmire. Additionally, if we are prone to having the amygdalae of the brain posteriorly activated, then this effect will also be strengthened resulting in greater negativity. However, if through such systems as Cabbalistic traditions which are more modern forms of the original Nazarene Cabbalah (called **Kabalta**) and inner alchemy among others, we are able to base our actions, emotions and thoughts in a more positive manner. Then the Gold ORMUS will bring us pleasure, enlightenment, increased cognition, health and spiritual awakening.

## Ancient Psychology and the Seat of the Soul

The techniques taught in ancient Inner Alchemy and Cabbalah act to anteriorly stimulate the amygdala and open the third eye which is the subtle eye of insight that is the pineal gland of the brain. The ancients were all too aware of this gland and its function and often referred to it most appropriately as the *Seat of the Soul.* The pineal has also often been associated with the eye, thus has been referred to as The Third Eye, the Ayin (All Seeing Eye), the Mind's Eye, and so forth. This is actually appropriate. The pineal structure is indeed a light sensing organ just as are the eyes, and is basically a visual organ like the eye. It has been supposed that the *fontanel* (soft spot) that we are all born with on the top of our heads, which is actually a temporary opening in the top of the skull, at one time in our human history never completely closed. This would mean that we could possibly have gone throughout our lives with this pulsating soft void in our crowns. It has been assumed that this might have allowed greater functioning of the Pineal Eye. In our time, the opening in the skull closes usually by the time we are toddlers. Due to the thick bone that covers the pineal eye of the modern human, the pineal has atrophied and withered. We now must rely on other methods to strengthen and revitalize the pineal gland. However, when children are under one year of age, especially when they are under six months of age, they see clearly with the pineal eye. When my son was a newborn he used to very obviously watch and react to things that were invisible to me and my wife. Sometimes he would laugh at and engage these visitors. Sometimes it was as if my wife and I were not even there as he interacted with his guests. Even when we were holding him this would occur. The most common time this would occur was during bath time when he would often have his attention captured by something above him. He would laugh and follow the visitor with his eyes and at times even reach for them. Sometimes when he would be sleeping in my arms, he would suddenly fling open his eyes, turn his head and look with his eyes for whatever he had sensed with his eye of insight. Unfortunately this sort of powerful pineal sensing often begins to wane by the end of the first year of life due to the closing of the fontanel. However there are those who remember and strive to keep the inner eye engaged and operable. These are our seers, those of powerful insight.

Traditions like Inner Alchemy and Cabbalah are also well-rooted in psychology. If one were to study either of these systems, one would see that modern psychology techniques such as cognitive therapy, briefest resolution therapy and psychotherapy techniques were actually practiced long ago. In fact, modern psychology and hypnotherapy draw heavily on other so called primitive and even shamanic techniques and traditions.

Many modern psychology and hypnotherapy techniques are drawn from a spiritual system of the Hawaiian peoples called **Huna** (hidden or esoteric). There is a tradition within Huna known as **Ho-o-ponopono** (to make right) which is a daily focus on forgiveness and emotional clearing. Ho-o-ponopono teaches us to let go of hurts and emotional baggage so that we can live in the present. This is most important for the evolution of the human spirit and these techniques are heavily drawn on in modern psychology. Huna is saturated with wonderful spiritual and emotional healing and strengthening techniques that mirror those of Cabbalah and Inner Alchemy. It is probably not often recognized how many of the modern psychology techniques draw from these wonderful time-honored traditions. Interestingly, the tradition of Huna was originally called **Ho' omana** which means "to make mana". The word mana to the Hawaiians means life force. Notice the similarity to the word **manna** (ORMUS of gold) which is believed to contain light and can strengthen the life force. When the word was spoken in full as **Ho'omana** it meant empowered, as one who has a strong life force is empowered. The Kahuna Kapihe in Kona in 1850 may have succinctly captured the essence of the science of Huna in the saying, "E iho ana o luna. E pii ana o lalo. E hui ana na moku. E ku ana ka paia." This translates to: "Bring down that which is above by means of the light. To ascend, take from darkness into light that which is below by means of light. This will transform the spiritual energy as it flows from the source and integrates all the islands (inside you), giving peace. This will affect you profoundly, and change your life bringing illumination, and you will feel the delightful supreme fire."

Notice the similarity to the Emerald Tablet that we discussed earlier and its hermetic axiom, "That which is above is like that which is below, and that which is below is like that which is above". People who practice Huna are called *Kahuna* (hidden light) and believe that all life force emanates from the one great source of all life known as I'o. It is believed by the Kahuna that this understanding was in ancient times taught all around the world. Due to the similarities I see between Huna and other systems practiced about the world, I am inclined to agree. It was the isolation of Hawaii which helped to preserve Huna when its counterparts around the world were being destroyed. In modern times only a few isolated, rediscovered or well-protected spiritual systems like Huna remain. It is my opinion that Huna would make a very wonderful and complete system to utilize as inner alchemy for one to make the appropriate transformations necessary to commence the use of the ORMUS or just for the simple healing and strengthening of the mind, body and spirit.

### Physics, Metaphysics and the Brain

Certain ORMUS compounds such as the *Red Lion* can really give the pineal gland a kick. When the pineal gland is so stimulated without proper preparation, it might be a very disturbing experience. The pineal gland creates and stores tiny crystals about its base known as *brain sand*. These crystals, which are comprised of a chemical known as DMT (Di-methyl-tryptamine), are an alkaloid substance which can, like other alkaloids, cause hallucinations in large doses as discussed earlier in this book. However, the natural DMT of the brain causes hallucinations or spiritual experiences that can often be verified as prophetic or even remote viewing. Additionally, these experiences have been shown to have great therapeutic value. For this reason it is obvious that these hallucinations are not mere fantasies or dreams. This chemical helps to create the conditions of awareness that allow us to experience higher dimensions. However, this dizzying experience can cause great disorientation for someone who is unprepared. Also, the psychic visions and experiences may be overwhelming to the unprepared user of the Red Lion in its full strength.

Inner alchemy differs in its approach to the transformation of consciousness in only one basic way than do most other methods; that is the use of the ORMUS substances in the proper successive order, proportion and amounts is one of the basic preparations for healthy and successful transformation. When done properly, there will be no big surprises to the consumption of the ORMUS elements and other associated compounds. The proper use of the elements also depends on the goals of the recipient. Someone who wishes to heal a dysfunctional immune system will need to work their way toward the regular consumption of platinum and iridium. Those who wish to heighten their psychic powers may work toward the use of various substances made of gold such as manna or Red Lion. However, this must be preceded by the proper usage of the fortifying rhodium, iridium and copper which in itself creates a condition of great knowingness. It has been my observation that many who take the gold eventually become afraid of the changes they are making and thus halt their supplementation. They often state that they were afraid that they were going into another dimension. Still others take but one dose and find themselves careening out of emotional control. This is a result of simply being unprepared. It never ceases to amaze me how different people can react to the gold ORMUS. I have other associates who have taken the gold and found it from the very first to be the most soothing, pleasurable and joyful experience. It all depends on one's base frame of mind. For those who normally have their amygdala anteriorly stimulated and who have a fairly functioning pineal gland, the experience can be quite joyous, mind expanding, and spiritual. For those who have a closed pineal eye and who are basically negative or aggressive, they may find the taking of gold in any form to be a bad experience, possibly even insufferable. And here we begin to gain a greater understanding of what it means to say that the ORMUS can be the greatest medicine or the most potent poison.

The Renaissance alchemist George Beatus describes the power of the stone and also grants a warning to those who are unprepared to receive it: *"I am a poisonous dragon, present everywhere and to be had for nothing. My water and fire dissolve and compound. Out of my body you shall draw the Green and Red Lion, but if you do not exactly know me, you will destroy your five senses with my fire. I give you faculties both male and female and the powers of both heaven and earth. I am the Egg of Nature. I am dark and bright; I spring from the earth and come out of heaven. I am the Carbuncle of the Sun. I am a most noble, clarified earth by which you may turn copper, iron, tin, and lead into most pure gold."*

Here Beatus tells us that the inherent water (the cleansing and purification ability) and fire (the active ability to transform) of the stone can dissolve and compound one's nature. He tells us that the stone's ability to actively transform can overwhelm one's senses if they are unprepared to receive. Modern quantum mechanics and metaphysics can lend a great deal to inner alchemy for it teaches us in scientific, concrete terms that we are co-creators of the reality in which we exist. A basic understanding of these theories can greatly enlighten and grant one a sense of magic. When we learn how we constantly affect our reality, we can learn how to affect it to our benefit. The most intimate aspect of our reality, and thus the most easily effected physical facet of our reality, is the condition of our bodies. Usually there is little more than our own input of thought toward our bodies and therefore we need not wrestle with the constant thoughts of others concerning our own physical condition. Other creations outside of ourselves such as the events of the day are affected by a soup of thoughts of other co-creators. Quantum mechanics shows us that everything in reality is not just connected but is in actuality an inseparable component of everything else. From this we can really understand the substance of the adage about a butterfly flapping its wings in the Amazon and how it spawns a storm in China. The great Magi of old knew this as did the **Wiccan** priestesses as well as the **Druid Bards.** The concepts of quantum physics are even found within Buddhism and within the early Nazarean teachings.

Any modern class on inner alchemy should hold central our modern knowledge and theories of physics and metaphysics. Why *metaphysics* (beyond physics) one might ask? Just remember that the metaphysics of yesterday is the physics of today. The Magi somehow knew the basic concepts of our most modern theories of physics on the basis of reality. These were the wise men of old who used the forces of nature and thought to transform their world and evolve toward a more positive and noble inner condition. This is the true meaning of magic. When the three Magi who traveled far to grant the gifts of Gold Frankincense and Myrrh, to the newborn Yeshua, they were in actuality proclaiming their support and acknowledgment of Yeshua as a *King Priest* or a *Melchi-zedek.* These three substances were the symbols of kingship, priesthood and righteous knowledge or wisdom. The very act of the Magi gifting Yeshua with these substances could have been considered a work of magic where upon the infant boy they bestowed their highest consecration helping to move the Universe in the sealing of Yeshua's reign for the benefit of good and peace. How did these men even know about Yeshua, being from so far away and of very different traditions than those of the land of Yeshua. Tradition says that they followed a star, but still they knew what they would find. The star they followed was likely the planet Venus, also known as Lucifer or the Morning Star, with which Jesus (Yeshua) has long been associated. And, if this was so, then the star had appeared before on a regular basis, although on certain circuits it appears brighter and closer. But this one time they followed Venus and found Yeshua. How did they know for sure when and how this birth would occur? This was the way of the Magi.

**Miracles or Magic: What is the Difference?**

The Magi were simply tapped into the all consciousness of the universal Lord and so they knew Yeshua and knew how to find their kindred. The magic of the Magi was the result of their dedicated Inner Alchemy practices and their usage of the ORMUS elements. The Magi were but one of many groups who held such practices central, but in modern times these practices have dwindled to the point that they are few and scattered.

However, with the resurgence of interest in such practices as Cabbalah, Huna, Gnosticism, and Celtic wisdom among others, perhaps we will regain some of our tools of enlightenment. So, I say learn to listen to the trees, the land and wind, hear the voice of the voice as you listen with the ear of your ear. Learn to see the matrix of which you are a part and feel the web of life that sustains you. Discover your own divinity as you co-create the world and enjoy your creation. Learn to cherish and appreciate the gifts you are granted by the all and know that you yourself are a gift. Feel the oneness of all things as we are all components of the All. And above all, remain steadfast in love for this is the force which births all goodness and light. Remember the three part philosophy of the universe which has been shown to us by Tjehuti (Thoth/Hermes) which insures the wholeness of all. In these practices you shall be one with the Lord, the light of the cosmos. In the Hermetica, Thoth tells us "If thou receiveth but one ray of the light of Adon, released thou wouldest be from the cycles and laws of the Cosmos". This declares that if we can experience but one pure thought from the mind of God, we ourselves would be released from the natural laws of God and would be as ascended masters who could choose our own fate, destiny, and nature. To some this might seem an impossibility, but long ago it was accomplish by a few who are still with us. May they speak with you often and teach you to hear the voice of Adoni.

## Final Thoughts

Many volumes can be written on the ORMUS elements without relating all of the known science, research, history and lore surrounding the subject. The story goes back beyond recorded history and so there is a great deal of information that has amassed over the millennia. It is also likely that much more historical documentation has been lost than retained concerning the ORMUS materials and their usage. The ORMUS may be one of the greatest discoveries of our times even if, in actuality, it is a rediscovery. The ORMUS elements may change the face of much that we thought we knew about many sciences including biology, chemistry, archeology and physics. We must begin to look at ancient stories and writings with new eyes, as they may possibly contain valuable knowledge of ORMUS and other forgotten truths, both scientific and historical in nature. If such an amazing thing as the ORMUS has been proven to be true, what other truths might be gleaned from the stories handed down through time? The industrial, scientific and healthcare applications for the ORMUS products are vast and growing as we learn more about this amazing state of matter. It is likely that, if we as a species follow course, our growing knowledge of ORMUS elements and their usage will change the face of humanity. Therefore, if we humans evolve to a higher state of awareness as the ORMUS demands, we will have little choice but to change the world for the better as we ascend to a greater state of grace.

As above, so below.

I bid you speed in light, love and peace!

**The vision of the seven candlesticks from the book of Revelation**
**(Image is in the public domain)**

# EPILOGUE

## Codes and Privileged Language

During the course of this book, I have often touched on the alchemical knowledge hidden in ancient texts, especially texts of religious foundation. It is true that the Bible contains a great deal of alchemical knowledge and reference, but there are two books within the Bible where perhaps this holds most true. These two books contain vastly coded sophists wording. There is thus vast untold knowledge hidden within these lines which is just waiting to be gleaned by those who are privileged to the wording and codes. Much of the information is hidden in plain sight so to speak as the esoteric references are open and blatant. Yet, there are few who would understand, thus many attribute such references to something which befits their religious dogma or doctrines rather than to search out the true meanings.

The first of these two books is *The Song of Solomon*. This book is perhaps the most unmolested of the biblical writings. By this I mean that its content has been the least tampered with, perhaps due to the fact that it is the least referred to at the pulpit. When one reads this book, one might wonder why this book was ever added to the Bible cannon at all. It appears at first read to be a love poem; in parts it seems nearly pornographic. The style and content of this book appears to be far removed from anything seen in the rest of the body of the Old Testament. There rarely even seems to be any religiosity within the book. So then why was it selected for the biblical cannon over countless other texts which might be more befitting in a religious context? I believe at least one reason lies hidden within the text. For those who understand, this text explains firstly the Messianic rituals of marriage within kingship from the line of David. Secondly, it encodes, as we have discussed in this book, the secrete starfire ritual which is the root of the Eucharist, and the inner and outer alchemy of the queen and king as they ascend to the high mental plain of the *Rose of Sharon*. Yet there is also another story told here perhaps even more obscured. Firstly, the original title of the book was *The Song of Songs*. It was always attributed to the love between the Messianic queen and king of the moment. In this particular instance in time, the story would be concerning Yeshua and Magdalene and the rites, rituals and transformation they endured as the Messianic couple of the day. It seems that the Roman Church wanted to firstly keep this entire knowledge close, and secondly, the coded information was likely important to the inner, more privileged circles of the church hierarchy just as it was to the early Nazareans. Perhaps the truth of the text was not fully understood by the early Catholic Church, however there must have been enough insight into its true meaning to have driven its selection for the bible cannon for there certainly seems to be little other religious reason for its selection.

You have now learned enough within this book to be able to glean much of this secret knowledge as you read such texts, thus you enter the ranks of the privileged. With this in mind, I will seek now to take a look at a few lines of the second of these two texts, *The Book of Revelations*. However, before beginning, take a minute to go back to the Preface of this book and read these texts to see how much of the secret information becomes clear to you now that you are more privy to the code words and alchemical language, then return here to see how close you were in your interpretations.

## The Book of Revelation

The Book of Revelation is literally filled with all sorts of code and hidden knowledge. One subject that has been a sore thumb to the church for some time concerns the possible marriage of Jesus to Mary Magdalene. However, those who know about the tarot will read portions of the text and easily see that the Book of Revelation blatantly uses the tarot code to tell the story of Jesus and Mary. But one must first be open to the idea that the tarot is used in this way and next one must be privy to the knowledge to understand the code. Since many Christians consider such things as the tarot to be evil or witchcraft, the consideration that the tarot is used as a code within the Bible might be offensive. Here is an excerpt to consider which illustrates my point. However it must be understood that this is only a brief explanation concerning the bloodline story, as the story is expansive and would be a subject for another book.

*And there appeared a great wonder in heaven; a woman clothed with the sun, and the moon under her feet, and upon her head a crown of twelve stars. And she being with child cried, travailing in birth.... And she brought forth a man child, who was to rule all nations with a rod of iron: and her child was caught up unto God, and to his throne. Book of Revelation (12:1, 2 & 5)*

It becomes clear here if anyone knows the tarot, that this description is that of the Empress card. The Empress card depicts a woman seated with the moon under her feet and a crown of twelve stars. This designates Mary as the Queen while Jesus is the King. The reference to being clothed in the sun is an alchemical one stating that she has completed her alchemical transformation. The text goes on to say that she had a son who would rule the world and that he was godly and took his kingship seriously.

It might also be considered that the High Priestess card also often depicts a moon under her feet. This might say that Mary is also the high priestess of the church of Yeshua which, as one researches the subject, there is substantial information to support this notion.

The text goes on to say that she is pregnant and is chased into the wilderness as she is in childbirth. We can explore many apocrypha to learn that Magdalene was chased into France by Rome and had a baby girl during the trip named Sarah. The Catholic tradition attempts to make this mystery woman out to be the Mother Mary as they continually hide the identity and works of Mary Magdalene by obscuring her with the Mother Mary.

However on a different topic, we also see that the Book of Revelation is also full of alchemical references and code. We may now explore a few of these verses and, as we do, the meaning of the title of this book will become perfectly clear.

*2:17: He that hath an ear, let him hear what the Spirit saith unto the churches; to him that overcometh will I give to eat of the hidden manna, and will give him a white stone, and in the stone a new name written, which no man knoweth saving he that receiveth it.*

When a verse starts out with "**He that hath an ear, let him hear**", this denotes that something important will be stated in code within the upcoming verses. Now that you are privy to the secret language, you too have ears to hear. The verse then states that the information is for the assemblies or churches. In alchemy the essence of something is always carried by the *Mercury* which is the *Spirit*. The phrase "**to him that overcommeth**" might leave one asking; to him who overcomes what? The meaning is: to he who overcomes the dogma and ignorance to truly understand. Now we see that the *hidden manna* will be given to the one who overcomes ignorance and he will be given a *white stone*. In fact as we have seen within this book, the manna is the white powder of gold and can be made into the white stone. The stone is the Philosopher's Stone imbued with all the natures we have discussed. Anyone who pursues the stone learns a great deal about self. In the discovery of the self, one finds new purpose. As we have learned, the manna holds one to delve deeply into self evaluation. We have also learned that the word **Shem,** which is almost always incorrectly translated in the Bible as **name,** actually has a far more complex set of meanings. In this case it would come to mean *fame* or **purpose.** So here we begin to see that the manna causes one to look within to receive a new purpose in life that no one else will know.

***21:21: And the twelve gates were twelve pearls; every several gate was of one pearl: and the street of the city was pure gold, as it were transparent glass.***

In the time period in which revelations was written, the word *pearl* was a metaphor for something precious. Here we see that the twelve gates are very precious. These twelve gates are twelve separate ways of alchemy. The twelve ways are twelve metals which may all be turned into white powders for bodily use, but the methods of confection and uses may vary. Each of these are equally valuable to the body, mind and spirit.

*"And the street of the city was pure gold, as it were transparent glass"* because, as we have learned, pure gold ORMUS can be turned into transparent glass. This is what paves the city street and thus the path upon which we walk within the city. We learn that we may enter the city through all twelve openings or gates. The *city* is a congregation of those who have overcome and succeeded. And the gold glass streets are thus paved as the use of gold ORMUS or manna is the pinnacle of the practice of alchemy which brings about the transformation of mind. This should excite you, for you are now equipped to pass through these gates, all who chose, and enter the city paved in gold for your pinnacle of work.

***22: 1: And he shewed me a pure river of water of life, clear as crystal, proceeding out of the throne of God and of the Lamb. 2: In the midst of the street of it, and on either side of the river, was there the tree of life, which bare twelve manner of fruits, and yielded her fruit every month: and the leaves of the tree***

*were for the healing of the nations.*

The pure river of the *Water of Life* is the liquid form of the ORMUS of gold which is the *Elixir of Life.* As the stone can be as clear as crystal, it issues forth from God and flows freely. The *Tree of Life* grows within the street, or the path bounds either side of the river. The *Tree of Life* in the earliest of times was the family tree who possessed the knowledge of the foods of the gods and, ironically as pointed out by David Hudson, the very word for Tree or Life in the Hebrew language is ORME (the name of his patent) which arose from similar yet much more ancient variations as we have discussed. Over time, the Tree of Life became synonymous with the specific knowledge of these food substances and their proper use. So, the knowledge is within the path and includes use and creation of the Water of Life.

This Tree of Life bears twelve manner of fruit. One might wonder about such a miraculous tree which bears apples, pears, oranges, peaches, etc. In fact, the twelve fruits are the twelve ORMUS elements. It takes roughly a month to make these elements by the lunar cycle and thus the tree bears monthly. The leaves of the tree are those who partake of the knowledge of the tree. They sprout from the tree so to speak and their knowledge passed out freely will heal the nations. It must be understood that not only will the alchemical knowledge help to heal the nations but the wisdom accumulated by those who overcome will benefit all nations.

**22: 14: Blessed are they that do his commandments, that they may have right to the tree of life, and may enter in through the gates into the city.**

This verse seems almost to be self-explanatory. However we need to realize that here the commandments referred to are those of Yeshua/Jesus not those of the Old Testament. And even the commandments of Yeshua found within the Bible have been changed to more closely suit the agendas of the early Catholic Church. So, in order to properly follow these commandments and thus gain the right to pass through the gates and have access to the Tree of Life, one must find the true commandments of Yeshua. Or, are the commandments in this case a formula for success? You be the judge, but do not forget that it also may be both.

***22: 17: And the Spirit and the bride say, Come. And let him that heareth say, Come. And let him that is athirst come. And whosoever will, let him take the water of life freely.***

Here we learn that the mercury/spirit will come forth along with the bride, which here is the moon and the feminine half of the equation, to those who have heard the word. Remember also that Yeshua often refers to himself as the bride of the church which proclaims his feminine powers. And the bride and the spirit which contains the essence say the ***Water of Life*** is offered freely to everyone who thirsts, and for everyone who wishes to take it.

Now that you are privy to the language, take the time to read through these books and others to see what you now can glean. The entirety of the Book of Revelation is chock full of such references and codes concerning alchemy, the bloodline of Yeshua and the tarot. There is little here to do with any prophecy for our time which foretells of the end of the world and a great deal to do with layers of hidden knowledge and dynamic history all wrapped in the trappings of a dream.

Now as you read the texts you may have read countless times before, you will see them in a whole new light and they will reveal to you their secrets that have been lying dormant and hidden for eons only to arise for a few who are privileged and who have overcome. Now that you have overcome, you have ears to hear, and now you have access to The Tree of Life and may take freely of the knowledge and the Stone of the Philosopher's.

# THE SUMERIAN KING LIST

There are a number of versions of The Sumerian King List which do not always agree with each other. This version, found in James W. Bell's *Ancient Sumeria: In the Days when Gods Walked Upon the Face of the Earth*, is based on an inscription on a block of stone found at the site of an ancient Sumerian city named Isin. It is an update of earlier Sumerian king lists, to add Isin's kings to Sumer's royal roster.

This list was inscribed during the reign of Damiqilishu of Isin (1816-1794 BCE). It presumed to be a list of kings from the beginning of history—when kingship was first handed down from Heaven. As the inscription was done only a few years before Hammurabi of Babylon captured the land in the first half of the 18th century BCE and added it as a province to his new empire called Babylonia, it is virtually a complete list of the kings of the land once called Sumer.

The Sumerian King List is a mixture of fact and fantasy, including many historical kings confirmed by archaeology, but omitting others, and listing some contemporaneous dynasties as if they followed each other. The list below is paragraphed and formatted in modern style for ease of reading.

## Kingship in Eridu

When kingship was first handed down from Heaven, the city of Eridu was chosen as the seat of kingship. In Eridu, Alulim ruled for 28,800 years as king and Alalgar ruled for 36,000 years. The two kings ruled a total of 64,800 years and then kingship was removed to Bad-tibira.

## Kingship in Bad-tibira

In Bad-tibira, Enmenluanna ruled 43,200 years, Enmengalanna ruled 28,800 years and Dumuzi, the shepherd, ruled 36,000 years. The three kings ruled a total of 108,000 years and then kingship was removed to Larak.

273

## Kingship in Larak

In Larak, Ensipazianna ruled 28,800 years before kingship was removed to Sippar.

## Kingship in Sippar

In Sippar, Enmeduranna ruled 21,000 years and then Sippar was abandoned and its kingship removed to Shuruppak.

## Kingship in Shuruppak

In Shuruppak, Ubartutu ruled 18,600 years and then The Flood came.

## The Flood

Eight kings in five cities ruled 241,200 years before The Flood swept over the land.

*It is important here to say that most of the kings who ruled before the flood were Anunnaki and not human. After the flood, kingship once again descends from heaven and at this point demigods and humans begin to rule. We can easily see the reduction in time periods of rule after the flood when compared to the lengths of rule prior to the flood. We also can see that after the flood the length of rule generally decreases as time goes on. Additionally, we see that there is also increased fighting after the flood and kingships are more often removed by weapons. And we now continue...*

## Kingship in Kish

After The Flood, kingship was handed down from Heaven a second time, this time to the city of Kish which became the seat of kingship.

In Kish, Gaur ruled 1,200 years; Gulla-Nidaba-annapad ruled

960 years; Palakinatim ruled 900 years; Nangishkushma ruled 670 years, 3 months and 3½ days;

Bahina ruled 300 years; Buanum ruled 840 years; Kalibum ruled 960 years; Galumum ruled 840 years; Zukakip ruled 900 years; Atab ruled 600 years; Mashda, the son of Atab, ruled 840 years; Arurim, the son of Mashda, ruled 720 years;

Etana, the shepherd who ascended to Heaven and made firm all the lands, ruled 1,560 years; Balih, the son of Etana, ruled 400 years;

Enmenunna ruled 660 years; Melam-Kish, the son of Enmenunna, ruled 900 years; Barsalnunna, the son of Enmenunna, ruled 1,200 years; Meszamug, the son of Barsalnunna, ruled 140 years; Tizkar, the son of Meszamug, ruled 305 years;
Ilku ruled 900 years; Iltasadum ruled 1,200 years; Enmebaraggesi, the king who smote the Land of Elam, ruled 900 years; Agga, the son of Enmebaraggesi, ruled 625 years.

All told, twenty-three kings ruled a total of 24,510 years, 3 months and 3½ days before Kish was defeated in battle and its kingship carried off to Eanna.

## Kingship in Eanna
(Eanna later became part of the city of Uruk)

After kingship was brought to Eanna, Meskiaggasher, the son of the Sun God, Utu (Shamash), ruled as both lord and king for 324 years during which time he entered the sea and climbed the mountains; Enmerkar, the son of Meskiaggasher, the king of Uruk who had founded Uruk, ruled for 420 years;

Lugalbanda, the shepherd, ruled for 1,200 years; Dumuzi, the fisherman who came from the city of Kuara, ruled 100 years; Gilgamesh, whose father was a nomad (?), ruled 126 years; Urnungal, son of Gilgamesh, ruled 30 years; Udulkalamma, the son of Urnungal, ruled 15 years;

Labasher ruled 9 years; Ennundaranna ruled 8 years; Meshede, the smith, ruled 36 years; Melamanna ruled 6 years and Lugalkidul ruled 36 years.

All told, twelve kings ruled a total of 2,310 years in Eanna before Uruk was defeated in battle and its kingship carried off to Ur.

## Kingship in Ur

After kingship was brought to Ur, Mesannepadda ruled for 80 years; Meskiagnunna, the son of Mesannepadda, ruled 36 years; Elulu ruled 25 years and Balulu ruled 36 years. All told, four kings ruled a total of 177 years before Ur was defeated in battle and its kingship carried off to Awan.

## Kingship in Awan

After kingship was brought to Awan, ..... (text destroyed) ..... All told, three kings ruled a total of 356 years before Awan was defeated in battle and its kingship carried off to Kish.

## Kingship in Kish (Second Dynasty)

After kingship was brought back to Kish, ..... ruled (more than) 201 years; Dadasig ruled 81 years; Mamagal ruled 420 years; Kalbum, the son of Mamagal, ruled 132 years; Tuge ruled 360 years; Mennumna ruled 180 years; Lugalmu ruled 420 years and Ibbi-Ea ruled 290 (?) years. All told, eight kings ruled a total of 3,195 years before Kish was defeated in battle and its kingship carried off to Hamazi.

## Kingship in Hamazi

After kingship was brought to Hamazi, Hadanish ruled 360 years before Hamazi was defeated and its kingship carried off to Uruk.

## Kingship in Uruk
(Including the ancient city of Eanna)

After kingship was brought to Uruk, Enshakanshanna ruled 60 years; Lugalure ruled 120 years and Argandea ruled 7 years. All told, three kings ruled a total of 187 years before Uruk was defeated and its kingship carried off to Ur.

## Kingship in Ur (Second Dynasty)

After kingship was brought back to Ur, Nani ruled .. , Meshkiagnanna, son of Nani, ruled .... (text destroyed) ..... All told, four kings ruled a total of 116 (?) years before Ur was defeated and its kingship carried off to Adab.

## Kingship in Adab

After kingship was brought to Adab, Lugalannemundu ruled 90 years before Adab was defeated and its kingship carried off to Mari.

## Kingship in Mari

After kingship was brought to Mari, Ilshu ruled 30 years; ..... , the son of Ilshu, ruled 17 years; Bazi, the leatherworker, ruled 30 years; Zizi, the fuller, ruled 20 years; Limer, the gudu priest, ruled 30 years and Sharrumiter ruled 9 years. All told, six kings ruled a total of 136 years before Mari was defeated and its kingship carried off to Kish.

## Kingship in Kish (Third Dynasty)

After kingship was brought back to Kish again, Ku-Bau, the innkeeper, she who made firm the foundations of Kish, ruled for 100 years as 'king' before Kish was defeated and its kingship carried off to Akshak.

## Kingship in Akshak

After kingship was brought to Akshak, Unzi ruled 30 years; Undalulu ruled 12 years; Urur ruled 6 years; Puzur-Nirah ruled 20 years; Ishu-Il ruled 24 years and Shu-Sin, son of Ishu-Il, ruled 7 years. All told, six kings ruled for a total of 99 years before

Akshak was defeated and its kingship carried off to Kish.

### Kingship in Kish (Fourth Dynasty)

After kingship was brought back to Kish, Puzur-Sin, son of Ku-Bau, ruled 25 years; Ur-Zababa, son of Puzur-Sin, ruled 400 years; Simudarra ruled 30 years; Usiwatar, son of Simudarra, ruled 7 years; Ishtar-muti ruled 11 years; Ishme-Shamash ruled 11 years and Nannia, the stoneworker, ruled 7 years. All told, seven kings ruled 491 years before Kish was defeated and its kingship carried off to Uruk.

### Kingship in Uruk (Second Dynasty)

After kingship was brought back to Uruk, Lugalzaggesi ruled for 25 years before Uruk was defeated and its kingship carried off to Agade.

### Kingship in Agade

After kingship was brought to Agade, Sargon, whose father (?) was a gardener, the cupbearer of Ur-Zababa, founded Agade and ruled for 56 years as its king; Rimush, the son of Sargon, ruled 9 years; Manishtushu, a son of Sargon and the older brother of Rimush, ruled 15 years; Naram-Sin, son of Manishtushu, ruled 56 years and Sharkalisharri, son of Naram-Sin ruled 25 years.

Then, who was king? Who was not king? Igigi, Nanum, Imi and Elulu, the four of them were kings but ruled for a total of only 3 years. Dudu took control and ruled for 21 years and Shudurul, son of Dudu, ruled 15 years. All told, eleven kings ruled a total of 197 years before Agade was defeated and its kingship carried off to Uruk.

### Kingship in Uruk (Third Dynasty)

After kingship was brought back to Uruk, Urnigin ruled 7 years; Urgigir, son of Urnigin, ruled 6 years; Kudda ruled 6 years; Puzur-ili ruled 5 years and Ur-Utu ruled 6 years. All told, five kings ruled a total of 30 years before Uruk was smitten by the Gutium Hordes and its kingship carried off by them.

## The Gutium Hordes

After the Gutium Hordes seized kingship, everyone was his own king for 3 years; then Imta ruled 3 years; Inkishush ruled 6 years; Sarlagab ruled 6 years; Shulme ruled 6 years;

Elulumesh ruled 6 years; Inimbakesh ruled 5 years; Igeshaush ruled 6 years; Iarlagab ruled 15 years; Ibate ruled 3 years; Iarla ruled 3 years; Kurum ruled 1 year; Apilkin ruled 3 years; Laerabum ruled 2 years; Irarum ruled 2 years;

Ibranum ruled 1 year; Hablum ruled 2 years; Puzur-Sin, the son of Hablum, ruled 7 years; Iarlaganda ruled 7 years; ..... ruled 7 years and Tiriga (?) ruled 40 days. All told, twenty-one kings ruled 91 years and 40 days before the Gutium Hordes were defeated and kingship carried back to Uruk.

## Kingship in Uruk (Fourth Dynasty)

After kingship was brought back to Uruk, Utuhegal ruled 7 years, 6 months and 15 days before Uruk was defeated and its kingship carried off to Ur.

## Kingship in Ur (Third Dynasty)

After kingship was brought back to Ur, Ur-Nammu ruled 18 years; Shulgi, son of Ur-Nammu, ruled 48 years; Amar-Sin, son of Shulgi, ruled 9 years; Shu-Sin, son of Amar-Sin (an error for 'son of Shulgi'), ruled 9 years and Ibbi-Sin, son of Shu-Sin, ruled 24 years. All told, five kings ruled for a total of 108 years before Ur was defeated and its kingship carried off to Isin.

## Kingship in Isin

After kingship was brought to Isin, Ishbi-Erra ruled 33 years; Shuilishu, son of Ishbi-Erra, ruled 10 years; Idin-Dagan, son of Shuilishu, ruled 21 years; Ishme-Dagan, son of Idin-Dagan, ruled 20 years; Lipit-Ishtar, son of Ishme-Dagan, ruled 11 years;

Ur-Ninurta ruled 28 years; Bur-Sin, son of Ur-Ninurta, ruled 21 years; Lipit-Enlil, son of Bur-Sin, ruled 5 years; Erraimitti ruled 8 years; Enlil-bani ruled 24 years; Zambia ruled 3 years; Iterpisha ruled 4 years; Urdukuga ruled 4 years and Sinmagir ruled 11 years—all told, fourteen kings who ruled a total of 203 years.

At this point, the Sumerian King List ends.

# BIBLIOGRAPHY

This bibliography contains a long list of textual information, research transcripts, lecture transcriptions and ancient text translations. Since there are few books currently written on this subject, there will be book references presented. The book references presented will be physics text books and books on historical subjects which refer to the historical references on the subject matter presented. All of these references have been gleaned by the author but in no way is this book a product only of these materials. The bulk of references which have been utilized during the study of the ORMUS elements is far too great to be included here. Additionally, many materials only contain smatterings of useful information. It is also important to note that the dates and/or authors of many of the texts presented here as reference materials are not all known, especially where more ancient texts are concerned. Website addresses are given where available so that the referenced text may be accessed, however websites often change and for this reason no guarantee can be made that the listed sites remain active.

## Physics and Alchemy Related Books

Holmyard, E.J. *Alchemy*. Pelican books, 1957. Penguin Books, 1968.

Lapidus. *In Pursuit Of Gold*. Great Britain. Neville Spearman Limited, 1976.

Sugomi, S. and H. Koizumi. *Microcluster Physics*. Springer Series in Material Science, 1997. Note: This is a text book for Microcluster Physics in Japan.

Zukav, Gary. *The Dancing Wu Li Masters*. Bantam New Age Books, 1979.

## Other Helpful Books
Szepes, Maria. *The Red Lion - The Elixir of Eternal Life*. Horus Publishing Inc., 1997.

Wize, Michael. *The Dead Sea Scrolls Uncovered.* Element Books Limited, 1992: Barnes & Noble Books, 1994.

Baigent, Michael, Richard Leigh, and Henry Lincoln. *Holy Blood Holy Grail.* Dell Publishing, 1982, 1983.

Sitchin, Zecharia. *The Earth Chronicles Series.* Avon Books. This series consists of 14 books. Most of these books are based on Zechariah Sitchin's interpretations of ancient textual information most of which is Sumerian.

Sitchin, Zecharia. *Genesis Revisited.* Avon Books, 1990.

Sitchin, Zecharia. *The Lost Book Of Enki.* Bear & Company, 2002.

Barker, Elizabeth Nazland. *The Mumies of Urumchi.* W.W. Norton & Company.

Gardner, Laurence. *Blood Line of the Holy Grail.* Barns & Noble, 1997.
Gardner, Laurence. *Genesis of the Grail Kings.* Barns & Noble, 2000.

Griffeth, Ralph T. H., trans. *The Rig Veda- Hinduism.*

*The Holy Bible*, King James Version

*The Amplified Bible.* Zondervan Publishing House. (Translated from Hebrew)

**The following is a list of references which includes papers and lectures presented by those in this or related fields. Not all have known authors.**

Historical references in David Hudson's presentations, www.subtleenergies.com

Other refernces at www.subtleenergies.com including Methods, Manipulating the ORMUS Elements, ORMUS and Quantum

Evolution, ORMUS Variations, ORMUS and Ozone and Cone Shaped Shewbread

Non-Metallic, Monoatomic Forms of Transition Elements. (This is David Hudson's patent on the making of ORME of Gold. The patent consists of Parts I and II.) www.monatomic.earth.com

Roth, Johannes, R. Schilling and H.R.Tribin. *Stability of Mon Atomic and Di-atomic Quasi-crystals and the Influence of Noise.* eds. Chr. Janot, J. M. Dubois, World Scientific, Singapore 1988.

Cole, K.C. "Putting DNA to Work as a Biomedical Tool." *Los Angeles Times* 29 December 1979. (Research conducted at Caltech and headed by Jacqueline Barton)

Duncan, Michael A. "Microclusters." *Scientific American* December 1987.

Burde, J. and R.M. Piamond. "Superdeformation." *Physics Review* August 1988.

Shemizu, Y.R. and R.A. Broglia. "Quantum Size Effects in Rapidly Rotating Nuclei." *Physics Review* April 1990.

Yam, Philip. "Spin Cycle, The Spectra of Super Deformed Nuclei." *Scientific American* October 1991.

Hudson, David. Presentation transcript. National Association of Transpersonal Hypnotherapists Conference, Virginia Beach, VA 1994.

Hudson, David. Interview. Internet source. May 31, 1996. "Biblical References To Manna." January 1999.

Hudson, David. "The White Powder Gold." Presentation. Internet source.

Champion, Joe. "Fundamentals of Commercial Precious Metal Synthesis". New Physics web page, 1996.

283

Patkanen, Matti. "Living Water, Vital Air".
www.subtleenergies.com

Patkanen, Matti. "Wormholes and Possible New Physics in Biological Length Scales". www.subtleenergies.com

Penrose, Hamerhoff, Sarfatti, Patkanen, and Deutsch. "Synopsis of Theories posed by New Physics- linking consciousness to ORMUS". www.subtleenergies.com

Patkanen, Matti. "Topological Geometrodynamics (TGD)". Essay 1998.

Gzarnecki, Ruth. "The Quantum Brain: Theory or Myth". Diss. http://serendip.brynmawr.edu/ 1998.

Lee, Virginia. "Science and Spirit: Conversations with Matthew Fox and Rupert Sheldrake, PhD". www.comngrnd.com

Nelson, Robert A. "Transmutation of Carbon". www.levity.com

"Transmutation of Radiation". www.subtleenergies.com

deVere, Nicholas. "The Origins of the Dragon Lords of the Rings, Technical Support Notes: The Royal Court of Dragons". www.dragoncourt.org, 1985-2002.

T.D.A. "Lingo and the Dormant Brain". Research and Development Laboratory (Location unknown, this paper was given to me as a gift.) Similar information can be found here http://www.neilslade.com/Papers/crazy.html

"Making High Temperature Superconductors". Diss. Colorado Future Science, Inc., internet source

http://www.huna.com/hunach1.html Teachings and information on Hawaiian Huna.

**The following list includes ancient texts that were among the many that were gleaned for information about manna and**

**ORMUS.** **Some of these texts are religious in nature while others are stories and still others are alchemical in nature.**

The books of the Nag Hamadi Library. The Nag Hamadi library contains such early Gnostic texts as listed below and many more. www.gnosis.org
The Gospel of Thomas
The Sofia of Jesus Christ
The Apocryphon of John (long version)
The Monichaean Psalms
The Spirit of the Paraclete
The First Book of Ieou
Pistis Sophia
The Gospel of Thomas Coptic Version.
The Gospel of Mary Magdalene
The Gospel of Bartholomew
The Gospel of Philip
The Gospel of Barnabas  http://www.sacred-texts.com/isl/gbar/
The Book of John

My research also includes a great number of the Dead Sea Scroll textual translations. These can be accessed on the web by typing "Dead Sea Scrolls" in a search engine. There are also many books on the Dead Sea Scrolls, none of which are all-inclusive.

The Talmud of Immanuel- The source for The Gospel of Matthew by Jim Deardorff, research Professor Emeritus, Oregon State University. Internet source.
The Book of Jasher
The Book of Enoch
The Second Book of Adam and Eve- Cain marries Luluwa and moves away.

The Vetas of the Hindu religion were a very good source for alchemical and scientific information. *The Vedas also contain great lore concerning the subject of ORMUS. The following texts are a few that were helpful. Unfortunatly, the bulk of Vedic texts have not been translated. Most serious scholars of Vedic texts study Sanskrit in order to delve seriously into these treasure troves of the past.*

Rigveda
Yajurveda
Samaveda
Atharvaveda
Upanishad
Mahabharata
Mahavira
Srimad Bhagavatam
Soma Pavamana
Samarabgana Sutradhara
Vymanira Shastra
*Gospel of the Holy Twelve* translated from the original Aramaic
by Gideon Jasper Richard Ouseley. First known as the Gospel of
Perfect Life. Also translated as The Gospel of The Nazareans.
This text is attributed to the Twelve Apostles. Here is a good
source- www.reluctant-messenger.com

The Writings of Abraham, www.earth-history.com *The Writings
of Abraham were as they are explained in this book, likely
channeled, however much of the information presented by
Joseph Smith in this work more closely parallels my work than
any of the currently widely accepted lore.*

The Apocalypse of Adam, translated by George W. MacRae,
www.gnosis.org

**Sumerian Texts**
One source of archived texts is
http://www.etcsl.orient.ox.ac.uk/catalogue/catalogue1.htm
The Eridue Genesis-Creation of Man by the Anunnaki
The Epic of Gilgamesh
Artra-Hasis, The Creation of Man and The Great Flood
The Celestial Battle

# GLOSSARY OF KEY TERMS

Below are selected terms and their definitions used throughout this book.

**Column force**: The screening potential which extends approximately 6 fermes from the nucleus to exclude certain electron orbitals from bonding. Those electron shells outside of the screening potential become valance electrons which are available for bonding.

**Di-atom and Di-atomic**: A pair of bonded atoms which are in the high spin state and remain as a pair due to the uneven number of electrons within the single atom. As in the mon-atom, the column force has extended beyond the valance shells to preclude the di-atom from further molecular bonding.

**High Spin State**: A state of high spin nuclear activity which deforms the atomic nucleus to an ellipse which in turn forces the column force beyond the valance electron orbitals, thus precluding the atom from molecular bonding.

**Microcluster**: The collection and aggregation of mon- and di-atoms existing in the high spin state due to an as yet unknown attracting force which holds the atoms together in a lattice structure. Microclusters may act as ceramic, metallic, liquid, or gas depending on certain environmental circumstances.

**Microfilaments**: The tiny twisted wire-like structures in cells that help to make up the structure of the cell or the cytoskeleton and are involved in the contraction of muscles in animals and the transport of nutrients through the cytoplasm in plants.

**Monatomic and Mon-atom**: Also spelled Monoatomic, a single atom able to reside alone due to the extension of the column force beyond the valance electron shell which disallows molecular bonding of valance orbitals.

**ORMES**: Orbitally Rearrange Monatomic Elements, a term

coined by David Hudson and used in his patent information concerning a process of monotonic element manufacture from gold.

**ORMUS**: Orbitally Rearranged Metallic Unit Structure, an ancient word and surname meaning serpent in some languages and tree in others. Both meanings are appropriate to the ORMUS materials as the tree relates to the Tree of Life and the serpent relates the greatest of the alchemist line of the Tree of Life known as the Serpent Clan which goes back to the original serpent of the Tree of Life. The serpent is a symbol of rejuvenation and the DNA molecule.

**Superconductivity**: As relating to mon- and di-atomics, superconductivity is the ability for a substance to conduct or absorb any given energy frequency with no net loss of energy.

**Superfluitity**: Super fluids may rise up the sides of a container even possibly spilling over the sides. Viscosity is zero so, when a container is rotated, the substance stays still. Super fluids may display other strange behaviors as well due to the lack of viscosity.

**Nada**: The origins of the word nada are Hindu meaning "Mother of the Universe". A similar form of the word is found in Arabic meaning "giving" and is a name often given to females. The word nada refers to the sound of the universe or the sound of life or of God. When one takes the ORMUS for a long enough period at high enough doses, one begins to hear the nada as a rushing sound or a gentle ringing outside of the head. In Hindu the word nada eventually became to mean simply "sound". Sound yoga or nada yoga is named from this effect.

**Hu**: Is much the same as nada. The sound Hu is the beginning and ending of all sound and is in the mysteries thought of as the sound of alpha and omega or God. The human is the man who can hear the hu. The hu was thought to be the name of God as it was the beginning and ending and the background as well as the spirit of all sound. The mystics also called this the Ismi-Azam, the name of the most high.

Made in the USA
Coppell, TX
12 April 2021

53613230R10177